KV-638-967

High-Frequency Trading Models

GEWEI YE, Ph.D.

WILEY

John Wiley & Sons, Inc.

EDINBURGH UNIVERSITY LIBRARY

WITHDRAWN

Copyright © 2011 by Gewei Ye. All rights reserved.

Published by John Wiley & Sons, Inc., Hoboken, New Jersey.
Published simultaneously in Canada.

No part of this publication may be reproduced, stored in a retrieval system, or transmitted in any form or by any means, electronic, mechanical, photocopying, recording, scanning, or otherwise, except as permitted under Section 107 or 108 of the 1976 United States Copyright Act, without either the prior written permission of the Publisher, or authorization through payment of the appropriate per-copy fee to the Copyright Clearance Center, Inc., 222 Rosewood Drive, Danvers, MA 01923, (978) 750-8400, fax (978) 646-8600, or on the Web at www.copyright.com. Requests to the Publisher for permission should be addressed to the Permissions Department, John Wiley & Sons, Inc., 111 River Street, Hoboken, NJ 07030, (201) 748-6011, fax (201) 748-6008, or online at http://www.wiley.com/go/permissions.

Limit of Liability/Disclaimer of Warranty: While the publisher and author have used their best efforts in preparing this book, they make no representations or warranties with respect to the accuracy or completeness of the contents of this book and specifically disclaim any implied warranties of merchantability or fitness for a particular purpose. No warranty may be created or extended by sales representatives or written sales materials. The advice and strategies contained herein may not be suitable for your situation. You should consult with a professional where appropriate. Neither the publisher nor author shall be liable for any loss of profit or any other commercial damages, including but not limited to special, incidental, consequential, or other damages.

For general information on our other products and services or for technical support, please contact our Customer Care Department within the United States at (800) 762-2974, outside the United States at (317) 572-3993 or fax (317) 572-4002.

Wiley also publishes its books in a variety of electronic formats. Some content that appears in print may not be available in electronic books. For more information about Wiley products, visit our web site at www.wiley.com.

Library of Congress Cataloging-in-Publication Data:

Ye, Gewei, 1971–
    High-frequency trading models / Gewei Ye.
        p. cm. – (Wiley trading series)
    Includes bibliographical references and index.
    ISBN 978-0-470-63373-1 (cloth)
    1. Investment analysis.   2. Speculation–Mathematical models.   3. Portfolio management–Mathematical models.   4. Financial engineering.   I. Title.
    HG4529.Y42 2011
    332.64'501–dc22

                                                                    2010024731

Printed in the United States of America

10 9 8 7 6 5 4 3 2 1

To my parents, Lei, Jessica, and friends

Contents

Preface

L et's start the book by explaining the title: *High-Frequency Trad-ing Models*. First, there are three types of models of high-frequency trading: revenue models, theoretical (including behavioral, quanti-tative, and financial) models, and computer models. Revenue models are strategies, means, and ways to generate revenue and profit for a financial institution. Theoretical models are foundations for building computer mod-els for high-frequency trading operations. Computer models refer to the computer algorithms (algos for short) that program the theoretical models and trading ideas. To summarize, the computer algos automate the trading ideas and the theoretical models with computer programming languages and technology infrastructure so that the revenue models of financial insti-tutions may be materialized in a systematic way.

Thus, the high-frequency trading models may expand to the following: (1) existing revenue models; (2) new revenue modes, for example, high-frequency trading in derivatives markets; (3) theoretical (behavioral, finan-cial, and quantitative) models for building unique investment strategies for high-frequency trading; and (4) computer algos for high-frequency trading and portfolio management. These four topics make up the central themes of the book.

Second, the high-frequency trading models belong to investment re-search and practice that are part of investment management. Investment management provides professional asset and portfolio management for financial institutions or private investors. As part of the functions of a financial institution, investment management provides the people, re-sources, and objectives to conduct high-frequency trading operations with the high-frequency trading models as the tools or goals. The advent of high-frequency trading may impact the investment management industry profoundly if not revolutionarily. As a result, investment management, in-cluding portfolio management, will benefit from computer algos e.g., Sen-timent Asset Pricing Engine (SAPE) designed for high-frequency trading operations.

To elaborate, SAPE is a unique set of computer algos that are built on top of several Nobel models such as modern portfolio theory (MPT) and the capital asset pricing model (CAPM), the Black-Scholes option pricing model, and the autoregressive conditional heteroskedastic (ARCH) model, by engaging a human behavioral factor, namely, traders' sentiment. Though the Nobel models have considered important elements such as risk and return, future-dated option pricing, and volatility clustering, traders' sentiment can also affect stock prices. As the Nobel models did not consider behavioral factors in asset pricing, SAPE fills in the gaps by adding traders' real-time sentiment to the equation. SAPE estimates future prices of individual assets by aggregating traders' real-time sentiment. Compared to the Nobel models that provide theories and formulas, SAPE provides an end-to-end solution to portfolio management, including a new theory on behavioral investing, a new formula on estimating future prices of individual assets, and a new computer system for real-time future asset pricing, asset allocation, and market timing.

At a higher level of abstraction, SAPE for portfolio management, with a collection of computer algos for high-frequency trading, represents technology as the driver of financial innovation and risk management. SAPE algos reflect the principle that technology may have a profound impact on new financial instruments and applications. Similar to the probability theory driving inventions in portfolio management, insurance, and risk management, the advent of high-frequency trading, with an emphasis on information technology, may give rise to more liquidity in securities (especially derivatives) markets, and to inventions in investment management and risk management.

High-frequency trading has swept Wall Street with the stunning profit generated by top tier investment banks. In the meantime, high-frequency trading has been mentioned repeatedly in headline news such as congressional hearings on the practices of Goldman Sachs, and the record-high market volatility on May 6, 2010.

Many financial institutions, regulators, and financial professionals would like to know how high-frequency trading works, how it profits, and what is needed to build the algorithms with technologies available in the public domain. There is a lot of demand in the financial services and regulatory community for an in-depth book on this topic.

The audience for this book includes traders, regulators, portfolio managers, financial engineers, IT professionals, graduate or senior undergraduate students in finance, investment analysts, financial advisors, investment bankers, hedge fund managers, and financial institutions.

This book may be instrumental to the effort of reforming domestic or global financial systems and improving financial regulations. Imagine if financial regulators could develop a new high-frequency trading monitoring system based on the theoretical models and computer algos of this book. The monitoring system might automatically detect the preconditions of market anomalies and prevent the occurrence of undesirable anomalies. It would be especially useful for financial regulators to use computer algos to monitor and regulate trading. As a result, abnormal market behaviors like the one on May 6, 2010, could be anticipated.

The book comprises four parts: Part I describes the fundamental revenue models of high-frequency trading; Part II discusses theoretical models as a foundation of the computer algos used in high-frequency trading; Part III creates a unique model of sentiment asset pricing engine for portfolio management and high-frequency trading; Part IV discusses new models and computer algos of high-frequency trading. The four parts are illustrated in this outline.

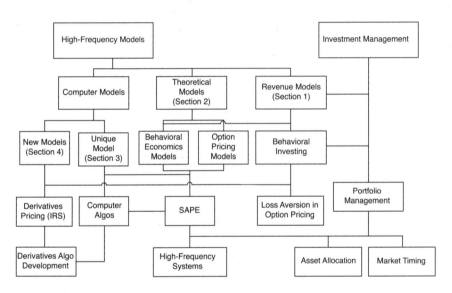

Yeswici.com provides ancillary materials for the computer algos mentioned in the book. It is a quantitative modeling and computing platform for innovative investment research. The platform transfers investment research to Internet and mobile apps.

Acknowledgments

I would like to thank Kevin Commins, Meg Freeborn, Michael Lisk, Pamela van Giessen, and other members of the team at John Wiley & Sons for their hard work to make this book possible.

Many thanks go to Dr. Fred van Raaij, Dr. Naresh Malhotra, Dr. Tracey King, and Dr. Curtis Haugtvedt for their help with the theoretical models (in Part II).

Many thanks also go to the colleagues and graduate students at Johns Hopkins University for their constructive feedback to the unique model and algorithms (in Part III).

Revenue Models of High-Frequency Trading

I n Part I, we cover the introduction to high-frequency trading and the existing revenue models of high-frequency trading. In addition, we discuss the roots, history, and future of the industry.

CHAPTER 1

High-Frequency Trading and Existing Revenue Models

I n this chapter, we discuss the basic concepts of high-frequency trading: what it is; why it is important; who the major players are in the United States; how it earns a profit; and how to categorize high-frequency trading operations.

WHAT IS HIGH-FREQUENCY TRADING?

High-frequency trading has swept Wall Street and made quite a few news headlines since 2008, with the stunning profit generated by top tier investment banks. Only a small percentage (about 2 percent) of all the trading firms operate the high-frequency trading business. So many financial institutions and professionals would like to know what high-frequency trading is. Let's answer the question here.

High-frequency trading extends program trading that normally uses computer algorithms to execute a collection of trading orders at fast speeds, boosting market liquidity (see Hendershott, Jones, and Menkveld, in press). The word *high-frequency* implies the boosting effect on market liquidity compared to manual trading practices. For example, as a liquidity booster, high-frequency trading operations may use sophisticated computer algorithms to analyze multiple markets and execute arbitrage strategies with many orders at the same time.

Based on the definition, there are four elements of a high-frequency trading system: computer algorithms (algos); market liquidity booster;

collection of orders; and faster speed than manual executions. Among the four elements, computer algos and liquidity booster are the necessary conditions to forming a high-frequency trading operation.

As there is not yet a widely acceptable definition of high-frequency trading among academia, practitioners, and regulators, we hope that the definition in this book will be adopted by many, as it addresses the benefit of high-frequency trading to market liquidity at a higher level of abstraction. This benefit is of critical importance to the existence of high-frequency trading practices, as regulators, who are the major force in monitoring and regulating high-frequency trading, have acknowledged the benefit of liquidity boosting of high-frequency trading to the securities markets. More on the concept of high-frequency trading may be found in Irene Aldridge's book *High-Frequency Trading* (2009).

Computer algos are programs written by financial engineers or software engineers that automate the trading activities or quantitative models that are traditionally conducted by human traders or researchers. Some of the algos are based on mathematical models and some are not. For example, a computer algo to compute the value at risk with Monte Carlo simulation uses statistical models. Another computer algo to get the real-time quote of a security over the Internet may not require statistical or mathematical backing.

Collection of orders refers to the grouping of buying or selling orders that are normally used for arbitrage operations that, for example, attempt to profit from price differences between securities or exchanges within a short period of time. Another example may be hedging: A trader may use computer algos to combine a long position of an underlying asset (stock or bond) and in the meantime hedge the risk of losing money by buying a put option on this asset. As a result, a collection of orders (buy the asset and the option) are formed as part of the automated trading strategy.

The advantage of speed has been the major factor of success for early high-frequency trading operations. This is enabled by super computing technology and sophisticated computer algos. For example, it has been reported that Goldman Sachs and IBM collaborated on this type of high-frequency trading to catch the price difference between buying and selling orders within milliseconds, which has delivered significant profits. In general, it is well received by the practitioners that the speed of order execution would position the trades with a better chance of profit-making. The principle of co-location, requiring that the trading servers be located as close as possible to an exchange, emphasizes this point for high-frequency trading. However, the speed of execution is not a required condition for a high-frequency trading system that may use advanced computer algos to outperform peers.

WHY HIGH-FREQUENCY TRADING IS IMPORTANT

Why is high-frequency trading so important today? First, from a functional perspective, high-frequency trading is a type of electronic trading that uses information technology to increase transparency and liquidity of securities markets. The primary benefit of engaging high-frequency trading is boosting liquidity for the securities markets. As such, according to Bloomberg news on May 13, 2009, Tim Geithner,[1] the U.S. Secretary of the Treasury, has urged electronic trading for over-the-counter (OTC) derivatives that lack liquidity and transparency (Leising and Seeley 2009). Note that the 2008 U.S. GDP is $14.4 trillion (data from the World Bank). The OTC derivatives market is a major part of the $600 trillion global derivatives markets that have been frozen due to the lack of liquidity, which was triggered by the financial crisis from late 2008 to the end of 2009.

The second reason for high-frequency trading's importance is its trading volume. According to the data circulating in the trading community, by the end of 2009, the high-frequency trading firms, approximately 2 percent of the 20,000 trading firms of the U.S. markets account for over 70 percent of all U.S. equity trading volume. These 2 percent of companies include proprietary trading desks for a few major investment banks, less than a hundred of the hedge funds, and hundreds of small trading shops. They all operate with one mission: maximizing profit by being smarter or faster than their peers.

An illustrative work by advancedtrading.com (citing the research by TABB Group's Iati) visualizes the three types of trading firms that create the over 70 percent trading volume of U.S. equity with high-frequency trading. First are the traditional broker-dealers who undertake high-frequency strategies, separate from their client business. Second are high-frequency hedge funds. Third are proprietary trading firms that are mainly using private money.

The third reason for high-frequency trading's importance is that it has produced a high-paying labor market that is hiring large numbers of traders, developers, strategists, and analysts, even in an economy in financial crisis with an unemployment rate of more than 10 percent in December 2009, when the recovery of the economy and employment situation was remote.

Here is a job posted in December 2009 by a Wall Street recruiter seeking a quantitative algo trader: "Looking for someone with a quantitative background who comes with/can create their own algorithms. Must have experience with putting algo's into a live production environment on equities, FX/futures or fixed Income. PhD in Financial Engineering, Physics, Chemistry, Economics, Finance, or similar preferred. Roles in NYC and Fairfield County, CT. Total compensation $350k–$750k+."

Apparently, this job posting is very attractive to students or experienced professionals, especially as it claims to pay three times the average salary of an equivalent employee in other fields such as technology consulting with similar technical skills, or scientific research with similar quant skills.

I teach graduate courses on Financial Engineering (with a focus on high-frequency trading algos, financial institutions, and derivatives) at Johns Hopkins University Carey Business School. One of the courses had an original limit of 30 enrollments. It was quickly wait-listed for the first time. The school then raised the enrollment limit to 40. Within weeks, it was wait-listed again with 40 graduate students enrolled. This happened three to four months before the start of the class.

These examples demonstrate the popularity and importance of high-frequency trading and financial engineering in the investment management industry. It has been perceived to be the future of major investing activities for private investors such as hedge funds, and for public investors such as investment banks and mutual funds.

MAJOR HIGH-FREQUENCY TRADING FIRMS IN THE UNITED STATES

In the United States, the major locations of the headquarters for some of the major high-frequency trading firms are New York City in the Northeast and Chicago in the Midwest. Part of the reason is the need for co-location; an important requirement for high-frequency trading is to place the algo trading servers as close as possible to the exchange. The New York Stock Exchange (NYSE) is located in New York City. CME Group is in Chicago, which operates two self-regulatory futures exchanges, the Chicago Mercantile Exchange (CME) and the Chicago Board of Trade (CBOT). CME Group is the result of a merger of CBOT and CME in 2007 that formed one of the largest derivatives exchanges in the world.

Table 1.1 shows a small portion of around 200 high-frequency trading firms in the United States as of 2009. The table displays the names of major high-frequency trading players in the United States, the location of their headquarters, and their main characteristics of trading.

TABLE 1.1 Locations and Characteristics of U.S. High-Frequency Trading Shops

Name	Headquarters Location	Characteristics
Goldman Sachs	New York, NY	Milliseconds advantage to see buy and sell orders
Citadel Investment Group	Chicago, IL	Hedging
Renaissance Technologies	East Setauket, NY	Superfast trading; started in 1982 by legend James Simons
Getco LLC	Chicago	Market maker
Jane Street Capital	New York, NY	Quantitative proprietary trading
Hudson River Trading	New York, NY	Advanced mathematical and statistical modeling; high-performance computing
Wolverine Trading	Chicago, IL	Derivatives; superior technology
Jump Trading	Chicago, IL	Sophisticated high-frequency trading strategies
Millennium	New York, NY	Strong quantitative models
D.E. Shaw	New York, NY	Large hedge fund
Worldquant	Greenwich, CT	Private institutional investment; trade automation
Susquehanna International Group	Philadelphia, PA	Algo trading and market making; comprehensive asset classes

Source: Most data were collected in August 2009 by Scott Patterson and Geoffrey Rogow for the *Wall Street Journal.*

EXISTING REVENUE MODELS OF HIGH-FREQUENCY TRADING OPERATIONS

In a recent *Wall Street Journal* article entitled "What's Behind High-Frequency Trading," Scott Patterson and Geoffrey Rogow (2009) investigated the goals and revenue models of high-frequency trading firms. For a multi-line firm that operates on financial products from stocks to currencies to commodities, the revenue model is to profit from fleeting moves in these products. The high-frequency trading operation looks for "signals," such as the movement of option prices, that indicates which way the market may move in short periods. Some other high-frequency trading operations attempt to profit from finding ways to exploit the defects in the network or computer infrastructure of trading.

Market making is another revenue model for some of the high-frequency trading operations. As a result of the frequent buying and selling, securities on both buy and sell side become easy to liquidate.

Given the assumption of an efficient market for financial markets and exchanges, some high-frequency trading operations exploit temporary "market inefficiencies" and trade in ways that can make money before the brief inefficiency disappears. This extends the traditional arbitrage practice that profits from opportunities such as temporary price difference of a financial product (e.g., gold) in two exchanges (e.g., New York versus Japan). If risk is not involved, such as buying and selling the product at the same time, it is called pure arbitrage; if risk is involved, such as holding the product with one's own capital, the operation is called risk arbitrage.

Detecting and taking advantage of the bid-ask spread is another revenue model for high-frequency trading operations. A bid-ask spread indicates the difference between investors buying and selling a security. A high-frequency operation, for example, a computer algo, may detect the difference in milliseconds while the trade between the buyer and seller is to be matched, and make the trade happen for the buyer and seller. As a result, the algo takes the tiny profit for the matching. With the algo working automatically, the tiny profit may accumulate to a large sum.

Many exchanges, such as the New York Stock Exchange, offer liquidity rebates of about one-third of a penny a share to high-frequency trading operations that are willing to make trades between buyers and sellers easier to complete. The exchange becomes more liquid than before due to the high trade volumes. The frequent trading volumes would produce profit for the trading firms as the exchange awards the trades with the liquidity rebates.

TABLE 1.2 Existing Revenue Models

Existing Revenue Model	Focus	Participants
Fleeting moves	Stocks; currencies; commodities	Institutions
Signal detection	Interest rates	Institutions; individuals
Infrastructure	Defects of computing environment	Institutions
Inefficient market	Tiny gains; financial models	Institutions; individuals
Bid-ask spread	Stock	Institutions
Liquidity rebates	Exchange offers 0.33 penny per share for improving market liquidity	Institutions

To summarize, we organize some of the existing revenue models of high-frequency trading in Table 1.2.

CATEGORIZING HIGH-FREQUENCY TRADING OPERATIONS

To further categorize high-frequency trading operations at a higher level of abstraction, let's discuss the two criteria that organize high-frequency trading operations, followed by the four types of high-frequency trading operations. The two criteria are (1) the types of financial markets (efficient versus inefficient) where a high-frequency trading operation produces revenue, and (2) the participants or actors of the high-frequency trading operations (institutions or private investors).

The revenue models of high-frequency trading firms may be categorized in two parts: Does the model produce profit in an efficient market, or an inefficient market? The notion of efficient versus inefficient markets comes from academic literature. An efficient market refers to the financial market that all players, institutions or individuals, can maximize the utility of their resources with super computing power and advanced intelligence. In reality, the efficient market assumption may not hold, especially for trades that are conducted by human traders. Therefore, some financial markets are inefficient in that the trading represents characteristics such as bias, overconfidence, sentiment-driven, rumor-led, and so forth.

The participants of a high-frequency trading operation may be loosely defined as two groups: financial institutions or private ("individual")

TABLE 1.3   Categorizations of High-Frequency Trading

	Efficient Market	Inefficient Market
Institutions	Examples: Liquidity rebates; infrastructure defects	Example: Tiny gains on pure arbitrage
Private investors	Example: Trades with signals	Example: Algo-trade with financial anomalies such as behavioral economics models

investors. Financial institutions refer to the entities that handle a large volume of financial resources that are pooled from the public. For example, investment banks, mutual funds, pension funds, and insurance companies are institutional investors. Private or individual investors, sometimes called retail investors, use brokerage services to invest their own financial resources in various financial instruments. For example, individual traders, family offices of high net worth investors, private equities, and hedge funds are private investors. A good example to clarify the criterion of institutions versus private investors is to compare mutual funds and hedge funds. Both funds pool financial resources from many people or institutions (e.g., commercial banks) and invest in various financial markets. However, the difference between the two kinds of funds is that mutual funds register with the U.S. Securities and Exchange Commission (SEC), while hedge funds normally do not register with the SEC. This distinction makes a mutual fund "institutional" or "public" and a hedge fund "individual" or "private."

Based on the revenue models and participants that a high-frequency trading operation has engaged, we may categorize high-frequency trading operations as one of four types: the high-frequency trading operation (1) in an efficient market with institutional investor; (2) in an efficient market with individual investors; (3) in an inefficient market with institutional investors; and (4) in an inefficient market with private or individual investors. Table 1.3 shows the categorizations.

CONCLUSION

In this chapter, we discussed the following topics:

- The definition and concept of high-frequency trading.
- Reasons why high-frequency trading is important.

- Major high-frequency trading firms in the United States.
- Basic revenue models of high-frequency trading firms.
- Four types of high-frequency trading operations.

In the next chapter, we trace the roots of high-frequency trading to one of the eight major functions of investment management, namely program trading.

Roots of High-Frequency Trading in Revenue Models of Investment Management

I n order to trace the roots of high-frequency trading, Chapter 2 looks at the eight functions of investment management, followed by a discussion of program trading, an extension of which is high-frequency trading.

What is investment management? Investment management is conducted by financial professionals for financial institutions or private investors. It refers to the professional management of institutional or private investors' assets to meet certain goals for the benefit of the investors. Financial institutions include commercial banks, investment banks and securities firms, insurance companies, pension funds, mutual funds and hedge funds, and finance companies. Investment managers may be the firms that provide investment management services, or persons who manage investors' assets. Investment managers are sometimes called money managers, portfolio managers, fund managers, or even financial advisors and planners.

In their book *Financial Institutions Management*, Saunders and Cornett (2008) organize the activities of the investment banking industry for financial institutions and individual investors into eight types of activities: investing, investment banking, market making, trading, cash management, mergers and acquisitions, back-office services, and venture capitals. It is a bit misleading to use the word "investment banking industry" to capture all the investment management services for financial institutions and individual investors because "investment banking" may have a specific meanings of underwriting public or private offerings to issue new securities. Therefore, I use investment management instead to refer to the

13

activities of the investment banking industry that Saunders and Cornett discussed that include the eight investment activities.

In the next section, we'll discuss eight revenue models of investment management firms. They are investing, investment banking, market making, trading, cash management, mergers and acquisitions, back-office activities, and venture capital.

REVENUE MODEL 1: INVESTING

Investing refers to a long-term act for investment managers to manage investors' asset. In this space, financial institutions such as mutual funds and ETF funds are commonly used by investment managers to pool the resources from investors and diversify the resources with various financial instruments for long-term gains and minimized risks.

The general revenue model of investing is the fees that investment managers charge to financial institutions, retail investors, or financial instruments such as mutual funds. For example, a pension fund may hire investment managers to choose A+ grade investment instruments for the safest and stable long-term stream of income for retirees. The investment managers may choose fixed income mutual funds. The U.S. Securities and Exchange Commission (SEC) allows mutual funds to pay for the sales and distribution of the funds with the 12b-1 fees. These fees may be part of the revenue model for the investment managers who specialize in investing.

Art versus Science: Three Levels of Abstraction in Investing and Trading

In my opinion, there are three levels of abstraction in investing pertinent to the goals and the level of certainty on predicting the result of investing activities. Here *abstraction* means the expected certainty of the outcome of the investment choice.

First, at the level of art, investment managers treat the process of investing as a black box. Knowing the input, which is the starting financial resources, the outcome of the investing bears the maximum uncertainty to the investment managers a priori. In other words, investing as art shows a sense that the beauty and appreciation of the activity lies largely in individuals' subjective judgment.

Second, at the semi-art and semi-science level, investment managers use only quantitative methods such as regression analysis to analyze the black box. Building on linear regressions, we may choose the capital asset pricing model (CAPM) for asset and portfolio analysis; or we may choose option pricing models such as the Black-Scholes model for nonlinear analysis for the asset selection or allocation. At this level, the certainty level of the expected result is quantified. For example, value at risk (VaR) provides risk confidence levels for a portfolio construction. When an unexpected event occurs, it is part of the anomalies and may be hedged with insurance or other risk management instruments. So it is not guaranteed that at the second level, it is a sure win for the investing choice or the chosen investment portfolio.

Third, at the science level, this is where quantitative analysis meets computer science. High-frequency trading belongs to this level of investing. With the requirement for speed and time limit to generate revenue, it also belongs to the trading universe. When computer science and statistical analysis are combined, the expectation level for the outcome and risk management is lifted, because in computer science, an unexpected event is not called an anomaly within the 5 percent or 1 percent significance levels—it is called a bug or defect that need to be fixed. Therefore, at the science level of investing, investment managers pursue the maximum certainty of the expected investment outcome. In most cases, the revenue model may engage countless automated trials with computer algos and as a result a sure win is expected as the outcome.

The expectation of the third level of abstraction may be the ultimate goal of risk management: The maximum certainty suggests the minimum risk. A financial invention in the past, driven by the probability theory, attempted to achieve this with diversifications in investment management and insurance instruments such as credit default swaps (CDS) for risk management. The probability theory comes from the quantitative universe. With the rapid growth of information technology, principles of computer science should contribute to risk management as well. The principle of "bug-free applications" may be one. Its implementation in high-frequency trading operations would be a novel case to demonstrate the contribution of information technology to financial inventions and risk management.

With the advent of high-frequency trading as the new paradigm for trading and investing practice, we will see that high-frequency trading may lead to an expanded finance discipline with computer algos being a necessity. With computer algos, the semi-art and semi-science trading paradigm, solely based on statistics, may be replaced with a new paradigm, namely investing and trading as science engaging computer algos and statistics.

Common Investing Vehicles

Mutual funds and hedge funds are common investing vehicles for retail investors or accredited investors to achieve specified investment goals with risks minimized or controlled.

For retail investors, regardless of the amount of capital, mutual funds may reduce risk to a minimum by diversifying the pooled capital to maximum independent asset classes. Based on the modern portfolio theory and the CAPM, portfolio managers of mutual funds may minimize the risk of their portfolios by expanding the total number of asset classes as much as possible. The statistical explanation for this is the formula to calculate risk or volatility of a portfolio. Assuming the independence of the assets of a portfolio, the risk of the portfolio positively relates to the volatility of an asset over sqrt(N). N is the total number of assets of the portfolio. Hence, when N increases, the portfolio risk decreases. When the assets of a portfolio are not correlated in returns, increasing N may not cost the portfolio returns. However, when the assets are correlated, increasing N would affect the portfolio returns as shown in a typical efficient portfolio frontier. This is because the expected portfolio return is a function of the portfolio risk (Markowitz, 1952).

The payment plans for mutual funds reflect the revenue models of mutual fund companies. On the other hand, the plans outline the cost for investors to invest in mutual funds. For most funds, there are three types of payment plans through three share classes (A, B, and C). Each share class has different sales load, management, and 12b-1 fees. Sales loads may be charged at the purchase of a fund as a percentage of the price, which is called front-end load. Back-end loads are charged when the fund is sold (i.e., at redemption). Management fee is also a percentage of the fund value, paying for the expenses to maintain the fund such as portfolio managers' salaries. 12b-1 fees, getting the name from the SEC's rule number, cover the sales and marketing of the funds to investors. Table 2.1 summarizes the three types of payment plans.

Hedge funds are designed for accredited investors who have to meet one of these two criteria according to SEC rules as of 2009: (1) an individual net worth of 1 million; or (2) annual income of U.S. $200,000 or annual household income of U.S. $300,000. Hedge funds charge high performance fees (e.g. 20 percent) if the net asset value of the fund increases from the previous assessment (i.e., high water mark), and an agreed absolute return rate (i.e., the hurdle rate) is achieved.

TABLE 2.1 Payment Plans of Mutual Funds

Share Classes	Front-End Load	Back-End Load	Management/12b-1
A	Yes	No	Yes
B	No	Yes	Yes
C	No	Yes	Yes

TABLE 2.2 Comparing Mutual Funds and Hedge Funds

Features	Mutual Funds	Hedge Funds
Load	Front-end and back-end	N/A
Management fees	Yes	Yes; 2/20 rule
12b-1 fee	Yes	No
Performance fee	No	Around 20% if satisfying high water mark and hurdle rate
Total fee charge	Less	More

We may compare the fee structures of mutual funds and hedge funds in Table 2.2 to better understand the two types of funds.

REVENUE MODEL 2: INVESTMENT BANKING

Broadly speaking, investment banking may refer to an industry that involves creating and trading securities of equity, debt, and derivatives. Investment banks and securities firms are the major institutions of the industry. Narrowly speaking, investment banking refers to a revenue model for investment banks to generate profit by underwriting and distributing new issues of debt (corporate or government bonds), equity (e.g., stocks), and derivatives (e.g., options and futures).

The most newsworthy revenue model in investment banking may be an initial public offering (IPO), the first-time offering of debt and equity by a company. Famous IPO stories include high-tech companies such as Google, Yahoo!, and Apple. Through IPOs, investment banks earn best-effort fees or profit from firm-commitment practice.

In a best-efforts underwriting, the investment banker acts as an agent of the company issuing the security and receives a fee based on the number of securities sold. With a firm-commitment underwriting, the investment banker purchases the securities from the company at a negotiated price and sells them to the investing public at a higher price. Thus, the investment banker has greater risk with the firm-commitment underwriting, since the investment banker will absorb any adverse price movements in the security before the entire new issues are sold.

Factors concerning the issuing firm include general volatility in the market, stability, maturity and financial health, and the perceived appetite for new issues in the marketplace. The investment bank may consider these factors when negotiating the fees and/or pricing spread in making its decision on the types of underwriting.

In order to practice investment banking, let's try this exercise. Let us assume that a company called NewBaidu is an international search engine company, seeking IPO with your firm. Your team is challenged to make a decision on choosing which type of underwriting for the IPO: best-efforts underwriting or firm-commitment underwriting. This requires you to create a decision matrix with a scoring mechanism to quantify the risk and reward of the two options. Let us also assume that you would have to present the result to the NewBaidu executives.

REVENUE MODEL 3: MARKET MAKING

Market making creates secondary markets for assets, thus increasing the liquidity of the markets. Similar to secondhand cars, financial securities in the secondary market are not sold by the IPO companies. Instead, the original ownerships of securities traded in the secondary markets frequently do not exist anymore.

One of the main benefits of market making is boosting the liquidity of the markets. High-frequency trading is perfect for this; thus, one of the revenue models of high-frequency trading derives from market making, that is, to profit from liquidity rebates, an incentive to increase the liquidity of the markets.

When a security market is frozen (not liquid) due to various reasons, the financial industry may be affected as is the overall economy. In this case, market making becomes critically important for economic recovery. During the financial and economic crisis of 2008–2009, derivatives markets valued at about $600 trillion globally were frozen, especially for the over-the-counter (OTC) derivatives. The OTC derivatives are not publicly traded; thus they lack transparency and liquidity. Note that the U.S. GDP is around $15 trillion in 2008, just a fraction of the size of the derivatives markets.

A possible solution to make the secondary markets for the derivatives is increasing the liquidity of the derivatives markets by pushing electronic trading and high-frequency trading for OTC derivatives. This has been discussed extensively in regulations by the U.S. Congress and the Department of the Treasury.

REVENUE MODEL 4: TRADING

Compared to investing that seeks sustainable stream of income for the long term with tools like asset allocation and security selection, trading tends to seek profit on a short-term basis with sophisticated tools or strategies such as leverages and market timing.

Trading properly by the rules is essential to the health of the securities markets, as it provides necessary liquidity and market making. As a part of trading, high-frequency trading inherits the characteristics of market making and the liquidity booster for the markets. However, we need to realize that some of the high-frequency trading practices may threaten the integrity and fairness of the markets. As such, when we build computer algos for high-frequency trading systems, abiding by the rules and regulations should be part of the specifications of the system development process.

In general, there are four types of trading; high-frequency trading extends one of them. The four types of trading are: position trading, pure arbitrage, risk arbitrage, and program trading. High-frequency trading extends program trading, involving computer algos to find opportunities and automate the trading process. Position trading takes positions over time with the hope that the price movement would go the way as expected. Pure arbitrage trading requires the buying and selling of securities at the same time for a profit, exploiting market inefficiency. Risk arbitrage engages the time or ownership of the security; thus the risk of loss is associated with the transactions.

REVENUE MODEL 5: CASH MANAGEMENT

Before 1999, investment management is separate from commercial banking, which manages consumers' cash with deposits and loans. With the Financial Services Modernization Act of 1999, the investment management industry may collect deposits from consumers. Thus cash management becomes another revenue model of investment banks and securities firms in addition to creating and trading securities.

Cash management blurs the distinction between investment management and traditional commercial banks. Large banks such as Bank of America and Morgan Stanley handle both investment banking and commercial banking operations. This has streamlined the securitization process of mortgage-backed securities.

Mortgage-backed securities for special-purpose entities (see Figure 12.1) are created by investment banks that buy packages of loans from the commercial banks that interface with mortgage debt owners. By combining the commercial banking function with the investment banking function, the creation of mortgage-backed securities becomes part of the intradepartmental transactions within a large bank.

REVENUE MODEL 6: MERGERS AND ACQUISITIONS

Mergers and acquisitions (M&A) has been a lucrative revenue model for investment banks. Similar to the idea of creating new securities of debt equity of a single new company, mergers and acquisitions form new companies by combining two or more existing companies, most times followed by issuing new securities or converting existing securities.

For a fee, analysts of investment banks may seek opportunities for companies to merge by proposing expected benefit of the merger. They may also be hired by a company to explore the disadvantages of an M&A proposal so that the company may argue against the proposal.

With a merger and acquisition, similar functions of the companies may be combined or consolidated for efficiency concerns. As a result of the merger, duplicate positions may appear which would give rise to layoffs or workforce reductions. Hence, news on mergers and acquisitions may benefit equity prices. Yet it is normally not good news for most of the employees of the affected companies.

REVENUE MODEL 7: BACK-OFFICE ACTIVITIES

The back-office functions of an investment management firm may be perceived as expenses for the firm. Yet these functions are necessary to operate the firm's day-to-day business. These functions include clearance and settlement, escrow services, and IT services such as new account setup and management.

Automating back-office activities with information technology has proved to be a long-term investment for the firms. The payoff may come from the savings of manual engagements and additional quality services offered to investors. For example, for querying his or her account balances, as opposed to scheduling appointments on weekdays to come to investor centers, an investor may use a Web-based account management service to access the accounts anytime at a convenient location.

REVENUE MODEL 8: VENTURE CAPITAL

Venture capital firms are a special type of investment bank or securities firm. They pool money from individual investors and other financial institutions (e.g., hedge funds, pension funds, and insurance companies) to fund relatively small and new businesses (e.g., in social media and biotechnology).

Normally, the revenue model of venture capital firms is to invest in startup companies for a part of the ownership of the companies. They may also provide cash to the companies as corporate loans. When the companies become successful and even go IPO, the venture capital firm would get extremely lucrative returns. For example, Sequoia Capital is a successful venture capital firm that has excellent returns on investing in high-tech firms such as Google, Apple, and YouTube.

CREATING YOUR OWN REVENUE MODEL

Creating your own revenue models has been the main task for entrepreneurs or corporate leaders. With brand-new technology or new product, a paradigm shift could happen to an existing consumer market to create a new market. As a result, the entrepreneurs or leaders may have a temporary monopoly with the new revenue model to produce a profit in the new market. When competition comes in, the revenue model may be copied by the competitors and the profit may decline.

As part of a case study for a financial engineering class, I ask graduate students to form groups of three to start new financial institutions. Each student in the group is assigned an executive role as chief executive officer (CEO), chief technology officer (CTO), or chief marketing officer (CMO). The setting of the case could be: "You and two friends have a meeting at Starbucks, talking about why Warren Buffett and Bill Gates can amass so much fortune and then give back to society. All inspired, you decide to start a new financial institution together with major financial institutions as the primary clients. Here are the questions to ask: (1) How will my business generate revenue? (2) How will I launch my business plan? (3) How can I get help and make connections?" Therefore, the first question for any new corporation is: What is our revenue model?

I have developed a conceptual framework to guide students through the process of creating new ideas and revenue models for new corporations.

The goal for entrepreneurs is to achieve success and happiness through a sound revenue model. The core of this conceptual framework stresses the use of novel means and approaches to deliver success (i.e., revenue and customer satisfaction) through innovation. The framework has three stages: goal, strategy, and execution. The goal is to deliver "painkiller-like" customer and investor satisfaction. The strategy is to expand the idea pool and process the selected idea. The idea pool comprises expanded knowledge, skills, and attitude in technology and business through learning and training. These ideas will be filtered as one and only one opportunity

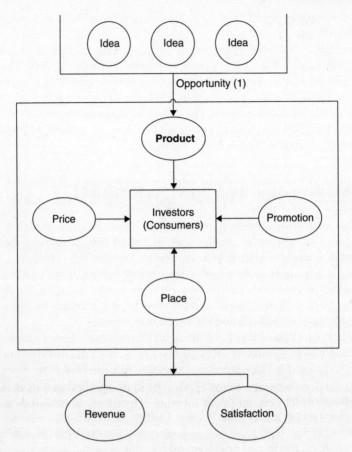

FIGURE 2.1 Generic Entrepreneurial Modeling

to enter a revenue model. The revenue model takes in the business opportunity and then converts it to a product or a service. Using processors such as price, promotion, and place, the revenue model will deliver profit and customer satisfaction as the output. Figure 2.1 illustrates the approach to creating a new revenue model.

HOW TO ACHIEVE SUCCESS: FOUR PERSONAL DRIVERS

Success is necessary for a person to be happier, which may be the ultimate objective of a person's lifelong pursuit. Happiness (and satisfaction) is a choice and relates to expectations. In other words, it is the result of

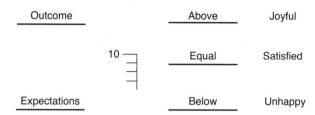

Outcome		Above	Joyful
	10	Equal	Satisfied
Expectations		Below	Unhappy

FIGURE 2.2 Relationship between Satisfaction and Expectations

a comparison between two entities: expectation and outcome. Say a student takes a final exam. If the outcome of the grade (e.g., C) is below his expectations (e.g., B), then he would be unhappy. If the outcome of the grade (e.g., B) meets his expectations, then he would be satisfied. If the grade outcome (e.g., A) exceeds his expectations, then he would be joyful. Figure 2.2 shows the relationship between satisfaction and expectations.

It is very important to manage reasonable expectations for investors. Otherwise, it would set up the business for failure even though the business may actually do very well. Look at this example. On February 1, 2006, the BBC published an analysis of Google's stock prices and its business performance. Google shares fell 7 percent the day after its earnings fell short of Wall Street expectations for the first time.

Why did Google shares fall? Compared with an average profit increase of 10 to 20 percent in the industry, Google is doing very well by delivering an outcome of 82 percent profit increase. However, as investors set very high expectations in the first place, this stellar business performance still does not meet the "very high" expectations. In other words, many investors are not satisfied and start to sell the stock. This results in a 7 percent drop in Google's stock price. Therefore, in order to make investors happy, reasonable expectations should be set as a proper reference point for them to compare to.

Knowing this principle, we may find a way to make people happy. Let us first start with ourselves. After we work hard and work smart, a reasonable lower expectation should be used to expect an uncertain outcome. If the outcome cannot be changed anymore, a relatively lower expectation would better prepare us to accept and be happy with the outcome. The principle is applicable to making others happy. The others could be our parents, partners, customers, and so forth. When others are happy, we will be more likely to be happy. Consciously framing the expectations of the outcome to properly set the expectations may give rise to a satisfactory response to the outcome, even if the actual outcome may not be that good.

The other two values related to business success are intelligence and truth. The more intelligent a person or a team is, and the more truth the person or the team knows, the more successful the person or team will likely be. Hence, intelligence and truth are the foundation for achieving success with a sound revenue model.

From a personal perspective, the four drivers of success with a sound revenue model are concentration, confidence, motivation, and persistence (CCMP). To achieve success, one has to concentrate on the objective of the revenue model. If you have too many ideas, then choose one after careful consideration and stick to that one. Concentrate on the one with all your energy and effort with 100 percent devotion because your competitors are strong and committed. If you invest just 50 percent of the effort, maybe because you have two projects going on at the same time, then you are using 50 percent of your strength to compete with others who are working at 100 percent strength. Unless you are super strong, you are unlikely to succeed in both projects.

A person's confidence on the subject matter comes from what he or she can offer in the competition. Usually a person's confidence is based on his or her knowledge, skills, and attitude (KSA). Knowledge means how much the person knows about the subject matter, the strengths and weaknesses of competitors, and so forth. Skills means what a person can do to deliver on expectations and promises, inclusive of technical skills such as developing a computer program or managerial skills such as leading a team of subject matter experts to success. Attitude means that a person should always stay positive even if things are not going as expected. This is especially crucial in a team-based environment. One team member's attitude can influence the others' motivation and effort in the completion of the group project. This is the foundation of leadership and teamwork skills.

To illustrate the relationship between success, confidence, and KSA, we look at a competitive analysis with KSA, competitors, and the needs and wants of customers (the market). Figure 2.3 shows three circles; the one on the left is for the market, which represents the needs and wants of customers or clients. The customers may be individuals who are using the products or services you are offering, or business customers as the clients or business partners of your company, or employers who are hiring talent with specific qualifications.

The circle on the right represents the KSA that we offer to customers. It may take the form of products or services that are built on the knowledge, skills, and attitude, or our qualifications for employers or clients. For example, one of the KSA constructs is the incremental creativity that a business student or entrepreneur may demonstrate in the offerings to clients. Incremental creativity suggests that the products or services of the offerings are relevant to the market's needs and wants, and depart from the

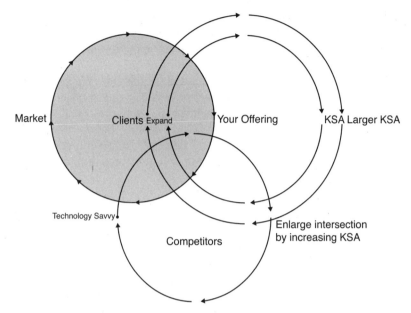

FIGURE 2.3 Competitive Analysis of Achieving Success

traditional offerings of competitors. A larger KSA circle gives rise to an enlarged intersection with the circle of the market, representing a greater likelihood of success.

The circle at the bottom of Figure 2.3 represents the competitors of the new business. Nowadays, the competitors are technology savvy in the sense that they are equipped with the advanced technologies to conduct business. For example, the competitors use web sites or blogs (Web logs) to market their products and services, and they use a cell phone or a PDA (personal digital assistants) such as a BlackBerry to communicate with business players. Some of the competitors have been around in the market for a while and have established a solid client base. To compete with them and achieve success, an even larger KSA powered by technology has to be delivered to the customers. The larger the KSA circle is, the more confident we will be, and the more likely we will be successful.

The third personal driver of achieving success is motivation. Motivation means how hard we want to produce the offerings and deliver them to market. Knowing the competition analysis, we must realize the gap between the current state and the state needed to beat competitors. As a result, we must be motivated to bridge the gap and get the job done at full strength. Compared to players without motivation, a motivated person achieves efficiency, effectiveness, speed, and quality of offerings, which gives rise to a greater likelihood of success. We will expand on the relationship between motivation and success (performance) in the next section.

The fourth personal driver of success is persistence. We keep in mind that for many people, the chance to get everything right on the first try is very slim or sometimes impossible. So be prepared for failure. It is said that failure is the mother of success. Persistence means that we need to keep trying with lessons learned from failed attempts. If the direction is right and we are competent and motivated, we will be successful in the end.

Understanding Motivation and Performance Maximization

Economics says that one should maximize the return on the investment. Normal people say one should do more with less. Both perspectives stress the idea of working smart in addition to working hard. Hence, performance may be assessed by the ratio of output (return) over input (investment).

Studies show that one's performance or the likelihood of success is affected by the mental state of the person, one of which is the level of motivation. A poor performance may result from a low level of motivation (e.g., a slacker's mind), or an over-motivated mind (e.g., a stressful state of mind). A strong performance results from a motivated and calm mind. Figure 2.4 illustrates the relationship between motivation and performance. A mind with moderate motivation maximizes performance.

In order to achieve more in learning and work, we may consciously adjust the state of mind to be at the level of moderate motivation in the long run.

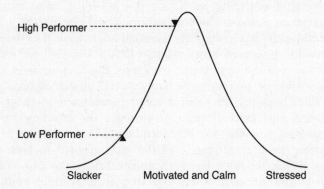

FIGURE 2.4 Levels of Motivation and Performance

CONCLUSION

In this chapter, we discussed the roots of high-frequency trading, that is, the program trading of investment management. The eight revenue models of investment management are directly or indirectly related to the program trading practice. In addition, we covered creating personalized revenue models, taking into account the factors for achieving success.

CHAPTER 3

History and Future of High-Frequency Trading with Investment Management

High-frequency trading may have a long history. We may trace its roots to the early days of electronic trading. However, the new term, high-frequency, was introduced more recently.

As high-frequency trading is an evolving concept that does not yet have a widely acceptable definition, we will take a quick survey of the different names that are relevant to the concept. As a result, we argue that high-frequency trading has gone by many names in the past.

For example, before the term "high-frequency trading" was created by an anonymous trading practitioner, similar operations carried the names such as program trading, electronic trading, algorithmic trading, automated trading, computer-aided trading, quantitative trading, and statistical arbitrage trading.

In standard finance textbooks, "program trading" is used to describe computer-aided trading that engages a collection of orders with a large amount of capital. For example, the NYSE defines program trading as transactions that have to engage at least 15 tickers and with a sum of $1 million. The word "program" in program trading has two meanings: (1) computer programs and (2) a program or collection of orders.

However, as there are so many different types of electronic trading practices, the strict definition of program trading is not applicable to all cases. For example, some high-frequency trading operations do not comply with the NYSE definition for program trading, as the number of orders and amount of capital engaged in a transaction may be less and flexible.

If we come back to our definition of high-frequency trading, then we look at two necessary questions: Does the trading require computer algos?

And does the trading boost market liquidity? If the answers are yes to both questions for an electronic trade, then we call it high-frequency trading.

REVENUE MODELS IN THE FUTURE

High-frequency trading has a bright future—not only has it already accounted for over 60 percent of the trading volume in the U.S. equities market, it is growing dramatically on a monthly basis. In the near future, we may see that most if not all of the U.S. equity market would be automated with high-frequency trading. We may also see it spread to other financial markets such as derivatives markets, including futures and forwards contracts, options, swaps, and credit derivatives. Let us look at the sizes of the different financial markets to understand the implications of the migration of high-frequency trading from the equity market to the derivatives markets.

The size of the world stock market was estimated at about $36.6 trillion at the beginning of October 2008. The *total* world derivatives market has been estimated at about $791 trillion at face or nominal value, 11 times the size of the entire world economy. If these data are stable to date, regardless of whether they are face versus hard values, globally the size of the derivatives markets may be roughly more than 21 times that of the equity market.

This may be derived from Saunders's data. In his *Financial Institutions Management*, the U.S. derivatives contracts with 25 major banks in September 2006 (in millions of U.S. dollars) are listed, along with the equity value of these banks. According to the data (Saunders and Cornett 2008, p. 692), the total assets of banks (about $8 trillion) equal a very small portion of the derivatives contracts (about $126 trillion).

Therefore, the migration of high-frequency trading from the equity market to the derivatives markets may imply a much bigger revenue pool. It would be reasonable to argue that the future revenue models for high-frequency trading would lie largely in the derivatives markets.

We may also see that high-frequency trading operations would go global. Similar to the United States, in Europe, electronic trading and high-frequency trading have been adopted as a major tool to improving the liquidity of the security markets.

One of the largest global markets in the future for high-frequency trading is emerging markets, including Asia, and especially China. Financial derivatives markets in China are not available, but the Chinese government is planning to create these markets in 2010 or later. Assuming the evolution of the Chinese financial derivatives markets would follow that of the United

States and Europe, we would see a lot of opportunities for high-frequency trading systems globally.

In the future, there are quite a few uncertainties for high-frequency trading. For example, we are not sure if flash order functionality will continue to exist. Similar to the traditional exchanges settings, a flash order is first exposed to members of the exchange a short time before it is dispatched to the world. The U.S. Congress and exchanges are investigating the flash order practice, and some have suggested that the flash order functionality should not be offered, as it is not fair to all investors.

NASDAQ offers flash orders and flash-enhanced routing strategies. This is especially beneficial for registered members of the exchange who are claimed to have access to the flash orders 30 milliseconds prior to other investors. According to NASDAQ (2009), the flash functionality provides additional order display opportunities for customers and makes routable orders more efficient and cost effective.

Before the high-frequency trading practice may hit most of the over-the-counter (OTC) derivatives, derivative securities in the United States has a lot of clean-up to do. For example, options, futures, and swaps are designed for risk management. Yet the abuse of these instruments contributed largely to the financial meltdown in 2008, starting from the bankruptcy of Lehman Brothers followed by the bailout of AIG. One of the major cleanups would be to reprice and improve the liquidity of the estimated $6+ trillion CDS (credit default swaps) market. This includes revising the CDS pricing software. To be specific, one may have to research the now open-source CDS software to reprice derivatives for trades, for over-the-counter CDSs at present, or possibly in the future through exchanges with high-frequency trading.

Knowing the history and future of high-frequency trading, the next question is how to position it in investment management. Let us look at the service providers of investment management, followed by the positioning of high-frequency trading in investment management.

INVESTMENT MANAGEMENT AND FINANCIAL INSTITUTIONS

Investment management is a service provided by and for financial institutions. In general, there are five types of financial institutions: (1) investment banks and securities firms; (2) depository institutions such as commercial banks; (3) insurance companies; (4) mutual funds and hedge funds;; (5) finance companies. All these institutions are related to investment management. We use Table 3.1 to illustrate the details.

TABLE 3.1 Financial Institutions and Investment Management

Financial Institution	Core Business	Relevance to Investment Management
Investment banks and securities firms	Issue new securities, e.g., firm-commitment underwriting	Core business of investment management
Commercial banks as depository institutions	Collect deposits and make loans, e.g., mortgage loans may be packaged and sold to investment banks to create mortgage-backed securities (MBS)	The capital collected from retail investors has to be invested properly to cover deposit interest and profit
Insurance companies	Collect premiums from policyholders and pay out for adverse events	The premium collected has to be invested properly to cover payouts, operation expenses, and profits
Mutual funds and hedge funds	Financial inventions to diversify pooled financial resource and invest with proper risk management	Both are investment instruments in which other institutions or individuals invest capital
Finance companies	Make loans to commercial or retail borrowers and collect repayment with interest	The institution is an investment practice itself

Based on Table 3.1, we find that the core businesses of the financial institutions are so closely related to investment management that without investment management, the core businesses may not exist. As a result, we may use investment management to capture the core activities of major financial institutions.

HIGH-FREQUENCY TRADING AND INVESTMENT MANAGEMENT

Summarizing previous discussions, we have seen that high-frequency trading extends program trading, which is one of the four types of trading transactions of investment banks or securities firms. The investment banks and securities firms are financial institutions that form the backbone of the investment management industry. Therefore, high-frequency trading is closely related to the investment management industry.

Figure 3.1 below illustrates the relationship between high-frequency trading and investment management. It also shows the connections between revenue models and investment banking, and the connections between mutual/hedge funds and investing/trading. The foundations of high-frequency trading are information technology for computer algos and statistical/quantitative models for formulas.

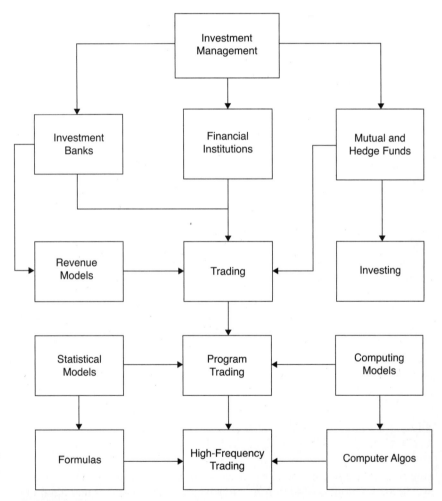

FIGURE 3.1 High-Frequency Trading and Investment Management

TECHNOLOGY INVENTIONS TO DRIVE FINANCIAL INVENTIONS

In history, technological innovations have driven financial inventions. For example, before the Internet era, U.S. billing systems relied primarily on the post office to send bills. With the advent of the Internet, more and more people pay bills online. The computer system built on the Internet is a technology-based financial invention that enables efficiency and convenience with online billing (a financial invention). Another example of financial inventions driven by technology is online banking, which becomes more and more important for consumers to check balances at will. These financial inventions are enabled by technological inventions such as the Internet and the new information technology for Web development.

The development of real-time computer algos is a technological innovation that explores new areas in securities trading systems where the developers of legacy financial models had no opportunities to explore. Technological innovation will give rise to financial inventions, such as the sentiment asset pricing engine (SAPE), which includes a new theory and a new formula on behavioral investing, and a new computer system for future asset pricing and portfolio management. We will elaborate on SAPE and its impact on portfolio and investment management in later chapters.

Writing this book gives me a good opportunity to think about the impact of technology for finance and investment at a very high level. With high-frequency trading representing the use of advanced technology for finance and investment management, it would be beneficial to assess the impact of high-frequency trading on the current industry and the future of the industry. I argue that high-frequency trading represents the future direction of finance and investment management in the sense that information technology may have a profound if not revolutionary impact on finance in academia and practice. It may turn investment management from an art, or a semi-art and semi-science, to a science that is fully based on mathematics and computer science.

THE ULTIMATE GOAL FOR MODELS AND FINANCIAL INVENTIONS

One may be a bit confused by the goals of learning these many revenue and financial models of high-frequency trading in investment management. It seems that the only goal is to maximize profit for a few rich people.

On the surface, the models that will be discussed in this book attempt to maximize returns at minimum risk. This is consistent with many other writings and theories in finance. However, we would like to point out that the ultimate goal of financial inventions is for people's well-being. It is for the happiness and well-being of the people that the financial industry is serving, and the financial practitioners, including financial education practitioners.

In many cases, like Hollywood movies, financial practitioners are portrayed as being cold-hearted people who care little about the well-being of others. In reality, this is not the case. There are a lot of good people in this industry. And believe it or not, about 20 percent of the northeastern economy of the United States is primarily related to financial practice such as investment management, insurance, and other financial institutions.

Another example of people-oriented financial activities is the philanthropists who achieved a great success in financial practice and in return give back to society. For example, Warren Buffett, an extremely successful private investor, and Bill Gates, an extremely successful information technology practitioner, donated more than 90 percent of their wealth to creating not-for-profit foundations to help society. In addition, many business schools are aware of the needs of humanity, especially after the financial crisis in 2008. The Johns Hopkins Carey Business School has the following slogan on its web site: Where business is taught with humanity in mind—to reflect that the ultimate goal of business and finance education is people's well-being and happiness.

The point, improving other people's happiness and well-being as the ultimate goal of financial and investment management, has its roots in psychology, religion, and even biological science. Let's look at a simple social experiment that I did with my students. As part of a homework assignment near the holiday season, students were asked to allocate a certain amount of money, say $20, then divide the money in half. They were then asked to spend one half on themselves, maybe watching a movie, buying clothes for themselves, and so on. The other half was to be spent on others, such as charitable donations or buying gifts for loved ones. When the students came back to class, I asked them to evaluate the happiness of their activities, which type of spending produced a happier result for themselves. More than 95 percent of the students responded that spending on others produced more satisfaction than spending on themselves. They also responded that the recipients of the spending were joyful, which doubled the sense of well-being from spending on others. I did this kind of social experiment in more than five business classes in finance or business technology, and each time a similar result was reported.

To elaborate on the point, here is a Johns Hopkins graduate student's thoughts on happiness and the social experiments:[1]

> *The Financial Institutions course has been a very interesting class to be a part of. The class went beyond its main topic, financial institutions, and touched on a bigger and more interesting topic, the reason why we're all here on earth and the purpose of our living experience. Extending such a course to cover real life was undone before, at least as far as I know. And it is what made the class mostly interesting.*
>
> *The reason we are all here is our individual pursuit of happiness. All the classes that we take to get us to the degrees that we need in order to get the jobs and careers that we want are to ultimately make us happier. I took away that true happiness is not material happiness. The things we acquire do not make us happy. Happiness comes from be[ing] at peace within oneself. I personally found the meditating exercise to be a particularly rewarding activity. Meditating helped me rechannel my thoughts and my energy. It brought me a sense of peace, which is a big part of happiness. I was happy within myself. Also we feel better, hence happier, when we belong to a community and positively contribute to its well-being. I drew this conclusion from the Thanksgiving assignment, which was to spend money on ourselves and someone else, and take note of which one of the two was more rewarding. The smile on that person's face immediately made me feel happy.*
>
> *Overall, I took from this course a valuable life lesson. This lesson extends beyond the topic of Finance. This is a lesson I won't forget and my goal is to pass it along to people around me and make the world a happier place.*

Not only were the recipients of the students' spending joyful, the initiators (students) were happier, too. This reflects a fundamental principle of human needs and the production of human well-being: Serving others would create much more output in human well-being as a whole than serving selves. We code this as the amplifying effect of happiness. Let's imagine that the world has a finite amount of wealth or spending capacity. If it is spent by the people who have access to it on themselves, then the summation of the well-being it generates is far less than the well-being it generates if the people spend it on others. Therefore, why not create financial instruments to motivate the spending on others in order to maximize the return of the finite financial resources as a whole?

The tax system in public finance does some of this, knowingly or not. But we have done very little in this arena as a whole, maybe partly because most of us are not aware of this principle of human needs and financial resource spending, namely the amplifying effect of happiness. Hence, new financial instruments and systems should be designed to maximize well-being as a whole as the result of spending the world's finite financial capacity on others.

To summarize, at a higher level of abstraction, the ultimate goal of financial models and inventions should be maximizing the well-being and happiness of people as a whole, by using new financial instruments to motivate the spending of the finite financial resource on others.

CONCLUSION

In this chapter, we discussed the history and future of high-frequency trading as it relates to the ultimate goal of innovation in investment management: improving human well-being as a whole. We also proposed that high-frequency trading, reflecting technological innovation in finance, would give rise to new forms of financial innovation as well.

Theoretical Models as Foundation of Computer Algos for High-Frequency Trading

I n Part II we introduce a series of behavioral economics models along with financial and quantitative models. As a result, a solid theoretical foundation for building behavioral investing and trading strategies for portfolio management is established. Building on this foundation, Part Three develops a unique set of computer algos to automate the process of building behavioral trading strategies for high-frequency trading and portfolio management.

Few writings in investment management have touched the fundamental principles of behavioral economics models. Behavioral finance, a subfield of behavioral economics, thus has not been supported rigorously by behavioral economics models. In Part II, we attempt to stress the rigorous modeling and empirical aspect of behavioral economics. We hope to build solid theoretical foundations for establishing a new subfield of behavioral finance, that is, behavioral investing. As a result, we may enrich high-frequency trading with computer algos that incorporate investors' psychological factors.

CHAPTER 4

Behavioral Economics Models on Loss Aversion

I n this chapter, we discuss a new theoretical model on loss aversion by linking the self-other asymmetry in judgment to the loss-gain asymmetry in choice. Part of the chapter adapts one of the author's journal articles (Ye, 2005).

WHAT IS LOSS AVERSION?

The central concept in behavioral economics is loss aversion of the prospect theory (Kahneman and Tversky 2000). Loss aversion suggests an empirical finding that losses loom larger than the same amount of gains (Kahneman and Tversky 1979). In their 1979 article that led to the Nobel Prize in 2002, Kahneman and Tversky described the finding in detail with experiments and mathematical formulas to support the finding. Ever since, the central concept evolves into a discipline that forms the foundation of behavioral economics, economic psychology, behavioral finance, and so forth.

THE LOCUS EFFECT

As a manifestation of loss aversion, an investor or consumer[1] tends to stay with the status quo (e.g., an owned fund) rather than switch to a new brand (fund) because losing the status quo looms larger than gaining the new brand.[2] Inertia equity assesses the difference between mental losses and gains, representing loss aversion in the brand switching context. It is the difference between the price that will induce an investor or consumer to switch to a competitor's brand and the price of the brand the investor has typically been using in the past (i.e., the anchoring price). We find that inertia equity is smaller when investors or consumers evaluate peer customers (locus of others), than evaluating themselves (locus of self) to switch brands, which is coded as the locus effect on inertia equity. The asymmetric value function postulated by the prospect theory is employed to describe inertia equity. The locus effect is then derived after linking the self-other asymmetry to the value function. The difference between valuing losses and gains in brand switching is larger for self-related than others' items because investors or consumers are more sensitive to self-related losses than others' equivalent losses. It is also found that the locus effect is applicable to brands with various anchoring prices.

Suppose you currently use Verizon (a major U.S. wireless firm) as your wireless service provider, with a monthly payment of $60 for 600 peak minutes and unlimited night and weekend minutes. For the same service, Cingular (another major U.S. wireless firm) would like to win you over by offering a price reduction. Suppose you have no financial obligations (e.g., year-long contracts) to stay with Verizon. How much reduction in price will induce you to switch to Cingular?

A small price reduction, say $1, may not be sufficient to induce consumers to conduct brand switching because consumers hold a propensity to stay with the status quo rather than change. This propensity is robust and is coded as the status quo bias (Samuelson and Zeckhauser 1988; Kahneman and Tversky 2000). According to Kahneman, Knetsch, and Thaler (1991, p. 205), "after more than a decade of research on this topic we have become convinced that the status quo bias, endowment effect, and aversion to losses are both robust and important."

What is the minimum price reduction, or the just noticeable difference of price between the price from competitor brands and the price of the brand the customer has typically been using in the past (i.e., the anchoring price), to induce consumers to switch? Say $15 will work in the case of switching wireless firms with $60 monthly payment. The amount of price difference to induce brand switching (e.g., the "15 dollars") is coded as the inertia equity. The term "inertia" means the propensity to stay with the status quo. The term "anchoring" comes from Tversky and Kahneman (1974) to reflect the biased evaluations toward reference points. Throughout the article, we also refer to the home brand (the status quo) as brand A, and the competitor brand as brand B.

From a macro perspective, inertia equity can be traced back to brand inertia (Guadagni and Little 1983), which is later used as a main predictor in the customer equity models that describe the various drivers of customer equity. Customer equity is defined as the total of the discounted (expected) lifetime values summed over all of the firm's current and potential customers. The "brand inertia" is a vital part of the switching matrix that forms the basis of the model to calculate customer equity (for a detailed description, see Rust, Lemon, and Zeithaml 2004). As the result of applying the customer equity model to the airline industry, the "inertia" driver explains a large portion of the variances to predict the magnitude of customer equity (Rust, Lemon, and Zeithaml 2004). Therefore, inertia equity is a vital part of customer equity.

From a micro perspective, inertia equity assesses inertia value, which is the difference of mental values for gaining the new brand and losing the home brand. Brand switching entails a process of losing home brands and gaining new brands (van Heerde, Gupta, and Wittink 2003). In separate articles, we have demonstrated that the behavioral source of "inertia equity" is the status quo bias (Samuelson and Zeckhauser 1988) that describes a robust propensity for consumers to stay with home brands rather than switch to competitor brands. The status quo bias is a manifestation of the principle of loss aversion (Kahneman and Tversky 2000), namely, losses loom larger than gains (Kahneman and Tversky 1979). Although we acknowledge potential alternatives to loss aversion to account for inertia (Casey 1995), the widely accepted principle of loss aversion and the status quo bias is more meaningful and parsimonious in fitting with the brand switching situation.

Due to the asymmetry of valuing losses and gains (Kahneman and Tversky 1979, 2000), the difference of the mental values ("psychologically richer" utility; Thaler 1985) between losses and gains is the source of inertia equity (the monetary difference). In other words, inertia equity assesses the magnitude of loss aversion, namely, the difference of mental losses and gains. Therefore, a congruent (e.g., log-linear) relationship holds true between inertia values and inertia equity. The larger the inertia value, the larger inertia equity will be, and vice versa.

Previous studies have identified several factors that influence inertia equity. The magnitude of the anchoring price is one. We find that the larger the anchoring price, the larger the inertia equity will be. This is consistent with what a principle of psychophysics of pricing (i.e., Weber's law) predicts for price sensitivity in a noncompetition environment (Monroe 2003; Nunes and Park 2003; Grewal and Marmorstein 1994). Weber's law predicts that the just noticeable difference of the price change of a single brand or product will increase as the magnitude of base price increases

(Monroe 1971). In a competition context (the brand switching entails at least two brands), we find that inertia equity, holding the property of a "threshold" (just noticeable difference), appears to also increase as the magnitude of anchoring price increases.

Another factor that influences inertia equity is the level of exposure. It has been extensively demonstrated that prior mere exposure to an item increases the affect to the item (Zajonc 1968; Bornstein 1989). We also find that previous overexposure to the item will decrease the affect and inertia equity. For example, frequently repeated (over) exposure (consumption) to the same product or item (e.g., restaurant) will induce a decrease in the affect toward the product or item (Howard and Sheth 1969; Bornstein 1989), thus a decrease in the inertia equity. In separate studies, we use experimental studies to empirically support that both the magnitude of the anchoring price and the level of exposure can affect the inertia equity.

Along the lines of investigating factors that may impact inertia equity, we study a new factor in the present study, the locus of evaluating self or others (Kruger and Dunning 1999; Pronin, Kruger, Savitsky, and Ross 2001). The locus of self means consumers consider a just noticeable price difference to switch brands for themselves (assuming themselves to be the consumers that use the home brand), while the locus of others means that consumers consider a just noticeable price difference for others to switch brands (assuming others to be the consumers that use the home brand).

The first question of interest is: Will the shift from the locus of self to others impact the magnitude of inertia equity? If yes, we will code it as the locus effect or the self-other asymmetry on inertia equity because various theories on the self-other asymmetry in judgment may serve as the antecedents. The second question is: Will anchoring prices affect the self-other asymmetry in choice?

These questions have not been investigated before but are of vital importance to the literature relevant to marketing management and prospect theory. This is because inertia equity (i.e., equivalent to "brand inertia" from a macro perspective) is a vital portion of customer equity, which becomes one of the top research priorities of marketing management (Rust, Lemon, and Zeithaml 2004). Investigating factors that impact the inertia equity will be instrumental to offering strategies to managing the customer equity in service-oriented firms.

Linking the self-other asymmetry to loss-gain asymmetry underscores and extends the literature relevant to prospect theory (Kahneman and Tversky 1979, 2000), especially to the principle of loss aversion. In an enhanced value function that describes loss aversion (see Figure 4.1), we demonstrate that the principle holds true in a new context. That is, we show that loss aversion occurs on the evaluation for peers as well as on the

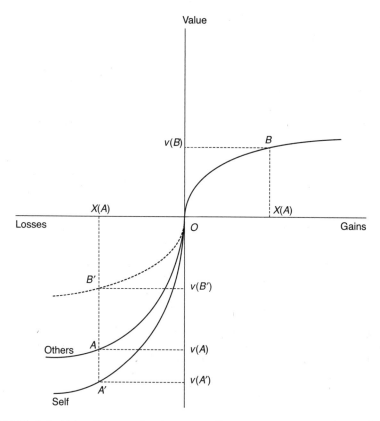

FIGURE 4.1 Value Function for the Locus Effect

evaluation for self. In the meantime, an alternate assessment approach on the magnitude of the loss-gain asymmetry is proposed. The magnitude of loss aversion is assessed by the difference between mental losses and gains with inertia equity, rather than the unequal relationship between the mental losses and gains. Further extensions of loss aversion include the self-other asymmetry on the losses of self-related items (e.g., the home brand) that reduces the inertia equity (i.e., the magnitude of loss aversion).

THEORY AND HYPOTHESES

Because the root of inertia equity is loss aversion, we will first analyze the questions and derive hypotheses from a theoretical perspective, based on the asymmetric value function postulated by prospect theory (Kahneman and Tversky 1979, 2000). Then we will design experiments to test the hypotheses. In previous studies, we derive predictions on anchoring price and inertia equity on the basis of the asymmetric functions and then support the predictions with the empirical data. This approach is used extensively in behavioral decision theory studies. For example, it has been used to report the status quo bias (Samuelson and Zeckhauser 1988), and provide evidence for loss aversion (losses loom larger than gains) (Kahneman and Tversky 1979, 2000) and mental accounting (a manifestation of loss aversion) (Thaler 1985). Hence, a similar approach is employed to derive and test the hypotheses in the present study.

The prospect theory is relevant to marketing and consumer research because it is the foundation of one of the two schools of consumer and marketing research, that is, behavioral decision theory (Simonson, Carmon, Dhar, Drolet, and Nowlis 2001). The other school is rooted in social cognition (Wyer and Srull 1986; Simonson et al. 2001). In general, the school of behavioral decision theory investigates choices (selections) with two or more options. On the other hand, the school of social cognition investigates judgments on or responses to an object (i.e., one option).

Self-Other Asymmetry and Loss Aversion

Several theories in the school of social cognition have documented the self-other asymmetry in judgments. For example, attribution theory postulates that people tend to attribute their own behavior to external factors, but attribute others' behavior to dispositional factors (Kelley 1973). Recently, the social cognition research has demonstrated the asymmetry in people's assessments of their own knowledge relative to that of their peers (Pronin, Kruger, Savitsky, and Ross 2001). Specifically, people tend to hold overly favorable views of their own abilities in many social and intellectual domains (Kruger and Dunning 1999).

We may speculate a self-other asymmetry on various domains (including inertia equity in the choice domain) on the basis of these theories. However, there are two aspects that the social cognition theories need help to go further with its application to the choice domain (i.e., on inertia equity in brand switching). One is the conceptualization of inertia equity, namely, what is the difference between self and others? The other is the direction of the asymmetry on inertia equity, namely, which one (self or others) needs a larger inertia equity to switch brands? This gives rise to the need to link the self-other asymmetry in judgment to the loss-gain asymmetry in choice. However, little research has documented the relevance of the self-other asymmetry in social cognition to the gain-loss asymmetry in prospect theory.

The conceptualization of inertia equity comes from the loss aversion that is postulated by prospect theory. Inertia equity is derived from status quo bias, which is a manifestation of loss aversion. The inertia equity reflects the difference between mental gains and losses. Therefore, the self-other asymmetry on inertia equity links the self-other asymmetry in judgment to the loss aversion that is assessed by inertia equity. As a result, the focus of the present study is not on the causes of self-other asymmetry in social cognition, but on the relationship between self-other asymmetry and the principle of loss aversion.

The directional prediction of the self-other asymmetry on inertia equity requires help from the value function of prospect theory, which conceptualizes the switch cost (i.e., the inertia equity) in brand switching. It is further explored as the locus effect on inertia equity.

The Locus Effect on Inertia Equity

As we know, the asymmetric value function of prospect theory has been used to derive predictions in the literature relevant to mental accounting and endowment effect (see Figure 1 of Thaler 1985). Similarly, the asymmetric value function initiated by Kahneman and Tversky (1979) is enhanced in Figure 4.1. It is then used to derive directional predictions for the relationship between self-other asymmetry and loss aversion.

In addition to the original curves (OB and OA'), two more curves (OB' and OA) are added to the Kahneman and Tversky (1979) function. In Figure 4.1, unsigned OB' is identical to OB (the concave curve for gains), that is, $v(B) = v(B')$, except drawn in the section of losses, for the purpose of comparison. OA is the convex curve of losses for the locus of others. OA' is the convex curve of losses for the locus of self. We assume that consumers are more sensitive to self-related losses (in terms of money or the value of the old brand) than to peers' equivalent losses. So the convex curve OA' (locus of self) is steeper than OA (locus of others).

We code the inertia value as the difference between valuing losses and gains, that is, $v(A') - v(B)$ or $v(A) - v(B)$. Consumers must overcome the inertia values psychologically to conduct a brand switching. Because OA' is steeper than OA, the inertia value, $v(A') - v(B)$, for the locus of self is larger than the inertia value for the locus of others, $v(A) - v(B)$. With a congruent (e.g., log-linear) relationship assumed between inertia value and inertia equity, we predict that inertia equity will be larger for the locus of self than others. In other words, consumers will estimate more price reductions for themselves than for others to switch brands. The difference will be coded as the locus effect, stated as H_1.

H_1: the magnitude of inertia equity for the locus of self will be larger than the locus of others

There is one assumption required to derive H_1, stated as A_1, that will be tested in study 2:

A_1: consumers are more sensitive to self-related (personal) losses than to others' losses of the same amount, that is, in Figure 4.1, $v(A') > v(A)$, a steeper loss curve for self (OA') than for others (OA).

Assumption A_1 describes a manifestation of the self-other asymmetry in judgment because it addresses responses to one option (i.e., loss of an object or a brand) rather than comparing two options.

The values in Figure 4.1, such as $v(A')$ and $v(A)$, represent the experienced utility, or the experience of pleasure and pain (Kahneman and Tversky 2000). Intuitively, A_1 is likely to hold true. It assumes that consumers are more sensitive (e.g., hurt or disappointed) to the losses of self-related (personal) items than the similar losses of others. In other words, the convex curve for the locus of self (losing my old firm), OA', is more distant than the locus of others (others losing their old firm), OA, for the same magnitude of losses (e.g., unsigned $X[A]$). Nevertheless, we attempt to test A_1 in study 2.

Anchoring Price and the Locus Effect

As the locus effect on inertia equity is a new effect derived on the basis of the prospect theory, little literature can be found to speculate the relationship between anchoring price and the locus effect. However, this relationship is practically important to marketing management. It answers the question: Will the locus effect exist in products and brands with various price ranges? In other words, what is the applicability of the locus effect?

We have to use common sense to derive the hypothesis on the applicability of the effect. When comparing trading a single-family house (a large price anchor) and trading a wireless service plan (a small price anchor), suppose you will estimate the switch cost from house A to B, and from plan A to B. Will the estimated cost be different between yours and others' (say, a friend's friend) for switching houses? Will the estimated cost be different between yours and others' for switching wireless service plans? Intuitively, we speculate that the difference between yours and others' (i.e., the self-other asymmetry) will occur regardless of the fact that the items are small (e.g., the plans) or large (e.g., the houses). Hence, we predict:

H_2: the magnitude of anchoring price will not affect the locus effect on inertia equity.

In the following sections, we design experiments to empirically test H_1 and H_2 in study 1, followed by an attempt in study 2 to validate the assumption A_1 to derive H_1.

STUDY 1: THE LOCUS EFFECT ON INERTIA EQUITY

The hypotheses are made that the inertia equity will decrease as the locus of evaluation shifts from self to others, and the locus effect will not be affected by anchoring prices. We will design an experiment to empirically test the two hypotheses. The methodology has been used in previous studies that are similar to the ones used in Samuelson and Zeckhauser (1988) on status quo bias and Thaler (1985) on mental accounting.

Respondents

Fifty undergraduate students from a U.S. university participated in the study. All students were aware of the service plans for wireless cellular and many of them were cell phone users.

Design

The base design was a 2 (locus: self versus others) by 2 (anchoring price: $30 versus $90) between-subjects factorial with both the locus of evaluation and the monthly service plan charges (anchoring prices) as the between-subjects factors. A total of four conditions were created. Students were randomly assigned to one of the four conditions. They were presented with a question and then prompted to provide estimates of just noticeable price differences for them or others to switch to competitor wireless firms.

For the locus of self, the question is "Let A and B be two similar wireless firms with equal offerings in everything except price. Assuming you are A's customer paying a monthly service charge fee (price) of $30. Firm B offers you a price reduction to win you over. Assuming you decide to switch to firm B at a minimum (threshold) price reduction, what would be firm B's price reduction to win you over?"

For the locus of others, the question is "Let A and B be two similar wireless firms with equal offerings in everything except price. Assuming a customer of firm A pays a monthly service charge fee (price) of $30. Firm B offers the customer a price reduction to win him (her) over. Assuming the customer decides to switch to firm B at a minimum (threshold) price reduction, what would be firms B's price reduction to win over the customer?"

The other two conditions of the factorial design varied the magnitude of the anchoring prices. One was with the locus of self and $90. The other was with the locus of others and $90. For all the conditions, all other factors that might impact the brand switching (e.g., transaction costs) except price were assumed to be invariant. For example, the mobile phone numbers were assumed to be portable.

Results

An analysis of variance (*ANOVA*) was performed with inertia equity (the just noticeable price reduction from competitor brands) as the dependent variable. Independent variables were locus of evaluation and anchoring price.

With inertia equity being the dependent variable, the main effect of locus (self vs. others) was significant ($F(1, 46) = 5.94, p < .05$), effect size (partial eta squared) $= .11$. The main effect of anchoring price was also significant ($F(1, 46) = 31.45, p < .05$), effect size (partial eta squared) $= .41$. The interaction between locus and anchoring price was insignificant ($F(1, 46) = 1.56, p > .05$), effect size (partial eta squared) $= .03$. According to Cohen (1988), an effect size is categorized as trivial if it is less than 0.1. The trivial effect size of interaction suggests that the interaction effect would be ignored because it is too small (i.e., only 3 percent of the variance is accounted for by the interaction). We use effect sizes (rather than the level of significance) to measure the association of strength between factors and dependent variables, especially when the effect sizes are trivial (Cohen, 1988).

In Figure 4.2, when the locus of evaluation shifts from self to others, the means (with standard errors in the parentheses) of inertia equity

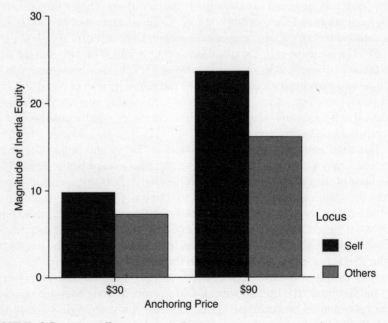

FIGURE 4.2 Locus Effect on Inertia Equity

decrease at the anchoring price of \$30 from 9.71 (1.72) to 7.27 (2.14); and at the anchoring price of \$90, from 23.75 (2.05) to 16.20 (2.25). Similarly, the larger the anchoring price, the larger the inertia equity will be, regardless of the locus of evaluation. The insignificant interaction suggests that the locus effect is not affected by the magnitude of the anchoring price (\$30 or \$90).

Conclusions

Both H_1 and H_2 are supported by empirical data. The main effect for the locus of evaluation empirically supports H_1 in that consumers need a larger price reduction from competitor brands if assuming themselves rather than others to switch brands. The insignificant interaction (between the locus and the anchoring prices) empirically supports H_2 in that the magnitude of anchoring price may not moderate the relationship between inertia equity and the locus of evaluation. In summary, the locus effect is supported analytically and empirically, and the locus effect is not affected by a change in the anchoring price.

STUDY 2: ASSUMPTION A_1 AND A_2

The goal of study 2 is to explore evidence to support A_1 and A_2 that have been previously used to derive H_1. The assumption A_1 to derive H_1 describes that consumers are more sensitive to self-related (personal) losses than to others' similar losses, for instance, in Figure 4.1, $v(A') > v(A)$. In other words, we assume that curve OA' is steeper over OA. Intuitively, A_1 appears to be consistent with common wisdom. For example, one would be more sensitive to losing their own books than the feelings on others' losing the same kind of books. We attempt to validate A_1 with a simple approach.

In addition to A_1, another assumption (A_2) states that the principle of loss aversion (people are more sensitive to losses than equivalent gains) will hold true if consumers assume others, as the customers, will make a brand switching choice. In other words, the loss and gain asymmetry holds true if consumers assume others to make the choice. Represented in Figure 4.1, OA (loss curve for others) is steeper than OB. As we know, OA' (loss curve for self) is steeper than OB, as postulated by prospect theory.

Respondents

Thirty-six undergraduate students from a U.S. Northeastern university participated in the study.

EDINBURGH UNIVERSITY LIBRARY
WITHDRAWN

Design

The base design was a paired comparison, with the dependent variable being students' rating of the feeling about their own or others' loss of a textbook valued at $100. The order of rating on themselves or others was counterbalanced, with half of the students rating themselves first, and the other half rating others first. This is to eliminate a potential order effect in ratings because we are not investigating order effect.

The elicitation question for the locus of self is "Suppose you lost a textbook valued at $100. Please rate your feelings on a scale of 1 to 10, 1 being extremely disappointed and 10 being extremely pleased." The elicitation question for the locus of others is "Suppose a student of the college of business lost a textbook valued at $100. Please rate your feelings on a scale of 1 to 10, 1 being extremely disappointed and 10 being extremely pleased." We expect that the ratings on self-related items will be lower than on others' similar items.

Results

A paired sample t-test was performed to compare the difference of the ratings on the self-related and others' losses. A significant difference was found between the means of the two ratings, $t(35) = -5.45$, $p < .05$. The mean of the ratings on self was 2.61 (1.86), and on others 4.75 (2.05), with standard deviations in parentheses.

Discussion on A_1

A_1 is validated with the empirical data from study 2. Consumers are more sensitive (hurt or disappointed) toward the loss of self-related items than the similar loss of the others. Therefore, assuming a steeper curve for OA' than OA (see Figure 4.1) is based on the assumption (A_1) that is validated by empirical data.

The causes of the self-other asymmetry in perceiving a loss may be relevant to various beliefs. For example, the endowment effect implies that the ownership of self-owned items can be assessed monetarily (Thaler 1985). Ownership may create more value for self-owned items than for others' items. Other variables might account for the self-other asymmetry in judgment as well. For example, the respondents perceived themselves to be not as well off financially as the others, or they felt that they were more disciplined than others, and so on.

However, the focus of the present study is not on the causes of the self-other asymmetry in judgment, but on the application of the asymmetry to inertia equity that assesses the magnitude of loss aversion. For study 2, we need empirical evidence to support A_1 that has been used to derive H_1. We achieve the goal of study 2 when A_1 and A_2 are supported.

Validation of A_2

Another implicit assumption (A_2) is used to derive H_1. A_2 states that the principle of loss aversion will hold true if respondents assess the inertia equity (i.e., the switch cost) for peers (others). This is shown in Figure 4.1 that curve OA (the curve of others) is more distant from OB'.

A_2 is validated with the data from study 1 that the values of inertia equity (if assuming others as the customers) are larger than zero ($t(49) = 10.43$, $p < .5$), rejecting the null hypothesis that the inertia equity is equal to zero. This is inferred from the fact that the inertia value is greater than zero ($v(A) - v(B) > 0$). As inertia values are equal to the differences between the values of losses and gains, consumers have shown more sensitivity (experience of pleasure or pain) to the losses than to similar gains ($v(A) > v(B)$) if assuming others as the consumers to switch brands. In other words, consumers follow the principle of loss aversion regardless of the locus of evaluation.

GENERAL DISCUSSION

We will discuss the implications of the locus effect to the literature relevant to prospect theory and marketing management in customer retention and acquisition, followed by a section on further research.

Theoretical Implications

The locus effect on inertia equity underscores and extends the literature relevant to prospect theory. It underscores the principle of loss aversion in choice contexts where peers' experience is considered. It also extends the understanding of the impact of the magnitude of loss aversion on the self-other asymmetry in judgment.

Little literature relevant to prospect theory has examined the influence of the locus of evaluation on the asymmetric relationship between losses and gains. In general, the literature relevant to prospect theory describes principles for choices on the locus of self (e.g., loss aversion on self's experiences). For example, consumers estimate their experience of pleasure and pain on their own gains and losses, coded as the experienced utility (Kahneman and Tversky 2000). Estimating the pain and pleasure of others' losses and gains uses a different angle. That is, the group-oriented choice considers peers' experience in a choice context.

With the loss aversion examined in peers' experience, we underscore the principle in a new choice context. We find that the principle of loss aversion (asymmetry of valuing losses and gains) holds true regardless of the locus of evaluation. In other words, loss aversion (losses loom larger than gains) occurs on evaluating self-related items. It occurs on evaluating peers' items as well (see assumption A_2).

The locus effect on inertia equity extends our understanding of the dynamics of the magnitude of loss aversion. First, inertia equity proposes an alternate assessment of the magnitude of loss aversion. It assesses the difference between the mental losses and gains, rather than describing the relationship between mental losses and gains.

Second, it demonstrates the impact of the locus of evaluation on the magnitude of loss aversion. On the basis of the asymmetrical relationship between self and others' experiences on one option (A_1), a new convex curve for others' losses is added to the asymmetric value function of prospect theory (see Figure 4.1). A steeper curve for self-related than for others' losses is validated with the empirical data. As a result, the locus effect (more value difference between losses and gains for self than for others) is derived with the added loss curve. It shows that the magnitude of loss aversion is reduced when the locus of evaluation shifts from self to others. Therefore, consumers estimate a larger switch cost for themselves than for others. With these findings supported analytically and empirically, the locus effect on inertia equity extends the literature relevant to loss aversion.

Further Research

The locus effect, which describes that consumers estimate more price reduction for themselves than for others to induce brand switching, is derived from linking the self-other asymmetry in judgment to the asymmetric value function of prospect theory.

One assumption (A_1) is that consumers are more sensitive to the losses of self-related than others' items. To simplify the derivation for the current study (H_1), consumers' sensitivity to gains is implicitly assumed to be invariant for the locus of self and others, coded as assumption A_3. This assumption may be relaxed and validated in further research. If A_3 is relaxed, then the sensitivity to gains varies for the locus of self and others, that is, $v(B)$ for curve OB' in Figure 4.1, may vary for self and others. Hence two concave gains curves may co-exist in the value function of Figure 4.1.

However, even if A_3 is relaxed, the relationship between the value differences, $v(A') - v(B)$ and $v(A) - v(B)$, will still hold true. This is similar to the situation (described in H_1) where $v(B)$ will not vary for self and others. It is because the curves are steeper for losses than gains for the locus of self and others as well, which is assumed and validated as A_2. As a result, the difference between the two loss curves (e.g., OA' and OA) should be larger than the difference between the two gains curves, which give rise to the same prediction (H_1) on the locus effect in the case of a changing $v(B)$ due to the shift of the locus. Provided that A_3 is relaxed, additional evidence to support the prediction (H_1) is the empirical data of study 1. It is inferred that the relationship of the value differences (H_1) will hold invariant regardless of whether $v(B)$ changes as the locus shifts from self to others.

CONCLUSION

Inertia equity is of vital importance to investor retention and acquisition, especially investor (customer) equity management. From a macro perspective, it is a vital part of customer equity. From a micro perspective, it assesses the asymmetry between mental responses to losses and gains. After linking the self-other asymmetry to inertia equity, we find that consumers estimate more price reductions from competitor brands for themselves than for others to initiate a brand switching. This is coded as the locus effect on inertia equity. In other words, the shift of the locus from self to others will give rise to a reduction in inertia equity. This effect is derived after linking the self-other asymmetry in judgment to the asymmetric value functions postulated by prospect theory. The locus effect results from the different value differences between losses and gains for self-related and others' items. The derived effect is later supported by the empirical data. We also find that the locus effect is applicable to brands and products with various anchoring prices.

CHAPTER 5

Loss Aversion in Option Pricing: Integrating Two Nobel Models

As we discussed, loss aversion is the central concept of the prospect theory and behavioral economics (Kahneman and Tversky 1979, 2000). It suggests that losses loom larger than gains. For example, losing $1,000 may cause a stronger mental response in an investor's mind than gaining the same amount of wealth. The empirical finding on loss aversion has been widely demonstrated, thus it is the classic principle of behavioral economics and the backbone for Kahneman's 2002 Nobel Prize.

Option pricing is a typical research and practical topic in financial economics. It refers to the valuation of options that are the right (not commitment) to buy or sell the underlying asset at a specific price in a fixed future date. The Black-Scholes model on option pricing (1973) has pushed the popularity of the option pricing research to a new level. Both the Black-Scholes model and prospect theory have won Nobel Prizes in economics.

However, do these two important topics connect? Little literature or practice has documented the existence of loss aversion in option pricing. In this chapter, we will provide repeatable empirical evidence to demonstrate that the two topics are connected. In other words, loss aversion exists in option pricing. I do this with the help of real-time computer algos.

DEMONSTRATING LOSS AVERSION WITH COMPUTER ALGOS

We use computer algos to demonstrate a real-time empirical finding that loss aversion (Kahneman and Tversky 1979, 2000; Ye 2005) may be observed in option pricing (Black and Scholes, 1973; Hull, 2008). This empirical finding occurs on strike-on-spot prices, which are the closest strike prices to the spot prices of the underlying assets.

The strike-on-spot prices are close to the at-the-money strike prices but the two are different. At-the-money strike prices suggest that the spot prices are equal to the strike prices. As the spot prices in reality change all the time, it is rare to find that at-the-money strike prices and spot prices are the same.

The context to discover loss aversion is with call and put options.[1] For call options, traders feel a gain when a strike price goes up, whereas they suffer a loss when the strike price goes down.

The computer algos are Web-based computer programs that collect real-time empirical data from a randomly selected sample with 32 tickers. The 32 tickers have call premium changes for loss and gain conditions. Call premiums reflect traders' mental evaluation to future events. Hence, the changes of call premiums would reflect the mental responses to the loss or gain conditions.

After collecting the data in real time, real-time t-tests are conducted on the data to check the significant difference in call premium changes between the loss and gain conditions (loss/gain ratio). The results have repeatedly demonstrated that loss aversion does exist in option pricing.

Here is an example. The data in Table 5.1 were captured on November 27, 2009, at 09:09:40:26. These data are generated by proprietary computer algos. A real-time significance test was conducted with this result: The mean of the ratios $= 3.09$; $std = 3.76$; t (31) $= 3.14$; p-value $= 0.00084481$. The result suggests that traders' mental response as call premium changes due to asset price drops is significantly larger than their response to the same price increases. This real-time trial may be repeated many times by refreshing the URL that triggers the computing. Therefore, the real-time computer algos have repeatedly demonstrated the empirical finding of loss aversion in option pricing.

We also found evidence for the case of put options. The data show that the put premium changes due to losses (price up) is significantly larger than the put premium change due to gains (price down).

If we change the locus of forming losses and gains conditions, namely, shifting the locus of strike-on-spot prices, the effect may disappear. So the moderator for loss aversion in option pricing may be the distance between the strike price and the current spot price of the underlying asset. The loss aversion may disappear when the strike price of the option is distant from the current spot price. This is consistent with the empirical finding in other contexts of the locus effect of loss aversion (see previous chapter). The locus effect of loss aversion suggests that the strength of loss aversion may be affected by the locus of evaluation on self or others.

TABLE 5.1 Real-Time Empirical Evidence—Call Options

Tick	Premium Change Due to Loss	Due to Same Gain	Ratio
ACH	0.35	0.40	0.87
ACI	0.55	0.35	1.57
ACL	1.70	1.67	1.02
GOOG	5.15	3.75	1.37
MSFT	1.40	0.32	4.38
ACO	1.75	0.95	1.84
ACS	3.80	1.35	2.81
IBM	4.21	2.46	1.71
MMM	2.90	0.55	5.27
C	0.92	0.23	4.00
CA	1.83	0.52	3.52
CAB	1.70	0.50	3.40
MOT	0.86	0.39	2.21
CAH	4.39	2.46	1.78
CAJ	5.50	0	0
CAL	0.80	0.50	1.60
CAT	3.19	0.76	4.20
CAM	1.95	1.15	1.70
FAZ	0.48	0.32	1.50
CAR	1.95	0.60	3.25
ORCL	0.57	0.28	2.04
DCI	3.65	0.55	6.64
T	0.70	0.35	2
CBS	0.88	0.26	3.38
BAC	0.64	0.34	1.88
AIG	0.46	0.34	1.35
L	5.20	0.9	5.78
IBM	4.21	2.46	1.71
INTC	4.23	0.19	2.26
GS	2.60	1.89	1.38
FAZ	0.48	0.32	1.50
FAS	0.45	0.55	0.82

VISUALIZING THE FINDINGS

We may visualize the finding with an options table as shown in Figure 5.1, which is captured from the Yahoo! Finance web site. The spot price of ticker C (for Citigroup, Inc.) is 4.06. The strike-on-spot price is 4, which is the closest price to the spot price. The computer algos automatically search for the strike-on-spot price using a proprietary sorting and comparing algo.

Options　　　　　　　　　　　　　　　　　　　　　　　　　Get

View By Expiration; Nov 09 | Dec 09 | Jan 10 | Mar 10 | Jun 10 | Jan 11

CALL OPTIONS					Expire at close Fri, Nov 20, 2009		
Strike	Symbol	Last	Chg	Bid	Ask	Vol	Open int
1.00	CKT X	3.00	0.00	3.00	3.10	8	165
2.00	CKU X	2.04	↓0.01	2.04	2.07	48	753
3.00	CKV X	1.05	↑0.02	1.05	1.07	1,475	9,454
4.00	CKW X	0.17	↓0.01	0.16	0.17	18,742	144,926
5.00	CKP X	0.02	0.00	0.01	0.02	9,571	434,916
6.00	CKX X	0.01	0.00	N/A	0.01	980	116,595
7.00	CKG X	0.01	0.00	N/A	0.01	1	10,718
8.00	CKH X	0.01	0.00	N/A	0.02	100	5,950
9.00	CKI X	0.02	0.00	N/A	0.01	17	472

PUT OPTIONS					Expire at close Fri, Nov 20, 2009		
Strike	Symbol	Last	Chg	Bid	Ask	Vol	Open int
2.00	CWU X	0.01	0.00	N/A	0.01	100	792
3.00	CWV X	0.01	0.00	N/A	0.01	1,634	89,839
4.00	CWW X	0.11	↓0.02	0.10	0.11	18,358	353,379
5.00	CWP X	0.98	↑0.02	0.95	0.97	9,570	118,214
6.00	CWX X	1.97	0.00	1.93	1.96	736	6,164
7.00	CWG X	2.96	0.00	2.93	2.96	29	394
8.00	CWH X	3.35	0.00	3.90	4.00	20	20

FIGURE 5.1　Options Data for Citigroup (C)

If the strike price changes from 4 to 5, the associated call option premium would change from 0.17 to 0.02. Thus the change in value is 0.15. This is a gain condition as profit may increase due to the strike price change. For the loss condition, when the strike price drops from 4 to 3, the call premium changes from 0.17 to 1.05, with the value of the change being 0.88. The change in the call premiums indicates traders' mental response to the underlying stock price change.

With the call premium change for the loss condition being 0.88, and that of the gain condition 0.15, we may compute the loss versus gain ratio,

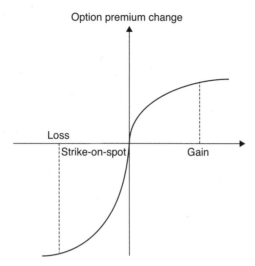

FIGURE 5.2 Loss Aversion Effect in Option Pricing

namely, loss/gain ratio = 0.88/0.15 = 5.87. This is much larger than 1. There-fore, we conclude in this case that loss aversion exists in option pricing.

Let us look at a case of put options. Similarly, traders feel gains as price goes down for a put option at the strike-on-spot price. For example, when the price goes down from 4 to 3, the put premium change is .11 – .01 = 0.1. When the price goes up from 4 to 5, traders feel a loss. Thus the put change is 0.98 – 0.11 = 0.87. The loss aversion ratio is .87/.11 = 7.9, where the put premium change due to losses is much larger than the change due to gains. Figure 5.2 visualizes the loss aversion effect in option pricing with a typical loss aversion diagram.

COMPUTER ALGOS FOR THE FINDING

The computer algos behind this finding are triggered by a URL from the Web. Let us look at part of the algos. In Part IV of the book, we elaborate the detailed infrastructure and technologies for developing these computer algos. Ideally, the reader may want to go through Part IV before diving into the following computer algos.

The computer algos are triggered by a call to testLossGainArr() that takes in a sample of 32 tickers and loop through each ticker to call testLossGain(). The result is displayed as data entries in an HTML table.

The function testLossGain() gets all the strike prices and the current spot price at first; then compares the spot price against the array of strike prices to find out the strike-on-spot price; and then it calls getLossGainNearCurrentPrice() that computes the option premium changes due to losses and gains.Yeswici.com provides a utility to test the effect with real-time data. Please e-mail info@yeswici.com for the specific utility.

```
testLossGainArr();
function testLossGainArr()
{
  $arr =
  array("ACH","ACI","ACL","ACM","ACN","ACO", "ACS","BYI","BZ","C","CA","CAB","CAG",
  "CAH","CAJ","CAL","CAT","CAM","FAZ","CAR","DBS","DCI","SPY","QQQQ","BAC", "AIG",
  "QQQQ","IBM","BAC","GS","GOOG","FAS");

  echo '<link href="../style.css" rel="stylesheet" type="text/css">';
  echo "<b>Empirical evidence for loss aversion in option pricing - case of call
  options</b>";
  echo "<table border=1>";
  echo "<tr><td>Tick</td><td>premium change due to loss</td><td>due to same
  gain</td></tr>";
  for($i=0; $i<sizeof($arr); $i++)
  {
      testLossGain($arr[$i], "");
  }
  echo "</table>";
}

function testLossGain($tick, $m)
{
  echo "<tr><td>$tick</td>";
  $arr_c_strike_premium = getCallOptionStrikesLastPriceByMonth($tick, $m);
  $currentAssetPrice = getCurrentPrice($tick);
  $closestStrike = getClosetStrikeToAssetPrice($currentAssetPrice,
   $arr_c_strike_premium[0]);
  $keyClosestStrike = getKey($arr_c_strike_premium[0],$closestStrike);
  $nearLossGain = getLossGainNearCurrentPrice($keyClosestStrike,
  $arr_c_strike_premium[1]);
  //print_r($arr_c_strike_premium);
}

function getLossGainNearCurrentPrice($k, $arr)
{
  $arr_r[0] = $arr[$k-1] - $arr[$k]; //loss
  $arr_r[1] = $arr[$k] - $arr[$k+1]; //gain
  echo "<td>$arr_r[0]</td><td>$arr_r[1]</td></tr>";
}

function getKey($arr, $val)
{
  for($i=0; $i<sizeof($arr); $i++)
  {
    if($val == $arr[$i])
    {
     $k = $i;
    }
  }
  return $k;
}
```

```
function getClosetStrikeToAssetPrice($cp, $arr_strike)
{
  $s = 0;
  $arr_d = array();
  for($i=0; $i<sizeof($arr_strike); $i++)
  {
      $sp = $arr_strike[$i];
      $diff = abs($cp - $sp);
      $arr_d[$i] = $diff;
  }
  sort($arr_d);
  $s = $cp - $arr_d[0];
  $k = array_search($s, $arr_strike);
  $z = in_array($s, $arr_strike);
  if($k==NULL && !$z)
  {
      $s = $arr_d[0] + $cp;
  }
  return $s;
}

function getCallOptionStrikesLastPriceByMonth($tick, $m)
{
  $arr = array();
  $res = getOptionPageByMonth($tick, $m);
  $size = getSize($res);
  $arr_calls = parseVol2PArr($res, $size);
  $tot_calls = array_sum($arr_calls);
  $arr_strikes = getStrikes($res, $size);
  $arr_premium = getPremiums($res, $size);
  $arr[0] = $arr_strikes;
  $arr[1] = $arr_premium;
  return $arr;
}
```

To reproduce the finding, a reader with extensive computer programming experience may integrate the algos with real-time ticker data feeds. The reader has to develop a mechanism to create the real-time data feeds for the algos.

EXPLAINING THE FINDING WITH THE BLACK-SCHOLES FORMULA

My graduate students and I have been looking into the mathematical mechanism of the empirical finding. One thought is to use the Black-Scholes formula to derive the relationship between option price changes for losses and gains. We started to take partial derivatives of the formula. The research is in progress. If you find a good or alternative solution to this, please let us know via e-mail: info@yeswici.com.

Since the empirical finding has been made available to the public, we have found that the variance of the loss-gain asymmetry increases over time, which may increase the p-values of the tests. This may reflect that the options market may self-adjust and become efficient once a systematic anomaly is detected and made known.

CONCLUSION

In this chapter, we found empirical data to demonstrate that prospect theory and option pricing are connected. In other words, we found loss aversion in option pricing on strike-on-spot prices. The finding may be repeatedly supported by statistical significance tests with real-time data. In addition, the computer algos for producing the empirical data are published.

CHAPTER 6

Expanding the Size of Options in Option Pricing

T he Black-Scholes option pricing model assumes a setting of a future-dated option for traders to estimate the option premium given present conditions. Therefore, from behavioral decision theory perspective, there are two options in the choice set: the option for now with spot prices and the option for the future with strike prices. What if there are three options (e.g., a spot price with two strike prices) for a trader to make a decision in pricing option premiums? Will the change of the size of choice set (e.g., from two to three or three to two) affect the choice behavior? Could new financial instruments be devised with an expanded number of options?

This chapter attempts to look at choice behaviors in choice sets with two to three options. These scenarios are hypothetical at present, and the empirical findings may serve as theoretical foundations for new financial instruments of option pricing. We use data from Web polls to derive the empirical findings.

When a third option is removed from a three-option choice set, its choice share can be distributed to the two remaining options in an asymmetric manner. This is coded as switchers' choice reversal. A switcher is a decision maker who may be a trader, an investor, or a voter in Web polls. The manner of the distribution depends on whether the relevant anchors of the two options are presented to switchers who have voted for the third option. Data from the Web polls on a blockbuster NBA event, the seven-player trade between the Houston Rockets and Orlando Magic (on June 29, 2004), have demonstrated the proposition. When the third option for the switchers (who originally vote for neither of the remaining two options) is removed from the choice set, most switchers vote consistently with the majority voters when they are anchored by relevant cues on NBA online. However, most switchers' choices are reversed to be irrational when the relevant cues are absent in the *USA Today* Web poll. In a controlled study, the data from formalized telephone interviews on the 2004 presidential election have underscored the findings on the asymmetric manner in distributing switchers' votes. The controlled study also shows that the switchers' choice reversal can be decisive in close competitions.

THE NBA EVENT

On June 29, 2004, two National Basketball Association (NBA) teams, the Houston Rockets and Orlando Magic, decided to switch their players (a total of seven players), involving Tracy McGrady (T-Mac, two-time NBA scoring champion) of the Orlando Magic and Steve Francis (NBA All-Star guard) of the Houston Rockets. Tens of thousands of online voters judged whether the blockbuster trade deal was a good one for Houston (where All-Star center Yao Ming shines) or Orlando. The *USA Today* web site, the *Houston Chronicle* web site, and NBA online asked voters similar questions, yet with differences in anchoring (framing) the questions.

The *Houston Chronicle* offered three options for voters to choose from:

A: The deal is good for Houston (voted by 69 percent of all voters).
B: The deal is bad for Houston (19 percent).
C: Other (e.g., more can be done for Houston) (12 percent).

NBA online and *USA Today* offered two options, namely, option *A* and *B*. However, the framing of the survey questions was different for the two Web polls. NBA online provided a detailed description for the relevant benefits for both teams due to the trade deal (e.g., T-Mac and Yao are the next Kobe-Shaq). The same relevant benefits are presented to all voters. However, *USA Today* provided a general question without offering relevant benefits for the teams (e.g., which team got the better deal: Houston or Orlando?)

The online voting result is intriguing. It shows reversed patterns of choice in different polls. That is, the 12 percent of voters who originally voted for neither team (i.e., the switchers who voted for the third option in the *Houston Chronicle* Web poll) has shown reversed patterns in choosing *A* or *B* in the Web polls where their options of choice were reduced to two. With NBA online, 9 percent of the 12 percent of switchers chose *A* and the remaining 3 percent chose *B*, which was consistent with the majority of the voters and experts' analyses (i.e., most voters and experts think it is a better deal for the Houston Rockets; see Appendix B for experts' opinions in the Associated Press and *USA Today*). However, in the *USA Today* Web poll, only 2.15 percent of the switchers chose *A* and 9.75 percent chose *B*. So a choice reversal occurs with the switchers; more switchers chose *A* on NBA online, while more switchers chose *B* (the opposite of *A*) in the *USA Today* Web poll. In other words, switchers made an irrational choice on *USA Today*'s web site because the majority of the voters and experts voted otherwise.

The switchers show a reversed choice pattern in distributing their votes to the two remaining options. On the one side, the switchers make rational choices (i.e., the deal is good for the Houston Rockets) when the relevant benefits of the deal are present on NBA online, for example, T-Mac and Yao are the next Kobe-Shaq (who won three NBA titles for Los Angeles). This is consistent with experts' opinion and the majority of voters. However, the switchers become irrational when the relevant benefits are not present in the *USA Today* Web poll: Most of them chose option *B* (i.e., it is a bad deal for Houston). This (USAtoday.com) reverses the rational choice. The rational choice is: Experts and the majority of the voters agree that it is a good deal for the Houston Rockets.

Why would the choice reversal (irrational choice) happen in the online voting? Following a detailed analysis of the data, we attempt to interpret it with behavioral choice theories on anchoring and uncertainty. A controlled test with formalized offline data on the 2004 presidential election will attempt to underscore the findings from the Web polls.

WEB DATA

We analyze further the data for the NBA Web polls, attempting to answer (1) who are the switchers in the two Web polls with just two options (NBA online and *USA Today*)? and (2) how large is the effect of the relationship between teams (Houston versus Orlando) and polls (NBA online versus *USA Today*)?

If we assume that the *Houston Chronicle* assesses the base data for the data analysis, then 69 percent of the 50,192 voters think that the deal is good for the Houston Rockets; 19 percent think it is good for the Orlando Magic; the remaining 12 percent chose neither Houston nor Orlando (as of June 30, 2004). The voters who were among the 12 percent had to choose Houston or Orlando when their option was removed in a two-option choice set that includes only the two options. In other words, the 12 percent of the voters are switchers. In a two-option choice, according to Simonson, Kramer, and Young (2004), "decision makers can be roughly divided into three groups"; "switchers" is defined as "decision makers (who are not prone to the first option or the second option) whose choices are contingent on particular conditions." The other two groups are composed of those who strongly prefer the first option or the second option.

On the NBA site, the 12 percent switchers split to 9 percent (for the Houston Rockets) and 3 percent (for the Orlando Magic), constituting 78 percent (69 + 9) in total for Houston and 22 percent (19 + 3) for Orlando. On the *USA Today* Web poll, the 12 percent switchers split to 2.15 percent (Houston) and 9.75 percent (Orlando), constituting 71.15 percent (69 + 2.15) for Houston and 28.75 percent (19 + 9.75) for Orlando, which seems to run counter to rational reasoning. The distributions of the votes for all voters (Figure 6.1) and the switchers (Figure 6.2) are displayed in the corresponding figures. Figure 6.2 shows the different distributions of the switchers to the two options in the two different polls.

Now we know who the switchers are and how their votes are distributed. The next question is: How large is the effect of the choice reversal? In other words, are these changed numbers of the switchers' choice shares meaningful beyond statistical errors?

This question can be examined by testing the relationship between teams (Houston versus Orlando) and Web polls (NBA versus *USA Today*). A χ^2 test uses the numbers of switchers (i.e., the products of sample sizes and percentages) to examine the relationship. The sample size is 42,609 for NBA online and 2801 for *USA Today* as of June 30, 2004. We calculate the value of the χ^2 test ($\chi^2(1) = 508.16$, $p < .001$). The effect is significant.

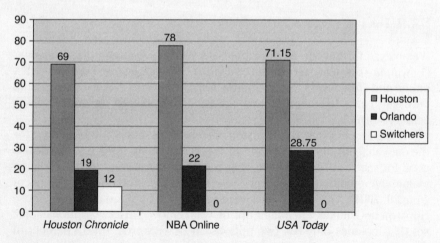

FIGURE 6.1 Vote Distributions for All Web Voters
Note: The numbers are percentages of all Web voters.

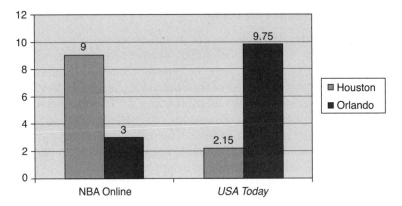

FIGURE 6.2 Vote Distributions for the Web Switchers
Note: The numbers are percentages of all Web voters.

This procedure of the test design is similar to Dhar and Simonson's (2003) study that examined the redistribution of the choice shares due to an increase of the choice set size from two to three. However, in the Dhar and Simonson (2003) study, the choice shares use an equal sample size ($n = 140$ for all conditions) and a logit model for all respondents. The present one has unequal sample sizes and a focus on switchers (a portion of all voters).

In addition, as the sample sizes are very large for the χ^2 test, the significance of the result may not be persuasive. So the effect size (the strength of the relationship) has been calculated for the χ^2 test, Phi (interpreted as a Pearson correlation r) = .28. According to Cohen's (1988) convention, this is a medium effect.

THEORETICAL ANALYSIS

In the theoretical analysis, we start with describing the resemblance in the procedures between the Web polls and a forced-choice experiment by Dhar and Simonson (2003). Then we focus the target population of the present research on switchers whose opinion is not strong enough to prefer either of the two remaining options. After that, we analyze the choice reversal and the irrational choice. Most certain switchers chose the rational option (Houston), while most uncertain switchers chose the irrational option (Orlando) that gives rise to the irrational choice. Finally, we use the uncertainty account on anchoring and the principle of loss aversion to explain the irrational choice.

Procedure and Choice Reversal

From the perspective of the procedure that changes the size of the choice set, the Web polls on the NBA blockbuster event resemble a "reversed" forced-choice experiment conducted by Dhar and Simonson (2003), yet in a reversed manner on how the size of the choice set changes. In their forced-choice experiment (study 1), the analysis starts with a forced-choice task where two options (an all-average option versus a mixed option) are presented for respondents to choose from. The mixed option has advantages on some dimensions and disadvantages on others, while the all-average option has average values with respect to various dimensions. Then a third option, namely, the no-choice option, is added to the choice set. This makes the set size three. Dhar and Simonson (2003) find that the all-average option loses more choice shares to the third option.

In contrast to the inclusion of the third option in the choice set in their study 1, the analysis of the present NBA polls starts with the *Houston Chronicle* poll, with three options, namely Houston, Orlando, and Other. Then the third option is eliminated from the choice set to make it a two-option task. There are two polls for the two-option choice task, namely the NBA poll and the *USA Today* Web poll.

The result of the reversed forced-choice analysis with the removal of the third option later on is consistent with and extends the findings from the forced-choice experiment with the subsequent inclusion of the third option. Dhar and Simonson (2003) find a one-way directional (i.e., asymmetric) movement of the choice share of the third option, with more shares moved from the all-average option to the third option. However, for the three online polls, a bidirectional movement to the remaining options from the choice share of the third option occurs. With the NBA Web poll, most switchers chose Houston, such that more choice shares for the third option moved to the Houston option. However, most switchers chose Orlando in the *USA Today* Web poll, such that more choice shares for the third option moved to the Orlando option. This is what is previously called the *choice reversal* due to the reduction of the choice set size. The voters who originally voted for the third option are switchers who are the key players to make the choice reversal happen.

In summary, the Web polls on the NBA event appear to be a reversed forced-choice experiment (i.e., study 1 of Dhar and Simonson, 2003). However, their study 1 predicts a one-way effect (more share reduction in the all-average option) on the choice shares due to the availability of the no-choice option. The Web polls, with the reversed manipulation of the no-choice option ("eliminated from" in contrast to "added to" the choice set), show that switchers distribute their choice shares in a reversed (bidirectionally asymmetric) manner.

Switchers

As defined in Simonson, Kramer, and Young (2004), the switchers are prone to choose neither option a priori. Here they are operationalized as voters whose opinions are not strong enough to prefer either of the two remaining options. The switchers constitute a small portion of the voter population (e.g., 12 percent of the population for the NBA event). However, the switchers' opinion can be decisive, especially in a marginally equal competition between two opponents. For example, the 2000 presidential election was very close between George Bush and Al Gore. The switcher state (Florida) determined the final outcome of the election.

Although the switchers do not change the asymmetric distribution of the Web polls for all voters on the NBA event, the movement of the switchers' choice share can help us understand how to influence the opinion of the switchers. When a marginally equal competition approaches, the strategies obtained from the NBA event polls may be instrumental in influencing the outcome of the votes for all voters.

Anchoring and Uncertainty

The switchers' choice reversal occurred in the Web polls for the NBA event. Why would this happen? In other words, what are the factors that give rise to the switchers' choice reversal? The availability of relevant benefit anchors seems to be the reason. Relevant anchors are defined as cues that are identical to many respondents, while irrelevant (or arbitrary) anchors are different for each respondent. Technically, relevant anchors and irrelevant anchors influence choice behavior in a similar manner.

The switchers' choice reversal occurs with the two Web polls: NBA online and *USA Today*. With large sample sizes for both web sites, the population of the NBA-savvy people (who are interested in NBA news) is impartially represented by both web sites. So sampling should not be an issue to cause the choice reversal. However, the difference between the NBA online and the USA Today polls is the framing of the survey questions, with (NBA online) or without (*USA Today*) relevant benefit anchors being presented to voters.

The presence of relevant anchors may influence switchers' choice outcome by reducing uncertainty about the choice context (e.g., the benefits of the NBA trade deal). When the relevant benefit anchors are absent, switchers do not know the real (relevant) benefit of the trade deal. As a result, they are more likely to be biased by arbitrary (irrelevant) benefit anchors generated on their own (e.g., Houston should not lose too many players) due to the arbitrary anchoring effect (Tversky and Kahneman 1974; Simonson and Drolet 2004).

Similar biases due to arbitrary anchors can be found in the literature. The bias can be systematically produced if the arbitrary anchors (e.g., the last two digits of respondents' social security numbers) are manipulated. For example, in Simonson and Drolet (2004), the last two digits of respondents' social security numbers are manipulated to anchor respondents' assessment of their willingness to accept (*WTA*) to give up and their willingness to pay (*WTP*) for a product (e.g., toaster). A systematical arbitrary anchoring effect has been found. Respondents uncertain about the desire to trade estimate a higher *WTA* and *WTP* value if their SSN digits are higher (> 50), compared to a lower value with lower SSN digits (< 50). When respondents are certain about the desire to trade or the market value of the product, the arbitrary anchoring effect disappears. So the arbitrary anchoring effect depends on one's uncertainty level about the choice context. This has been coded as the uncertainty account in Simonson and Drolet (2004).

Alternative accounts to the uncertainty account on anchoring effects have been proposed, such as the adjustment account (Tversky and Kahneman 1974) and the activation account (Chapman and Johnson 1999). The original explanation for the anchoring effect is the adjustment account. It postulates that people provide estimates on the basis of accessible information in mind (i.e., the anchor) and adjust their responses in a direction that seems appropriate (Tversky and Kahneman 1974; Epley and Gilovich 2001). The activation account suggests that anchors affect judgments by increasing the availability and construction of features that the anchor and judgments hold in common (Chapman and Johnson 2002).

Both the adjustment account and the activation account focus on the general process of how the anchoring effect occurs. The uncertainty account, however, focuses on one specific condition (i.e., uncertainty) for the arbitrary anchoring to appear. In the Web polls on the NBA event, the availability of the relevant benefit anchors induces a manipulation of the uncertainty about the choice context (the trade deal). When the switchers are presented with relevant anchors, they are certain about the benefits of the trade deal to both teams. When the relevant anchors are absent, the switchers are uncertain about the deal. This manipulation of certainty about the choice context affects the outcome of switchers' choice. In other words, it gives rise to the switchers' choice reversal under uncertainty. Therefore, the switchers' choice reversal is more relevant to the uncertainty account on anchoring.

THE NBA EVENT AND THE UNCERTAINTY ACCOUNT

The uncertainty account on anchoring and price perception suggests that consumers' judgment is anchored by irrelevant cues, and this anchoring effect occurs only when consumers are uncertain about the trade (Simonson and Drolet 2004). For example, an arbitrary cue (e.g., the last two digits of respondents' social security numbers) anchors consumers' willingness to pay and sell when they are uncertain about the desire to trade. However, this anchoring effect is debiased when consumers become certain about the trade.

From the perspective of the uncertainty account, the analysis of the NBA trade deal underscores and extends the uncertainty account by varying the context (e.g., from consumers' price perception to switchers' online voting) and the target of uncertainty (e.g., from "about the desire to trade" to "about the benefits of the trade deal").

We assume that the relevant reason for making the choice is the articulated relevant benefits (e.g., T-Mac and Yao would win the NBA title for Houston as Kobe and Shaq did for Los Angeles) and that irrelevant reasons are various arbitrary benefits generated by switchers to justify their choice. When the benefits are not explicitly articulated (e.g., in the *USA Today* Web poll), the 12 percent switchers are uncertain about the benefits such that they come up with various arbitrary (irrelevant) benefits of their own (e.g., Houston Rockets should not lose too many players at once). With various arbitrary benefits generated by the switchers who are uncertain about the trade deal, according to the uncertainty account, the switchers' judgment should be biased to various directions set by the various irrelevant reason anchors. As a result, the tendency for the rational choice is weakened and the choice can be reversed to be irrational.

In summary, NBA online provides the switchers with certainty about the trade deal, while the switchers of *USA Today* are uncertain about the benefits. The uncertainty account on arbitrary anchoring by Simonson and Drolet (2004) plausibly accounts for the choice reversal under uncertainty.

Irrational Choice and Choice Anomalies

There are three Web polls: *Houston Chronicle*, NBA online, and *USA Today*. In addition to the two options offered by NBA online and *USA Today*, the *Houston Chronicle* provides a third option (similar to a no-choice option in Dhar and Simonson, 2003) that identifies 12 percent of the voters as switchers (Simonson, Kramer, and Young, 2004). Then the question of the present study is: How would the switchers (who voted for a third option a priori) distribute their votes when they have to choose from the two remaining options?

This research targets the switchers who made the choice reversal happen. An approach used in Dhar and Simonson (2003) observes the distribution of total respondents when the size of the choice set increases from two to three. However, using the "total respondents" approach for the present study (see Figure 6.1), the choice reversal is hardly apparent in a meaningful manner. Therefore, we need to refocus the target population of the research, from total voters to switchers. In other words, we observe the choice reversal on switchers rather than on total voters. The similar refocus of the target research population to switchers can be found in Simonson, Kramer, and Young (2004).

The choice reversal shows that the switchers make rational choices (the trade deal is good for the Houston Rockets) when the relevant benefits of the trade deal are articulated and presented (on NBA online, e.g., T-Mac and Yao are the next Kobe-Shaq), which is consistent with experts' analyses and the votes of majority voters. According to the certainty rule of rationality for normative models (e.g., game-theoretical and probabilistic models), decision makers should choose the outcome of an option with the largest payoff (Simon, 1955). In the case of voting on the NBA event, the normative models predict that switchers should choose the rational option (Houston). The rational choice option is: It is a good deal for the Houston Rockets, which is agreed on by experts and the majority of the voters.

However, the switchers become irrational when the relevant benefits are not articulated in the *USA Today* Web poll. This (USAtoday.com) reverses the rational choice (i.e., more switchers choose that it is not a good deal for the Houston Rockets). This is because of the absence of relevant anchors and the presence of the anchoring effect due to irrelevant (arbitrary) anchors.

The relevant anchors, analogous to the market value of a product in Simonson and Drolet (2004), are articulated relevant benefits. The irrelevant anchors are various arbitrary benefits generated by switchers to justify their choice. When the benefits are not articulated and presented (e.g., *USA Today*), the switchers are uncertain about the benefits such that they come up with various arbitrary/irrelevant benefits of their own (e.g., the Houston Rockets should not lose too many players at once). With various arbitrary benefits generated by the switchers who are uncertain about the trade deal, according to the uncertainty account (Simonson and Drolet, 2004), the switchers should be biased to various directions set by the various irrelevant anchors. As a result, the rational choice is reversed to give rise to the irrational choice that is contrary to the majority votes and experts' analyses.

The irrational choice violates principles of normative choice models (i.e., the certainty rule of rationality), which predict that people make rational and calculated decisions under all conditions. This presents an example of "bounded rationality" (Simon, 1955), which postulates that people must be boundedly rational, namely, rational within certain limits. When switchers are certain about the choice context (i.e., the benefits of the trade deal), they act rationally. However, the switchers may act irrationally in a systematic manner if they are uncertain about the choice context.

The irrational choice is sometimes referred to as anomalies to normative economic choice models (Thaler 1980, 1993). The choice reversal (irrational choice) of the present research adds new evidence to the group of anomalies including the endowment effect, loss aversion, status quo bias, and so on (Kahneman, Knetsch, and Thaler 1991). The anomalies suggest that normative choice models are not sufficient to account for all choice scenarios and it is possible to systematically violate their predictions.

Irrational Choice and Loss Aversion

The endowment effect postulates that consumers' willingness to pay for an item should normally be smaller than their willingness to accept to give up the same item (Thaler 1980). The status quo bias suggests that people tend to stay with the status quo rather than change because the expected loss from the change looms larger than the expected gains from the change (Samuelson and Zeckhauser 1988). Both anomalies are manifestations of loss aversion that suggest losses loom larger than gains for the same amount of change (Kahneman and Tversky 1979, 2000). Analogously, can this choice reversal (the switchers' irrational choice) be interpreted as being relevant to loss aversion?

The normative choice models predict that most switchers should choose the rational option (Houston Rockets). However, this prediction does not hold true when the switchers are not presented with the benefit anchors for the trade deal. If the relevant benefits are absent (e.g., *USA Today*), the switchers' choice share for Houston drops sharply from 9 percent to 2.15 percent.

With the uncertainty account, when the relevant benefit anchors are absent, unarticulated random irrelevant anchors may bias the votes to different directions. As a result, switchers should split the 12 percent roughly evenly between Houston and Orlando, say 6 percent apiece. The uncertainty account can explain why and how switchers do not make a rational choice, with an average choice share for the rational option.

Assuming statistical errors are controlled, the outcome for switchers making an irrational choice (namely, the choice reversal) entails two scenarios on the choice share of the rational option (Houston): an average choice share (e.g., about 6 percent) or a below-average choice share (e.g., below 6 percent). The uncertainty account can explain the scenario for the average choice share. However, in the case of the *USA Today* Web poll, the switchers' choice share for the rational option (Houston) drops sharply to 2.15 percent, below the average 6 percent. The uncertainty account alone cannot explain this scenario. So what else is needed to explain the below-average scenario?

Considering other anomalies such as the endowment effect and the status quo bias, is the principle of loss aversion functioning in the below-average scenario? The answer seems to be positive.

Suppose that the irrelevant anchors are equally framed on losses and gains of the trade deal for the rational option (Houston). Also suppose that the irrelevant anchors are equally generated and equally distributed among the switchers to justify their choice when the relevant anchors are absent. In other words, half of the irrelevant anchors are generated about the gains of the trade deal for Houston (e.g., T-Mac will shine in Houston) and the other half about the losses for Houston (e.g., Houston loses too many players at once).

On the basis of the uncertainty account in that the irrelevant anchors are effective to bias switchers' choice, switchers may show loss aversion in further valuing the self-generated irrelevant anchors. As the losses are valued more than the gains, more uncertain switchers would consider that Houston has lost more than it has gained. The uncertain switchers tend to choose that it is a bad deal for Houston (good for Orlando). As a result, the uncertain switchers' choice share for Houston (the rational option) becomes below average.

In summary, the irrational choice of uncertain switchers can be explained with the uncertainty account and the principle of loss aversion. The uncertainty account alone accounts for a scenario in which the uncertain switchers distribute an average choice share to the rational option (Houston). Under additional assumptions, the combination of the uncertainty account and the principle of loss aversion has introduced a scenario in which the uncertain switchers choose the rational option with a below-average choice share.

Summary

Based on the procedure to change the size of the choice set, we position the research design for the Web polls on the NBA event as a reversed forced-choice experiment that resembles and reverses Dhar and Simonson's (2003) procedure. Switchers' choice reversal is observed with the reversed procedure. Switchers are voters whose opinion is not strong enough to prefer either of the two remaining options. Most certain switchers chose the rational option (Houston), while most uncertain switchers chose the irrational option (Orlando) that gives rise to the irrational choice. The uncertainty account on anchoring with (or without) the principle of loss aversion has explained different scenarios for the irrational choice. The irrational choice is part of choice anomalies that systematically violate the predictions of normative choice models.

CONTROLLED OFFLINE DATA

The findings on switchers' choice reversal (i.e., the asymmetric distribution of switchers' votes) come from studying the Web polls on the NBA blockbuster trade deal. Can it be underscored in a controlled study such that it can be generalized to other domains such as political choice and option pricing in financial derivatives?

In order to underscore the findings and test whether the switchers' choice reversal can be reproduced, we attempt to do a controlled research study with respondents sampled from the same population and the framing variations controlled. The data have been obtained from the CNN/*USA Today*/Gallup instant reaction poll and the *USA Today*/CNN/Gallup comprehensive poll on the 2004 Kerry/Bush presidential election.

The basic findings from the Web polls on the NBA event can be summarized in H_1. We attempt to test H_1 with the poll data on the 2004 election.

H_1: The availability of relevant anchors impacts the manner for switchers to distribute their votes to the two remaining options when the third one (which the switchers choose a priori) is eliminated.

Respondents

The respondents were 909 registered voters from the *USA Today*/CNN/Gallup comprehensive poll and 553 registered voters from the CNN/*USA Today*/Gallup instant reaction poll. All of the registered voters for the two polls were interviewed by telephone; interviews were conducted between June 21, 2004, and July 6, 2004. For the *USA Today*/CNN/Gallup (abbreviated as *USA Today*) poll, the maximum margin of sampling error is ±4 percentage points. For the CNN/*USA Today*/Gallup (abbreviated as CNN) poll, one can say with 95 percent confidence that the margin of sampling error is ±5 percentage points. So both samples represent the same population: registered voters.

Design: The research design was constructed in a way that follows and extends the procedure of Dhar and Simonson (2003) in a reversed manner. For the *USA Today* poll, the respondents made a three-option choice (i.e., similar to the *Houston Chronicle* Web poll on the NBA trade deal). The telephone survey asked the respondents about their possible votes for Kerry (the Democrat), Bush (the Republican), and Nader (the independent). For the CNN poll, the respondents made judgments on Kerry and Bush with the third option (Nader) removed from the choice set. Both polls used formalized telephone interviews.

The voters in the CNN poll made judgments about Kerry and Bush with a shift of concentration (anchoring) on the candidates. The respondents were either favorable or not favorable ("unfavorable" or "don't know") to the candidates. The candidates were anchored with their relevant cues (i.e., similar to the NBA online poll on the NBA trade deal) when they were being judged, while their opponent was not anchored (i.e., similar to the *USA Today* poll on the NBA trade deal). Therefore, the availability of relevant anchors was manipulated. When Kerry was being evaluated, the relevant anchors were Kerry's attributes such as his potential to handle the economy and terrorism (where Bush's relevant anchors were absent). Similarly, when Bush was being evaluated, the relevant anchors were Bush's cues such as his handling of the economy and terrorism (where Kerry's anchors were absent).

Results

Due to the reduction of the choice set size from three to two, the choice share for Nader and others (i.e., switchers with total 9 percent of the population) was distributed to Kerry and Bush when the set size was two. When Kerry was being evaluated (anchored alone), 4 percent of the total 9 percent switchers voted for him, while the remaining 5 percent voted for Bush. Conversely, 8 percent of the total 9 percent switchers' votes moved to Bush (1 percent to Kerry) when he was being evaluated (anchored alone). See Table 6.1 for the data and Figure 6.3 for the vote distributions.

Similar to the test for the Web polls on the NBA trade deal, the χ^2 test was used to examine the relationship (H_1) within the election polls. The

TABLE 6.1 Votes for Kerry and Bush when the Set Size Reduces from 3 to 2

Votes (with Nader)	Default on Kerry	Default on Bush	
USA Today ($n = 09$)	CNN ($n = 553$)	CNN ($n = 553$)	
Kerry	46 (418.14)	50 (for Kerry)	47
Bush	45	50	53 (for Bush)
Nader	6		
Others	3		
Switchers	9% (81.8) total	Switchers' Distributed Choice Share	
Kerry	4 (22.12)	1 (5.53)	
Bush	5 (27.65)	8 (44.24)	

Notes: (1) The numbers are percentages of all voters with the numbers of votes in parentheses (product of sample sizes and the percentages). (2) Data were collected between June 21, 2004, and July 6, 2004.

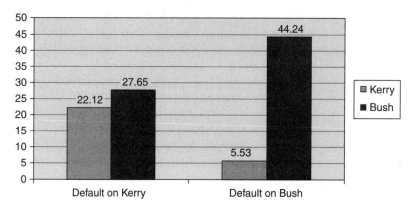

FIGURE 6.3 Switchers' Vote Distributions for Presidential Candidates
Note: The numbers are votes (product of sample sizes and the percentages of all voters).

relationship entails two variables: candidates (Kerry versus Bush) and the default positions of relevant anchors (default on Kerry versus default on Bush). The result shows that the relationship between the two variables is significant ($\chi^2(1) = 13.78$, $p < .001$, r(Phi) $= .37$). See Figure 6.3 for the switchers' vote distributions.

We also used a different categorization (definition) of switchers (i.e., using 6 percent of Nader's votes in the *USA Today* poll as the total switchers for the third option); a significant relationship was also found ($\chi^2(1) = -46.12$, $p < .001$).

Discussion

Derived from the analysis to the Web polls on the NBA trade deal, H_1 states that the availability of relevant anchors moderates the pattern on how the switchers' votes move to the two remaining options. The 2004 election poll data support this statement. It does so in a controlled manner in the sense that (1) the population for the two polls is identical, namely, registered voters; (2) the framing variations on the survey questions are controlled by the formalized telephone interviews.

The switchers' choice reversal (i.e., the asymmetric manner in distributing votes) on the NBA trade deal is underscored by the data from the formalized polls on the presidential candidates. In the *USA Today* poll that includes the third option (Nader), switchers' (the voters for Nader and others) percentage is identified at about 9 percent. In the CNN poll that includes only two options (Kerry and Bush), the switchers' votes are distributed between Kerry and Bush. However, the distribution shows an asymmetric pattern. When Kerry is being evaluated (i.e., the default anchor is on Kerry), switchers' votes are almost equally distributed between Kerry and Bush. However, more switchers' votes (8 percent of the total 9 percent) move to Bush when Bush is being anchored for evaluation.

The switchers' choice reversal can be decisive in presidential elections. In the present data (Figure 6.3), the total votes favor neither Kerry nor Bush (50 percent versus 50 percent) when Kerry is anchored and the switchers distribute their votes in a relatively equal manner. However, the total votes favor Bush (53 percent for Bush versus 47 percent for Kerry) when Bush is anchored and the switchers distribute their votes in a different (asymmetric) manner.

GENERAL DISCUSSION

Anchoring on switchers' choice has been underinvestigated, as the systematic examinations on "switchers" have just begun in the behavioral choice literature (Simonson, Kramer, and Young, 2004). The specific focus of the present study (anchoring on switchers under uncertainty in a reversed forced-choice task) has not been examined in the literature. Evidence for the anchoring effect (e.g., on all respondents) has been documented in various cases, from judgment and estimations (e.g., estimating the percentage of African countries in the United Nations; Kahneman and Tversky 1974) to consumers' assessments of their willingness to accept (*WTA*) and their willingness to pay (*WTP*) for a product (Simonson and Drolet 2004). However, little has been reported for switchers in Web polls and the polls on political elections in a scenario when the size of the choice set decreases. In the meantime, this topic is of vital importance to behavioral choice theory and practice.

Theoretical Implications

In theory, the impact of reducing the size of a choice set is as important as the impact of an increase of the set size. The impact of the increase of the set size has been documented extensively and highly valued in the literature, such as the attraction effect (Huber, Payne, and Puto 1982), the compromise effect (Simonson 1989), and the effect of a no-choice option on forced choice (Dhar and Simonson 2003).

We find that the size reduction is not just a simple reversal of the size increase. For example, the one-way effect of a no-choice option on the forced-choice task (i.e., more choice shares of all-average options move to the third option) is found when the choice set size increases (Dhar and

Simonson 2003). However, a bidirectional effect on switchers (e.g., the choice reversal) is found in the present study when the set size decreases. In other words, the impact of the set size reduction on switchers' choice can be moderated by variables such as the uncertainty about the choice context (e.g., the availability of relevant anchors) in a way that is different from the choice behavior due to the size increase. Therefore, understanding the impact of the reduction of the choice set size is important theoretically.

Managerial Implications

Practically speaking, switchers' choice reversal matters greatly to marketers, politicians, sports management, and so on. For example, in a close competition between two opponents, the switchers' choice reversal can be decisive in determining the outcome of a presidential election (e.g., see the elections in 2000 and 2004). Hence, factors that can impact the switchers' choice and choice reversals are extremely important and instrumental to strategists who want to gain an edge in close competitions.

Another aspect of the practical implications for choice reversal affects marketing strategies. We first use an example in the Web browser industry to illustrate choice reversal in marketing and then describe its marketing implications.

In the Web browser industry, there were three major groups of players: Internet Explorer (IE) versus Netscape versus other browsers (e.g., Lynx for Unix). In the past, Netscape dominated the browser market, with the largest choice share in all browser users. Switchers were composed of users of other browsers and new users. The switchers were considering a switch to Netscape or IE because of their advantages in functionality and reliability over the other browsers. If the status quo (the old competition environment) would remain, most switchers would be likely to choose Netscape because of its larger share. This is similar to the NBA case of the present study in that the switchers tend to choose Houston with larger choice share in population when the relevant benefit anchors are available. Another benefit anchor for switchers to choose Netscape was that the superiority in product quality of Netscape over Internet Explorer was apparent then (e.g., more reliable in handling Web plug-ins such as JavaScript). The relevant benefit cues of Netscape were supposed to anchor the switchers to choose Netscape.

However, Microsoft (the producer of IE) implemented a new marketing strategy and changed the status quo environment by bundling IE with its dominant desktop operating system, Windows. This created a default browser option (anchor) for all users. In other words, the bundling introduced a stronger relevant anchor than that of Netscape for the switchers.

Similar to the switchers choosing their default political candidate, the browser switchers were anchored by the default Internet browser from Microsoft and reversed their original choice of Netscape. Later on, even the original users of Netscape joined the switchers to use IE. As a result, IE dominates the present browser market, with about 80 percent or more of the market share.

The marketing implications of the switchers' choice reversal focus on guiding effective marketing strategies to gain a stronger presence of relevant anchors over competitors to influence switchers. The relevant anchors can be differentiable product benefits (like the NBA case) or the default options for the switchers to act on (like the cases of the elections and the Web browsers). Switchers are more likely to choose the products or brands that are anchored by the relevant cues. As a result, much of the choice (market) shares of the switchers would flow to the anchored products or brands. It is even possible to lure the customers of competitors to switch.

Further Research

More relevant information can be disclosed if we run controlled experiments to obtain respondents' individual data (in addition to the percentage of the samples). In that case, logit models (see Simonson 1989; Dhar and Simonson, 2003) for all respondents can be constructed. The switchers' logit model may be a submodel of the all-voter models that leaves out the variance of nonswitchers.

Using the logit models, we may validate the relationship between the availability of relevant anchors and choice outcome. We may also examine whether the relationship can be moderated by other variables such as the manipulation of the all-average/mixed options.

CONCLUSION

In contrast to an increase in the size of a choice set, the decrease of the set size gives rise to switchers' distribution of their votes to the remaining options. Switchers are prone to choose neither of the two options a priori. When they have to choose one of the two options, they distribute their votes in an asymmetric manner. In other words, the distribution of the switchers' choice share depends on whether the relevant anchors (the benefit anchors or the default anchor option) of the two remaining options are available. More choice shares are distributed to the option with relevant anchors, while less choice shares move to the option without relevant anchors. The Web polls on a blockbuster NBA trade deal between the Houston Rockets and the Orlando Magic demonstrate that the proposition holds true in Web voting. The findings from the Web polls are underscored in a controlled study with data from the polls on the 2004 presidential election. The controlled study also shows the decisive role of switchers' choice reversal on total votes in close competitions.

CHAPTER 7

Multinomial Models for Equity Returns

T he two important option pricing models are the Black-Scholes model and the binomial option pricing model. The binomial model offers a generalized approach to pricing options including bond options, while the Black-Scholes model may not price bond options (Black, Derman, and Toy 1991). However, the binomial model does not consider goodness-of-fit testing with techniques such as maximum likelihood estimation. Therefore, the validity of the model is not empirically corroborated.

In this chapter, we discuss a new modeling technique called multinomial modeling that incorporates the maximum likelihood estimation for goodness-of-fit testing. The context of the discussion is linking equity returns and consumer sentiment from a macro perspective. We hope that the multinomial modeling technique may someday extend the binomial modeling technique in pricing derivatives and debts with a robust empirical testing strategy. I would like to thank Dr. Fred van Raaij, Dr. Naresh Malhotra, and Dr. Tracey King for their valuable comments on earlier versions of this chapter.

Consumer sentiment indices assess consumers' perception of economic health, including consumers' self-report evaluation and judgment under uncertainty. The uncertain judgment involves operations of mental processes that are beyond awareness. Financial market dynamics reflect investors' judgment under uncertainty. Consumer sentiment and financial market are then linked through the investors' mental operations beyond awareness, namely, the implicit consumer (investor) components. This proposition is demonstrated with (1) the correlation and regression models between implicit consumer confidence (ICC) ratio, estimated from consumer confidence index, and S&P 500 stock returns; and (2) the significant relationship between two constructs in a structural equation model. The two constructs are implicit consumer decision (ICD) and implicit investor decision (IID). These are based on the use of historical (1985–2002) consumer sentiment data and stock return data ($n = 179$). As a result, we bridge the gap between consumer constructs and financial metrics from an aggregate perspective.

As we know, an important financial metric of interest to management, shareholders, and other constituencies of a firm is stock returns. The compensation of top management, the retirement of employees, and the wealth of shareholders are all significantly linked to stock returns (Keown, Martin, Petty, and Scott 2003). Yet, an attempt to understand and predict stock returns in terms of marketing-related variables is lacking. However, similar attempts have been made in other fields such as behavioral finance, which prove to be insightful to this research.

The origin of linking consumer decision variables with financial metrics can be traced back to utility theory (Bernouli 1738) and prospect theory (Kahneman and Tversky 1979) where mental utilities or values are modeled as a function of financial wealth or changes in wealth such as a gain or a loss. Behavioral finance, an emerging field of research that uses behavioral theories such as the prospect theory to model financial decision making, relies heavily on linking financial variables to conceptual consumer variables such as mental accounting (Thaler 1991a) and overconfidence (De Bondt and Thaler 1985; Shiller 2000a).

In general, a consumer decision includes both judgment (made on one single option) and choice (the selection of one option from two or more alternative options). Consumer decisions constitute many major activities of a person's daily life. For example, a consumer may choose from many options on a breakfast menu (e.g., eggs or pancakes) in the morning, choose what form of transportation to take (e.g., bus or car) to get to work, and make a number of choices among stocks to purchase (e.g., technology or oil) in the office.

The dominant paradigm in consumer research accepts consumers as normative decision makers who are assumed to be aware of choice options and to consciously evaluate these options (Bargh 2002; Bettman 1979). However, economic and marketing-related anomalies such as the endowment effect, where people tend to sell more (at a higher price) and buy less (at a lower price) during a stock market bubble and panic (Thaler 1980; Shiller 2000a), cannot be explained with theories based only on conscious decision processes. The type of consumer behavior mentioned above encompasses both conscious and unconscious decision processes, which means that a consumer may or may not be aware of his or her choice options or aware of engaging in a choice-making process in the first place. Hence, reliance on conscious decision processes alone is insufficient to describe and predict the outcomes of consumer decisions (i.e., stock returns) soundly. To reconcile this problem, implicit consumer decision processes should be included in consumer choice models to incorporate the unconscious motives underlying a consumer decision.

In this chapter, we will describe the ICD theory along with laying out the computational framework for the ICD process. Also, we will illustrate how one should estimate the ICD component in general and more specifically with consumer confidence data. We will then explain how the ICD process can be linked to stock returns and test hypotheses derived from the ICD theory with empirical data using regression and structural equation models.

LITERATURE REVIEW

Literature from the aforementioned two schools of consumer research (behavioral decision theory and social cognition) provides the theoretical roots for the four general components of consumer decision making that we used in our theorization and modeling—explicit components, implicit components, affective components, and guessing components. We organize the literature review based on the four components, which will also be represented in a computational model used to measure ICD processes.

Implicit Components

As we defined earlier, implicit decisions occur when consumers are not able or willing to access or retrieve information pertaining to the options available for evaluation. One example of an implicit component that influences the consumer decision-making process is implicit memory (Schacter 1987).

In a simple model of consumer decision making, retrieval of information concerning the attributes of alternative options is assumed to precede evaluation processes. Studies conducted on memory typically consider both the information encoding and retrieval processes (Roediger 1990). Under the framework of the process dissociation procedure, which separates automatic (implicit) memory processes from controlled (explicit) memory processes (Jacoby 1991, 1998), it is postulated that implicit memory processes have a significant influence on judgments of alternative evaluation options (Yonelinas 1994).

The idea of implicit memory was initially developed in the 1980s (Graf and Schacter 1985) and refers to the memory trace one has of an object in memory when intentional retrieval of information pertaining to the object fails. In other words, it is the implicit (automatic) mental representation of an object that exists beyond awareness (Ye 2000). Based mainly on the methods used to measure and estimate implicit memory, this area of research can be separated into three categories: (1) the phenomenon school, whose goals are to define the concept of implicit memory and provide direct evidence of its existence (Schacter 1987); (2) the conceptual exploration school, whose goals are to explore the mechanisms underlying implicit memory processes and provide indirect evidence of the implicit components of information retrieval (Roediger 1990; Jacoby 1991); and (3) the computational modeling school, whose goals are to estimate the value of implicit components of information retrieval using mathematical equations, the objective of which is to identify and predict implicit decisions (Jacoby 1998).

Explicit Components

Although the concepts of implicit memory and social cognition have been recognized for more than 15 years in experimental and social psychology research (Schacter 1987; Bargh 2002), most consumer decision research focuses mainly on explicit decision making (Bargh 2002). When engaging in the process of making a choice, decision makers are assumed to be able to retrieve information pertaining to the options available for evaluation and use this information to decide between various alternatives. For example, in a preference reversal scenario, when two options (A and B) are compared against a reference point R, A is preferred to B. If the reference point were to shift to R', it is possible that the preference may be reversed; therefore, B may be preferred to A (Tversky and Kahneman 1992). During this decision-making process, evaluations are formed using information pertaining to both options and the reference point as long as they are accessible in memory. If an individual is not aware of the shift in reference point from R to R', then the preference reversal would most likely not occur.

Affective Components

Research examining affective influences on choice has a long history (Howard and Sheth 1969; Zajonc 1968; Kahneman and Tversky 1979, 2000; Loewenstein, Weber, Hsee, and Welch 2001). It has been well established that consumer judgment and choice are based on both cognition and affect;

however, there is still much debate on the order in which the two components, affect and cognition, influence information processing (Zajonc and Markus 1982; Bornstein 1989; Lazarus 1991). Affective components encompass both primary affective reactions that occur with little awareness (Zajonc and Markus 1982; van Raaij 1989) and subsequent affective evaluations that occur in a more elaborate manner (Lazarus 1991). Primary affective reactions may be perceived as low-order affective responses to a stimulus that arise from automatic processes (van Raaij 1989; Shiv and Fedorikhin 1999; Fitzsimons and Shiv 2001). More elaborate affective evaluations are typically thought to be constructed with conscious involvement. In addition, the "experienced utility" that we mentioned earlier may in itself be thought of as an affective reaction (pleasure or pain) to choice options (Kahneman and Tversky 2000).

Guessing Components

When we have no information (anchors, heuristics, prior exposures, and so forth) available for judgment and choice, it is intuitive to assume that we guess. In other words, the guessing component in the decision-making process reflects the base rate of our responses with no prior contact to the options. "Base rate" is a common concept and is typically used as a basic reference point to measure the effect of certain factors in experimental settings (Kahneman and Tversky 1979). For example, in Zajonc's (1968) mere-exposure effect experiments, the "base rate" was the response rate ("preferred over peers") to neutral items that were not previously exposed to respondents (e.g., irregular figures). The guessing component of the decision-making process is the underlying mechanism that determines the "base rate."

A COMPUTATIONAL FRAMEWORK: THE MDP MODEL

In order to measure ICD processes, we must use equations from a computational model, specifically the multinomial decision process (MDP) model. In this section, we describe the MDP model equations relevant to ICD measures, and the process of deriving the ICD measures from the MDP model equations.

Research using multinomial choice experiments and multinomial logit models has a long history and is still very active (Guadagni and Little 1983; Ben-Akiva and Lerman 1985; Ashok, Dillon, and Yuan 2002;

Kanninen 2002). Related to but not actually the same as these research methods, multinomial modeling is a statistically based technique that involves estimating parameters (latent variables) that represent the probabilities of unobservable events (Riefer and Batchelder 1988; Batchelder and Riefer 1990).[1] It is an extension of structural equation modeling, which is based on linear equations, that uses multinomial distributions to analyze models based on more sophisticated nonlinear equations formed with decision trees. Multinomial modeling has been applied to the study of implicit (automatic) processes, which serves as a more general model than the process-dissociation procedure (PDP) (Buchner, Erdfelder, and Vaterrodt 1995; Xu and Bellezza 2001). See Figures 7.1 to 7.3 for a multinomial model developed for liking and recognition judgments under uncertainty (Ye, 2000).

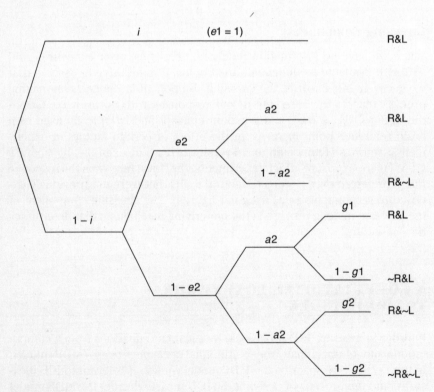

FIGURE 7.1 Structure of the MDP Model: Attended Stimuli
Notes:
R: Participants responding YES in the recognition tests
~R: Participants responding NO in the recognition tests
L: Participants responding YES in the liking tests
~L: Participants responding NO in the liking tests

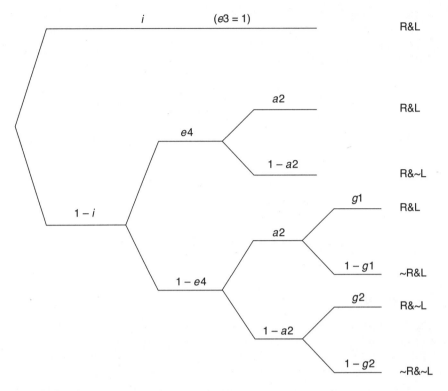

FIGURE 7.2 Structure of the MDP Model: Unattended Stimuli

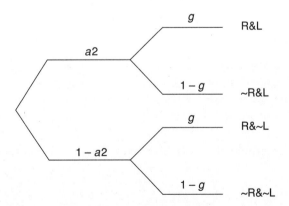

FIGURE 7.3 Structure of the MDP Model: New Stimuli

ICD Measures

Derived from Ye (2000), we have the following equations (a_2 stands for affective components):

$$a_2 = \frac{N_{31} + N_{33}}{N}, 1 - a_2 = \frac{N - (N_{31} + N_{33})}{N} = \frac{N_{32} + N_{34}}{N} \qquad (7.1)$$

Equation 7.1 is used to deduce the equation to estimate the implicit component (i), that is:

$$i = \frac{(N_{11} + N_{13}) - (N_{31} + N_{33})}{N_{32} + N_{34}} \qquad (7.2)$$

Therefore, the implicit component of judgment under uncertainty may be estimated with observed frequency values.

Transformation of the ICD Measures

The implicit component may be measured with observed frequency data in Equation 7.2. We may transform the frequency numbers to percentages of the total trial number (N). These observed percentages correspond with the conditional probabilities of each cell (judgment outcome).

So with Equation 7.2, we divide each frequency number with N, and get

$$i = \frac{\dfrac{(N_{11} + N_{13})}{N} - \dfrac{(N_{31} + N_{33})}{N}}{\dfrac{N_{32} + N_{34}}{N}}$$

Since the probability of liking given an attended option (liking| attended) is equal to the summation of the probabilities of liking and recognized given an attended option ($R\&L$|attended) and liking and not recognized given an attended option ($\sim R\&L$|attended), we have:

$$p(\text{liking}|\text{attended}) = p(\text{R\&L}|\text{attended}) + p(\sim\text{R\&L}|\text{attended})$$

$$= \frac{N_{11}}{N} + \frac{N_{13}}{N} = \frac{(N_{11} + N_{13})}{N}$$

Similarly, the probability of liking given a new option (liking|new) is the summation of the probabilities of liking and recognized given a new option ($R\&L$|new) and liking and not recognized given a new option ($\sim R\&L$|new), so we have:

$$p(\text{liking|new}) = p(R\&L|\text{new}) + p(\sim R\&L|\text{new})$$

$$= \frac{N_{31}}{N} + \frac{N_{33}}{N} = \frac{(N_{31} + N_{33})}{N}$$

On the other hand, since

$$N = N_{31} + N_{32} + N_{33} + N_{34}$$

We may derive the equation for the probability of not-liking options given that they are new:

$$p(\text{not liking|new}) = p(\sim L\&R|\text{new}) + p(\sim L\& \sim R|\text{new})$$

$$= \frac{N_{32}}{N} + \frac{N_{34}}{N} = \frac{(N_{32} + N_{34})}{N}$$

$$= 1 - p(\text{liking|new})$$

Finally, we have the transformed equation to measure the implicit component with conditional probabilities that may represent observed percentages.

$$i = \frac{p(\text{liking|old \& attended}) - p(\text{liking|new})}{1 - p(\text{liking|new})} \tag{7.3}$$

Interpretation of the ICD Measures

The conditional probabilities in Equation 7.3 may represent rating percentage data. For example, in a time period starting at time o and ending at time n, a rating scale R is used to measure consumers' evaluation (rating) outcomes. Let R_n stand for the rating at time n that may be perceived as new time, and R_o for time o that may be perceived as old time. Then we may assume R_n to be in line with the rating for new options and R_o for old options. Therefore, we have:

$$i = \frac{R_o - R_n}{1 - R_n} \tag{7.4}$$

Where $R_o = p(\text{liking|old \& attended})$ and $R_n = p(\text{liking|new})$

A typical rating scale technique is to ask individuals to estimate their likability, satisfaction, or preference on a scale of 1 to 100. Using Equation 7.4, which was derived from the MDP model (Ye 2000), we may transform the rating data to observed frequencies so that the implicit component may be estimated. We believe that individuals' rating responses reflect various components that are involved in the evaluation process, including an implicit component. The classic self-reported or explicit measures of behavior actually contain implicit influences, but we lack a technique to separate the implicit processes from the other components. This gap in the literature may be rectified with the ICD measure, which is derived from the MDP model.

To summarize, so far we have described our conceptualization of an ICD, the importance of ICD processes, and the way to measure ICD processes with MDP model equations. In the following sections of the chapter, we will apply ICD measures to stock market and consumer confidence evaluation data. We will then propose an ICD theory of stock returns, which is based on the notion that implicit decisions made by consumers and investors are linked to stock returns (i.e., a financial performance variable). Finally, we will test hypotheses that were derived from the ICD theory with a regression model and a structural equation model.

IMPLICIT CONSUMER DECISION THEORY

In general, the implicit consumer decision (ICD) theory postulates that a consumer variable, implicit consumer decisions, can be linked to stock returns. The rationale behind this proposition is that stock returns are seen as aggregated outcomes of implicit investor decisions that are actually a subset of implicit consumer decisions, which predict consumer confidence evaluations. Thus, using the ICD measures we developed, which give rise to an implicit consumer confidence (ICC) ratio, we expect to find an association between stock returns and implicit consumer confidence. Stock returns may be calculated with stock market indexes such as the S&P 500 index. The ICC ratio may be measured with consumer confidence data such as that found in the Michigan Index of Consumer Sentiment.

In the following sections, we will first propose the general relationships behind the ICD theory. We then describe the theoretical foundation for the ICD theory, which is followed by an examination of the equations that we use to estimate the two observable variables of the ICD theory: stock returns and ICC ratios.

The ICD Theory

First, the ICD theory postulates that implicit consumer decisions and stock returns may be linked (see Figure 7.4).

Second, most consumer judgments under uncertainty are made without the intentional retrieval of information pertaining to alternative options available for evaluation (Bargh 2002; Bargh and Chartrand 1999.) Consequently, most of the decisions that consumers make on a day-to-day basis are based on impulses or habits. In other words, many consumer decisions are made without conscious involvement, which implies the importance of studying implicit consumer decisions as an integral part of the overall decision-making process. As a result, implicit consumer decisions may be linked to overall consumer decisions.

Third, as a subset of the consumer population, financial investors make decisions to buy or sell stocks in the market. Hence, aggregated investor decisions may be viewed as a subset of aggregated consumer decisions. Most economists agree that investors should be viewed as irrational decision makers (Shiller 2000a). In other words, most investors make a number of decisions that deviate from predictions made by normative economic theories or financial fundamentals (Lei, Noussair, and Plott 2001; Daniel, Hirshleifer, and Subrahmanyam 1998). Hence, these irrational decisions made by investors may be viewed as constituting implicit decision making processes, which makes them a subset of implicit consumer decisions. As a result, implicit investor decisions may be linked to overall implicit consumer decisions.

Fourth, as advocated by behavioral finance research, stock returns reflect aggregated investor decisions (Shiller 2000a). In other words, as the number of investors who decide to buy a certain stock increases, the price of the stock (stock return) will increase. Since most investor decisions may be implicit, determined by irrationality (Shiller 2000a) or unawareness of information (Bargh 2002), this means that implicit decisions will have an influence on stock returns. Thus, stock returns may be linked to implicit investor decisions.

As shown with the above four steps, we are able to link implicit consumer decisions to stock returns. In summary, implicit consumer decision may assist in bridging the gap between consumer sentiment and financial performance of firms from an aggregate perspective. See Figure 7.4 for the theoretical framework of the ICD theory.

Based on the ICD theory, implicit consumer decisions and implicit investor decisions are related. As a result, the observed variables (indicators) of these two constructs should be correlated. The implicit consumer confidence ratio, which measures the implicit components of consumer confidence using the ICD measures, will serve as an indicator of implicit consumer decisions. The S&P 500 stock return index will serve as an indicator of implicit investor decisions since stocks returns are the results of irrational investor decisions in the market (Shiller 2000a). Therefore, the ICD theory predicts that the ICC ratio and S&P 500 stock returns

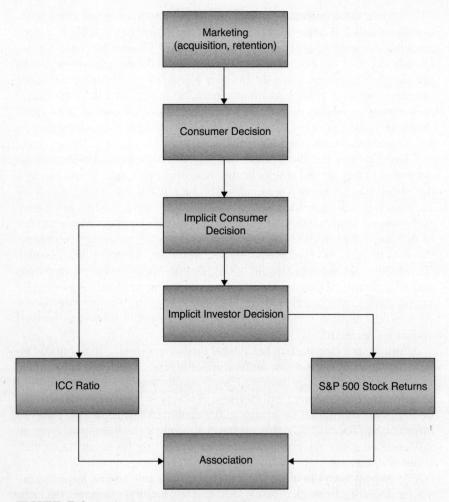

FIGURE 7.4   Implicit Consumer Decision Theory

will be correlated. We will go over these measures (indicators) in detail later in this chapter.

Theoretical Foundation for the ICD Theory

The theoretical foundation for the ICD theory includes three aspects: (1) an implicit component of consumer confidence measures, (2) implicit investment decisions that underlie stock market returns, and (3) the link between consumer constructs and financial metrics.

Implicit Component of Consumer Confidence

Since the ICD measure provides an estimate of the implicit component of information retrieval of alternative options available for evaluation, the availability of rating or evaluation data may be sufficient to estimate the value of the implicit component. The consumer confidence index, which is the outcome of consumers' evaluations of the current and future economy (including stock market performance), is one example of rating or evaluation data that would allow us to estimate the value of the implicit component of consumer decisions.

Consumer confidence data is primarily collected through household surveys. Two major measures of consumer confidence are available, one from the University of Michigan and the other from the Conference Board. The Conference Board's index is called the Consumer Confidence Index (CCI), while the University of Michigan's index is called the Index of Consumer Sentiment (ICS). To minimize confusion, we will refer to these two measures as the Conference Board index and the Michigan index, which allows us to use the term "consumer confidence" in a more generic sense (Garner, 2002).

Implicit consumer decisions may influence consumer confidence evaluations measured via telephone surveys (Michigan index) or mailed questionnaires (Conference Board index). In other words, the implicit component of information retrieval of alternative options may have an effect on consumers' evaluations of the current and future economy, including stock market performance. With our algorithm, we are able to estimate the implicit component of a consumer decision using an evaluation measure (i.e., consumer confidence), leading to the estimation of an implicit consumer confidence (ICC) ratio, which represents the implicit component included in a consumer confidence evaluation.

Implicit Investment Decisions That Underlie Stock Returns

The stock market often exhibits irrational behavior that is beyond the explanation of economic indicators and firm fundamentals. One example is the dot-com bubble that occurred at the end of last century where stock prices of Internet startup companies skyrocketed although the companies had zero or even negative earnings (i.e., the stocks were overvalued). Another example is the market crash at the beginning of this century where stock prices dropped drastically due to corporate scandals (e.g., Enron and WorldCom), which led to the undervaluation of stocks. In an emerging research field, behavioral finance, these irrational market behaviors are ascribed to psychological phenomena such as investor over- and underconfidence (Shiller 2000a; Daniel, Hirshleifer, and Subrahmanyam 1998). Psychological influences on investors' decisions may be further interpreted as the processes that occur automatically without the involvement of cognitive awareness, which in turn lead investors to make implicit decisions. Thus, the implicit decisions made by investors have an effect on the value of stock return indexes.

Link between Consumer Constructs and Financial Metrics

Since investor decisions are a subset of consumer decisions, implicit consumer decisions should relate to implicit investment decisions. As a result, the outcomes of implicit consumer decisions, implicit consumer confidence ratios, should relate to the outcomes of implicit investor decisions, namely, stock market indexes. With these propositions, the foundation of the ICD theory is formed, which suggests that implicit investor decisions predict stock market returns of major composite indexes such as the S&P 500, Dow Jones, and NASDAQ and implicit consumer decisions predict ICC ratios. Evidence for the expected association between the outcomes of consumer and investor implicit decisions, implicit consumer confidence, and stock market performance would be a significant step toward the discovery of a link between abstract consumer constructs and financial metrics.

Stock Returns

An important financial metric of interest to management, shareholders, and other constituencies is stock returns. The compensation of top management, the retirement of employees, and the wealth of shareholders are all significantly linked to stock returns. Yet, an attempt to understand and predict stock return in terms of consumer-related variables is lacking. In an effort to bridge this gap, we investigate how the implicit consumer confidence ratio, a consumer variable dependent on implicit consumer decisions, is linked to stock returns, a financial metric.

Following the definition of the arithmetic rate of return (Goetzmann 1996), stock returns, denoted as r, may be operationally defined as the proportion of price fluctuation (between the ending and starting prices) to the starting price.

$$r = \frac{Pn - Po}{Po} \tag{7.5}$$

Where Po is the starting (old) stock price at time o and Pn is the ending (new) stock price at time n.

The return rate may not only be influenced by risks (covariance of the portfolio) but also by financial data of corporations such as firm size, book-to-market ratios, and earnings (Daniel and Titman 1997). However, many market anomalies and even controlled laboratory results cannot be explained with financial data and risk assessments (Lei, Noussair, and Plott 2001). In addition, in consideration of market dynamics, relatively static corporate financial data (e.g., quarterly earnings and firm size) and assessments of risks may not be timely or useful to assist in accounting for monthly trading results. Therefore, the return rate may reflect psychological and consumer factors such as the implicit decision processes of investors and consumers.

For example, Alan Greenspan, the Chairman of the Board of Governors of the Federal Reserve System, spoke in January 2002 and announced publicly that there were more risks ahead for the economy. Stock markets, such as the S&P 500, dropped sharply after his statement concerning the future of the economy. Similar to the effects of corporate accounting scandals on consumer confidence, this "Greenspan effect" on the stock market cannot be reasonably explained by static financial data of corporations. Greenspan's prediction substantially influenced investors' implicit mental decision processes, which was illustrated by a sharp drop in the market that was not supported by financial indicators. This effect suggests that investors may have been unaware of or uncertain about certain information they had accessible to them to assist in forming evaluations of the future economy and stock market (i.e., financial indicators), which led to their decisions being influenced by implicit processes.

Included in the ICD theory, we argue that investors' aggregate implicit processes (i.e., their mental representations of market uncertainty and irrationality) contribute to the dynamics of stock returns in addition to the financial data of corporations.

Implicit Consumer Confidence Ratios

Consumer ability and willingness to buy or to save are the two major determinants of consumer expenditure and saving. The ability to buy or save refers to the consumer's level of discretionary income. The willingness determinant of consumer expenditure and saving is typically examined through consumer confidence research (Katona 1975; Garner 2002; van Raaij and Gianotten 1990) and is measured by an index of consumer confidence or sentiment. The consumer confidence index, which summarizes consumers' evaluations of economic expectations, is one of the prime indicators used to predict upcoming business cycles and is also used to determine the overall health of the economy. Since the 1950s, consumer confidence has been measured in the United States using household surveys such as the Index of Consumer Confidence of the Consumer Confidence Board or the Index of Consumer Sentiment (ICS) of the University of Michigan. In the European Union, a similar index has been in use since 1972. Survey questions regarding consumer sentiment in the Netherlands have been analyzed in the past by van Raaij and Gianotten (1990) and Nijkamp, Gianotten, and van Raaij (2002); however, a major proportion of consumer sentiment may be determined by implicit processes, which occur without consumer awareness and certainty about information pertaining to the market and the economy. These implicit determinants of consumer confidence or sentiment create the need for alternative measures of consumers' evaluations of the market and the economy.

Traditionally, consumer confidence has been measured by asking consumers to evaluate the economy and the stock market using household surveys. These evaluations reflect the contributions of both conscious (explicit) and unconscious (implicit) mental components. A consumer's explicit evaluation is based on successful information retrieval of alternative options; therefore, the evaluation is viewed as a rational observation and reaction to the current state of the economy. A consumer may also be influenced by implicit processes, which results in an irrational evaluation of the economy that is based on unsuccessful information retrieval of alternative options. In other words, consumers may be unaware of or uncertain about alternative options of current economic status and economic predictions that are available for them to consider. Assuming that consumers make explicit evaluations of consumer confidence, we are led to believe that they would also make explicit (rational) decisions such as engaging in spending and saving activities that follow fundamental financial principles. On the other hand, if we assume that implicit consumer evaluations also influence measures of consumer confidence (i.e., implicit consumer confidence, we are led to believe that consumers may not be aware of or may be uncertain about the alternative options that are available for their financial decisions. For example, consumers may spend their income or buy stocks based on impulsive decisions, which occur without the awareness of alternative options and budget planning or a concern about the return rate of their investments.

A measure of aggregate implicit consumer confidence should reflect the implicit evaluations of all consumers including investors and may be estimated from the Michigan index and Conference Board index. The specific equation used to measure the implicit component of consumer confidence may be derived from the ratings equation (see Equation 7.4), which was derived from a frequency equation (see Equation 7.3) rooted in the MDP model. Hence, based on the general algorithm (Equation 7.3) derived from the MDP model, an algorithm for implicit consumer confidence is described below, which is used to estimate the aggregate implicit mental component from the consumer confidence indexes:

$$i = \text{ICC ratio} = \frac{Vo - Vn}{N - Vn} \qquad (7.6)$$

Where Vo is the index value at the beginning of the period or time o.

This represents p(liking|old) in the general algorithm (Equation 7.3). Vn is the index value at the end of the period or time n. This represents p(liking|new) in the general algorithm. N refers to the reference point of the rating scale (Ye and van Raaij 1997; Ye 2000; Ye and van Raaij 2002). Extended from conditional probabilities of referenced ratings and evaluations such as the ICS, we use the reference point 100 as N.

The number 100 is used because it is the most practical reference point available at this time that may be used to estimate N (e.g., 100 is the beginning score of the confidence indexes; Garner, 2002; van Raaij and Gianotten 1990). The use of this reference point may induce concern that the ICC ratio will be greater than 1 or less than zero. Since N is a reference point, the value of the ICC ratio is considered to be relative to zero impact on decisions due to implicit information retrieval. So an ICC ratio value that is greater than 1 would indicate the distance away from zero impact on decisions due to implicit information retrieval. When the ICC ratio is negative, this may be interpreted as the implicit component having a negative influence on evaluation and decision, for example, a negative priming effect (Roediger 1990). Recall that negative priming results in inhibitions pertaining to the processing and evaluations of alternative options; this effect is due to prior subliminal contact with the option or its associates.

There are several empirical alternative options that may be used to approximately estimate $N - Vn$. One option is to use $Vo - N$; thus the ICC ratio may be approximated using the following equation:

$$i = \frac{Vo - Vn}{Vo - N} \qquad (7.7)$$

In practice, Equations 7.6 and 7.7 have both been used to estimate the ICC ratio (Ye, 2003). The one that illustrates a closer relationship (e.g., larger correlation coefficient) with other ICD constructs will be chosen as the ICC indicator because it has better construct validity.[2] In this case, the ICD construct that is correlated with the approximated ICC ratio is represented by stock returns, which indicate implicit investor (consumer) decisions.

To summarize, we described an ICD theory that links implicit consumer (investor) decisions to stock returns. We also described the equations used to obtain measures of implicit consumer decisions and implicit investor decisions with consumer confidence and stock returns data. In the following sections, we carry out two empirical analyses to test the hypotheses derived from the ICD theory, one using regression analysis and the other using structural equation modeling.

EMPIRICAL APPROACHES

Based on the ICD theory, we expect to find a link between stock returns and the implicit consumer confidence ratio. There are two approaches that may be used to test this association: exploratory and confirmatory. The exploratory approach (Analysis 1) involves examining correlation and regression coefficients between the Michigan ICC ratio (i.e., monthly aggregate implicit processes [MAIP] of the Michigan index) and the S&P 500 returns (i.e., monthly arithmetic rate of return [MARR] of the S&P 500 Index). On the other hand, the confirmatory approach (Analysis 2) involves measuring the association using a structural equation model (SEM) that includes two latent constructs, that is, implicit consumer decisions and implicit investor decisions. In the SEM model, implicit investor decisions predict observed stock returns of the S&P 500, Dow Jones, and NASDAQ indexes whereas implicit consumer decisions predict the ICC ratio of the Michigan index and/or the Conference Board index.

ANALYSIS 1: EXAMINATION OF CORRELATIONS AND A REGRESSION MODEL

In Analysis 1, we first propose two empirical hypotheses based on the ICD theory. One hypothesis concerns the predicted association between the ICC ratio (estimated using the algorithm based on the Michigan index) and S&P 500 stock returns. The alternative hypothesis is that the Michigan index, without the use of the algorithm, will not correlate with the S&P 500 returns. Using data we collected, we tested the two hypotheses with simple correlation coefficients. Finally, we integrated the S&P 500 index, the Michigan index, the ICC ratio, and their interactions into a multiple regression model with S&P 500 returns as the dependent variable.

Empirical Hypotheses

We believe that ICC ratios and stock return rates are under the control of related forces, specifically, implicit consumer decisions and implicit investor decisions. Thus, we predict that ICC ratios and stock returns will be correlated with one another. The hypotheses below summarize our expectations for the empirical investigation:

H_1: The ICS index reflects contributions of both conscious (explicit) and unconscious (implicit) processes and should not be correlated with the return rate of the S&P 500 index, which mostly reflects implicit mental processes of investors.

H_2: Implicit mental processes of consumers and investors influence both consumer confidence evaluations and stock market returns, so the ICC ratio (measured by the ICS or MAIP) and return rates (MARR) of the S&P 500 index should be correlated.

H_3: A significant partial correlation between the ICC ratio and S&P 500 returns is expected along with a significant partial correlation between the original index values (ICS and S&P 500 index).

H_1 states that a simple correlation between the ICS and the S&P 500 returns will not be significant; this is mainly because the underlying components of the two indices are too complex to eliminate each other's variance. H_2 purifies the implicit mental processes underlying the ICS index and the return rates of the S&P 500 index. Since the two indicators (ICC ratio and return rate) represent the same underlying source (implicit mental processes), they are expected be correlated. H_3 attempts to test the relationship between ICC ratio and S&P 500 returns conditioned on the original values of the indexes.

Method

Following the procedures listed below, we obtained the data and then performed the analysis, which is described by the following steps. First, we collected monthly ICS data (data archive of the University of Michigan) and S&P 500 index data (Yahoo! Finance) from June 1985 to February 2002. Next, we estimated the monthly aggregate implicit process data with Equation 7.1 and the monthly arithmetic rate of return data with Equations 7.2. Then we performed a regression analysis with MAIP and MARR. Note that for each year, we removed 17 January data points (the stock index values of January) due to the "January" or "Calendar" effect (caused by economic factors such as tax reasons), which describes that stock prices rise between December and January.[3] This is an anomaly of the stock market described by Shiller (2000a, p. 183), so we treat it as a special case and do not include it in the stock market data for the rest of the months. Finally, we performed a regression analysis with the ICS and S&P 500 indexes.

Examination of Correlations

We found an insignificant correlation between the ICS and the return rate (MARR) of the S&P 500 index ($r = 0.03$, $n = 183$, $p = 0.682$), but the correlation between the ICC ratio (MAIP) estimated with Equation 7.7[4] and the return rate (MARR) was significant ($r = 0.209$, $n = 183$, $p = 0.005$).

The strength of the association between the two indicators is shown to be stronger with the most recent data. The correlation coefficient between MAIP and MARR with monthly data from June 2001 to June 2002 is 0.68 ($df = 11$), $p = 0.01$, with adjusted R^2 being 41 percent, which shows a large effect size according to Cohen's convention.

There are a number of reasons that the relationship between the ICC ratio and the stock return index has not been uncovered until now. First, the previous understanding of implicit consumer confidence was premature and not yet modeled as an algorithm or as a statistic derived from the MDP model (Ye, 2000; Ye and van Raaij, 2002). In addition, there has been no solid evidence until recently showing evidence for speculation that market dynamics (stock returns) may be due in part to investor sentiment or even *implicit* investor sentiment (Shiller, 2000a). Also, data that were biased as a result of the "January effect" had not been separated from the rest of the monthly data.

Multiple Regression Analysis

To examine the partial correlation between the original index values (ICS and S&P 500), a backward multiple regression analysis was performed with expected MARR as the dependent variable (DV) and ICS (*IV1*), S&P 500 (*IV2*), MAIP (*IV3*), MAIP × ICS (*IV4*), S&P 500 × MAIP (*IV5*), and ICS × S&P 500 (*IV6*) as independent variables. All of the six independent variables were entered into an initial regression model. After examining their partial correlations and F values, we removed those with insignificant F values from the model and continued the analysis. The independent variables featured in the final regression model are MAIP, MAIP × ICS, and MAIP × S&P 500. S&P 500 and S&P 500 × MAIP failed to enter the final regression model because their F values exceed the criteria (0.09). The coefficients and t-values of the independent variables included in the final model are listed in Table 7.1.

TABLE 7.1 Coefficients of the Final Regression Model

Variable	Unstandardized Coefficient	t-value	p-value
Constant	0.009826	2.982	0.003
MAIP	0.232	2.694	0.008
MAIP × ICS	−0.00247	−2.609	0.010
MAIP × S&P 500	0.00002733	1.726	0.086

Notes:
UM_ICC = MAIP = Michigan ICC ratio
ICCPROUM = MAIP × ICS
ICCPRO50 = MAIP × S&P 500
ICS = Index of Consumer Sentiment (Michigan index)
SP500 = S&P 500 index stock returns

The F value of the final model is $F(3,178) = 5.184, p < 0.01$. Therefore, the model may be presented as:

$$\text{Expected (MARR)} = 0.00983 + 0.232\,(\text{MAIP}) - 0.00247\,(\text{MAIP} \times \text{ICS})$$
$$+ 0.0000273\,(\text{MAIP} \times \text{S\&P\,500}) \tag{7.8}$$

Equation 7.8 suggests that (1) the partial correlation between the ICC ratio and S&P 500 returns is also significant (Table 7.1), so H_3 holds, and (2) the association between the ICC ratio and S&P 500 stock returns is moderated by the Michigan index and the S&P 500 index values.

As we have previously demonstrated, the expected MARR can be estimated with Equation 7.5. We let the new stock price (Pn) represent future S&P 500 index values and the old stock price (Po) represent historical values (i.e., values for previous periods) of the S&P 500 index. This means that the expected S&P 500 index in Equation 7.8 is a predicted variable. We insert Equation 7.5 into Equation 7.8 and get the following equation:

$$\frac{Pn}{Po} - 1 = 0.00983 + 0.232\,(\text{MAIP}) - 0.00247\,(\text{MAIP} \times \text{ICS})$$
$$+ 0.0000273\,(\text{MAIP} \times Pn)$$

After assembling the same elements with Pn (i.e., $\frac{Pn}{Po}$ and $(\text{MAIP} \times Pn)$), we get an equation that represents the expected S&P 500 index (Pn),

$$Pn = \frac{1.00983 + 0.232(\text{MAIP}) - 0.00247(\text{MAIP} \times \text{ICS})}{\dfrac{1}{Po} - 0.0000273\,(\text{MAIP})} \tag{7.9}$$

In Equation 7.9, the expected S&P 500 index is a function of the MAIP (ICC ratio), the ICS (index of consumer sentiment), and the S&P 500 index value of the last period (Po).

Discussion

From the analysis described above, we have supported H_1, H_2, and H_3 with real-life data. Thus, we conclude that implicit mental processes underlying measures of consumer confidence (e.g., ICC ratio and ICS) and implicit decisions underlying measures of stock returns (e.g., S&P 500 index) are significantly correlated. The ICD theory assists in explaining how this correlation is due to the related underlying sources, the implicit mental processes of consumers and investors that influence measures of consumer confidence and stock market returns.

The final model resulting from the multiple regression analysis suggests that the partial correlation between the ICC ratio and the S&P 500 index is significant. It also discloses the relationship between S&P 500 return rates (MARR) and the ICC ratio (MAIP) and the interactions between the ICC ratio and S&P 500 index and between the ICC ratio and ICS index. In other words, the association between the ICC ratio and stock returns is moderated by the Michigan index and the S&P 500 index.

ANALYSIS 2: STRUCTURAL EQUATION MODEL

In Analysis 1, we found that two observed variables, the Michigan ICC ratio (an ICD indicator) and the returns of the S&P 500 index, are significantly correlated. The next question we ask is: Can we retest and identify the causal relationship between implicit consumer decisions and stock returns with multiple measures representing the two constructs? The ICD theory provides the conceptual foundation for the causal relationship; that is, the underlying construct influencing the Michigan ICC ratio (i.e., implicit consumer decisions) and the underlying construct influencing S&P 500 returns (i.e., implicit investor decisions) are associated. This proposition serves as a means to bridge consumer sentiment to financial performance. To retest this proposition from a broader perspective, we employ structural equation modeling, which allows us to model the causal relationship while also using more indicators for the two constructs.

We start our analysis by collecting multiple measures of the two constructs included in the structural equation model, specifically, implicit consumer decisions and implicit investor decisions. Then we used a structural equation model to retest the causal relationship between the two constructs using five observable variables. The data collected for the five observable variables ranged from the year 1985 to 2002. The two observable variables of the ICD construct are the Michigan index and the Conference Board index. The three observable variables for the IID construct are the S&P 500 composite index, the Dow Jones composite index, and the NASDAQ composite index. The data were transformed to ICC ratios or stock returns with the algorithms that were proposed earlier (see Equations 7.5 and 7.7). Finally, the ICC ratios and stock index returns were used to test the association between the two constructs with a structural equation modeling (SEM) analysis.

Empirical Hypotheses

In Analysis 1, the data supported H_2, which indicated that there was a significant correlation between the ICC ratio of the Michigan index and the S&P 500 stock returns. It also confirmed the prediction made by the ICD theory that implicit consumer decisions influence stock market performance through implicit investor decisions. To speculate how this causal relationship may occur, the ICD theory suggests that there are two associated factors that underlie the relationship between the two indexes. One of these factors includes the implicit investor decisions (IIDs) that influence stock returns. The other factor includes the implicit consumer decisions (ICDs) that influence the implicit component of consumer confidence evaluations, which are measured by the Michigan index or the Confidence Board index. The relationship between the constructs (ICC and IID) is conceptualized by a two-factor causal model of implicit consumer decisions.

H_4: There are two connected factors underlying the relationship between implicit consumer decisions and stock returns: (1) the implicit investor decision, which is observed with stock returns of the S&P 500, Dow Jones, and NASDAQ composite indexes and (2) the implicit consumer decision, which is observed using the ICC ratios of the Michigan index and the Conference Board index.[5] We expect to find a significant path coefficient between the ICD and the IID constructs (see Figure 7.5).

Testing the strength of the relationship between associated causal factors in consumer research with causal modeling may be traced back to the 1980s (Burnkrant and Page, 1982; Bagozzi, 1982). The first goal of this SEM analysis is to examine the strength of the relationship between ICDs and IIDs.

Since ICC ratios are calculated in the middle of the month when consumer confidence data are released and stock index returns are calculated at the end of the month, then we predict that there may be a

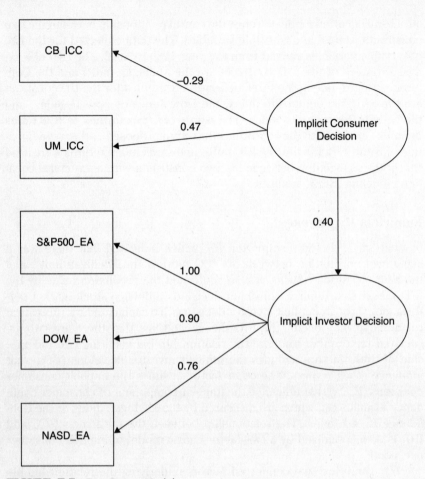

FIGURE 7.5   Two-Factor Model

causal relationship between the two, where the ICC ratio predicts the index returns. The second goal of the SEM analysis is to test this causal relationship.

H_5: The ICC ratio has a direct influence on stock index returns; this relationship is directional.

Method

The same data-collection method used in Analysis 1 was used to collect monthly index data ranging from June 1985 to February 2002 for five observable variables, which resulted in a total of 200 data points collected.

The difference between the two analyses is that data for only two variables (Michigan index and S&P 500 index) were collected in Analysis 1, but data for five variables were collected for Analysis 2. The five observable index variables we used were the Michigan index, Conference Board index, S&P 500 composite index, Dow Jones composite index, and NASDAQ composite index. We collected archived Michigan index data using the University of Michigan web site and Conference Board index data using the Federal Reserve Bank of Boston web site.

We transformed the Michigan index and Conference Board index data to implicit consumer confidence ratios with the algorithm described in Equation 7.7. The stock market composite indexes were transformed into stock returns (earnings) with Equation 7.5. We eliminated several outliers from the data set of the transformed ICC ratios of the Conference Board index because the ICC values exceeded the outlier boundary. After the elimination of outliers and data that were biased by the January effect, a total of 179 data points were entered into LISREL 8.5.

Results

A measurement model representing the associations between the latent variables (factors) and their respective measures was conceived and tested with a confirmatory factor analysis. The ICD factor has two indicators, specifically, the ICC ratios representing the University of Michigan and Conference Board indexes. The IID factor is measured with three indicators, which are the returns of the S&P 500, Dow Jones, and NASDAQ indexes.

As expected, two factors (ICD and IID) were extracted from the data with a principal-component analysis, resulting in the cumulative percentage of variance accounted for being 74.28 percent. The indicators corresponding to the three indexes converged on one factor (IID), with loadings 0.978 (S&P 500 returns), 0.935 (Dow Jones returns), and 0.870 (NASDAQ returns). The two ICC ratios converged on the second factor (ICD), with loadings 0.859 (Conference Board ratio) and −0.536 (Michigan ratio). Hence, the measurement model exhibits acceptable construct validity with respect to two factors (ICD and IID), which allowed us to proceed with our analysis of the SEM model.

We found that the Michigan and Conference Board ICC ratios had, respectively, positive (.47) and negative (−.29) loading values on the ICD construct, which indicates that there are differences between the two measures and their associations with the ICD construct. Why?

We speculate that different mental processes may be employed in the formation of consumer confidence evaluations with the use of different survey approaches. For example, the University of Michigan index is created using telephone surveys, whereas the Conference Board index is created using mail surveys that require consumers to provide written responses to the survey questions (Garner, 2002). We believe that consumer confidence evaluations collected by using telephone interviews are more sensitive to ICD processes, which would lead to a positive relationship between the Michigan ratio and the ICD construct. On the other hand, written responses illicit more elaborate and conscious mental processes so that ICD processes have less of an influence on consumer confidence evaluations. Since written evaluations are mostly influenced by cognitive rather than implicit components, this would help to explain the negative relationship between the Conference Board ratio and the ICD construct. In sum, the Michigan and Conference Board ratios, intended to measure the ICD component of consumer confidence indexes (i.e., ICC), exhibit varying degrees of association with the ICD construct. However, both loaded in a common component (construct).

The two-factor SEM model, which includes measures representing various ICC ratios and stock return indexes (see Figure 7.5, H_4, and H_5) is examined below. The fit of the model is indicated by $\chi^2 (4) = 2.58$,[6] CFI = 1.00, GFI = 0.99, AGFI = 0.98, and RMSEA < 0.001, $p = 0.63$. Therefore, the hypotheses that we developed pertaining to the two-factor causal model with two indicators representing ICC ratios and three indicators representing stock index returns (H_4, H_5; see Figure 7.5) are retained. The standardized LISREL estimates for the causal path coefficients, which relate measures that are used as indicators in the fitted model to their respective latent factors, are displayed in Figure 7.5. The path coefficient representing the relationship between the two factors is equal to 0.40, which is significant with a t-test ($t = 2.49$, $p < 0.05$).

Discussion

The SEM analysis described above was conducted primarily to assess the strength of the relationship between the ICD and IID constructs. The two-factor model hypothesis (H_4), which asserts that there are two connected latent factors (i.e., ICDs and IIDs), is retained in Analysis 2. Therefore, we are able to conclude that ICC ratios and stock returns are associated through two connected constructs. In other words, the implicit consumer decision (predicting implicit consumer confidence ratios) is strongly associated with the implicit investor decision (predicting the stock returns of three composite indexes).

The fitted two-factor causal model (Figure 7.5) helps further explain the relationship between the Michigan ICC ratio and the S&P 500 returns that we discovered in Analysis 1. That is, it illustrates the underlying processes that provide a conceptual explanation for the significant correlation between the two measures. Specifically, the Michigan ICC ratio is associated with a latent factor (ICD) that directionally correlates (0.40) with another latent factor (IID), and this other latent factor (IID) predicts the S&P 500 returns. Thus, the positive relationship between the Michigan ICC ratio and the S&P 500 returns that we discovered in Analysis 1 was also supported using a SEM analysis.

CONTRIBUTIONS OF THE ICD THEORY

In order to bridge the gap between consumer constructs and financial performance and respond to the call for the inclusion of implicit components in consumer decision-making research (Bargh 2002; Loewenstein 2001; Simonson et al. 2001), we propose a new concept, ICD, and postulate that many consumer decisions are influenced by automatic or implicit processes that occur without the intentional retrieval of information pertaining to alternative options available for evaluation. The conceptual foundation for this construct is grounded in research on affect (Howard and Sheth 1969; van Raaij 1989; Shiv and Fedorikhin 1999), implicit memory (Schacter 1987; Jacoby 1998), and implicit social cognition (Greenwald, McGhee, and Schwartz 1998; Bargh and Ferguson 2000). After reviewing the literature, we concluded that the quest to disentangle the roles that implicit cognition (memory) and implicit affect play in consumer decision making is crucial yet unresolved (Loewenstein 2001; Bargh 2002; Simonson et al. 2001); therefore, we attempted to isolate and assess the influence that implicit consumer decisions have on stock market performance.

To measure the ICD, we described a multinomial decision process model (Ye and van Raaij 2002), which derives a general algorithm to estimate the implicit component of consumer evaluation. The algorithm can be applied to many evaluation and decision practices, one of which is the implicit consumer confidence evaluation, namely, the implicit consumer confidence ratio.

The contributions made by the ICD theory fall into three categories: (1) extending the consumer decision-making model to include implicit components, (2) providing a framework linking consumer constructs to financial performance with supportive data, and (3) advancing the behavioral finance literature.

Extend Consumer Decision Making to Incorporate Implicit Components

Research on consumer decision making has a long history focusing on explicit decisions where respondents are aware of choice options and then make selections. An emerging direction of research in this field proposes that implicit components (such as implicit memory) play an important role in judgment formation and choice (Bargh 2002; Lee 2002). Extending the MDP model, which describes the preference (experienced utility) formulation process (Kahneman and Tversky 2000), we incorporate the influence of implicit components on consumer evaluations. Specifically, we consider the implicit processes that underlie consumer confidence evaluations (i.e., ICC) and derive an equation that measures the ICC ratio. As a result, implicit consumer decisions, which are central to the ICD theory, are represented using the ICC ratio. Thus, in an attempt to extend the use of implicit components in consumer decision-making research, we consider implicit consumer decisions, which are reflected in implicit consumer confidence ratios.

Since stock market behavior is in part attributable to investor psychology or irrational sentiment (Shiller 2000a; Daniel, Hirshleifer, and Subrahmanyam 1998), we formed a basic assumption that implicit consumer decisions influence investment decisions. This basic assumption is the core idea behind the implicit consumer decision theory that links consumer confidence to stock returns. Specifically, the ICD theory predicts that the ICC ratio and stock returns will be significantly correlated, which we supported with empirical data using the ICC ratio of the Michigan index and S&P 500 stock returns. To retest this relationship, we employed a structural equation model and tested the relationship between two latent factors, ICD and IID. The model included the ICD construct, which predicted two ICC ratios, and the IID construct, which predicted stock returns of three major composite indexes. A fitted two-factor causal model is supported with the data ($n = 179$), which discloses a significant association (standard path coefficient $= 0.40$) between the ICD and the IID constructs.

Our results in support of the ICD theory provide managerial value in the sense that by extending models of consumer decision making to include implicit components (i.e., ICD), we are able to link consumer sentiment to financial performance from an aggregate perspective. For example, positive news released (e.g., more federal funding injected in the defense industry) that is pertinent to an industry gives rise to a higher ICD level, which increases the stock returns of that industry. This chain reaction would occur because the ICD construct (represented by ICC ratios) is correlated with the IID construct that underlies the values of stock returns.

Link between Consumer Sentiment and Financial Performance

With an individual (micro) perspective, the second contribution falls within the recent gap-bridging movement in the consumer research community to link consumer constructs to financial metrics of firms. Within the ICD framework, we linked a financial metric (stock returns) to a consumer decision construct (the ICC ratio) with the discovery of a significant correlation between them. In addition, the ICD theory proposes a conceptual process that links implicit consumer decisions (reflected by ICC ratios) to implicit investor decisions (reflected by stock return indexes), which further bridges the gap between consumer constructs and financial performance indicators. We found support for the ICD theory through two empirical studies, thus supporting the argument that consumer sentiments are reflected in financial performance indicators. According to our findings, a one-point increase in an aggregate measure of consumer sentiments (the ICC ratio of the Michigan index) leads to roughly a 23 percent increase in S&P 500 stock returns, provided that the other two variables in the regression equation are controlled (see Equation 7.8).

By discovering the relationship between stock returns and ICC ratios, we feel that marketing campaigns such as advertising and sales promotions may be used effectively to increase consumer confidence regarding the firm's product or brand, which in turn will increase the ICC ratio. This increased ICC ratio may lead to an associated increase in level of stock returns of the firm through increased implicit consumer and implicit investor decisions. In future studies, one may focus on designing an individual (micro) measure of the ICC ratio for a particular product or brand of a firm, rather than using the aggregate ICC ratio of the Michigan index, which would be beneficial to firm-level practitioners.

Behavioral Finance Studied with an Aggregate Perspective

Another major contribution of the ICD theory involves conducting behavioral finance research with an aggregate perspective. The recent effort in consumer research to link consumer variables with financial metrics is a natural extension of work on utility theories, such as prospect theory, and behavioral finance. Branching off of behavioral economics research, behavioral finance research considers elements of investor psychology as essential for analyzing financial behaviors. Proponents of behavioral finance research argue that some financial phenomena may be better understood using models in which agents are assumed to be not fully rational (Barberis and Thaler 2001). De Bondt and Thaler (1985) proposed that psychological properties such as under- and overreactions to the stock market and mental accounting processes (Thaler 1991a) would have a significant influence on investor decisions. Also, prospect theory (Kahneman and Tversky 1979; Tversky and Kahneman 1992) was proposed to account for irrational decisions made by investors, which serve as important determinants of asset (stock) returns and portfolio management activities. A number of these psychological and consumer-related variables such as biased self-attribution and overconfidence have been incorporated into security market models (Daniel, Hershleifer, and Subrahmanyam 1998). These models are well accepted in the financial world.

There are two major financial theories that are undergoing extensive remodeling involving the inclusion of investor psychology factors. The first model is the capital asset pricing model (CAPM; Sharpe 1963), which originally argues that asset returns are determined only by economic factors such as risk (i.e., portfolio variance-covariance). The second model is the efficient market hypothesis (EMH; Fama 1970), which argues that the stock market is inherently unpredictable. To include behavioral assumptions in these two models, one must first consider constructs and theories originating from various areas of research. In this case, it is wise to consider both financial and economic ideas in an attempt to understand demand from a financial perspective. The second step involves also considering the unique and core contributions that psychological and consumer constructs may have on these behavioral finance models. For example, in this study, consumer confidence serves as a consumer variable, which we propose has an influence on stock returns (through implicit investor decisions) and that serves as the counterpart from the financial world, allowing the integration of the two research fields. We found that stock returns are correlated with the ICC ratio of consumer confidence. In other words, stock returns may be predictable if one considers consumers' implicit mental representations of economic uncertainty and unawareness. We also derived Equation 7.9 to provide a means to estimate the future S&P 500 index using historical ICC ratio, ICS index, and S&P 500 index data.

From an aggregate (macro) perspective, our findings contribute to behavioral finance research by challenging both the CAPM and EMH models. First, our results challenge the capital asset pricing model by arguing that psychological factors that influence investors' decisions, specifically implicit mental decision processes, are correlated with stock returns. In other words, stock returns may not be determined solely by economic variables such as the variance-covariance of asset portfolios or the characteristics of firms as the CAPM assumes (Fama and French 1992), but they may also be determined by psychological and consumer factors such as the implicit mental components of consumers' and investors' evaluations. Secondly, our findings also challenge the unpredictability hypothesis of the EMH model by demonstrating that it is possible to forecast stock market returns with ICC ratios.

CONCLUSION

The relationship between implicit consumer confidence ratios and stock returns was discovered using the multinomial decision process model and the algorithm of the ICC ratio. This relationship provides support for the ICD theory, which describes the process by which consumer sentiments are translated into financial performance indicators, mainly through the implicit consumer decision construct. The theory suggests that stock market behavior is irrational and influenced by investors' implicit decisions, which occur when they are not able or willing to or it is not necessary to retrieve information pertaining to alternative options available for evaluation. By fitting a two-factor causal model with the data ($n = 179$), we discover that the construct underpinning implicit consumer confidence and the construct underpinning stock index returns are closely related. As a result, this relationship underscores the linkage between investor sentiments and financial performance indicators (i.e., between ICC ratios and stock indexes).

CHAPTER 8

More Multinomial Models and Signal Detection Models for Risk Propensity

I n this chapter, we extend the use of multinomial modeling to understanding the growth of retail investors for a stock or a fund. We also look into how the mind of an investor operates with unconscious (aka implicit) processes. In addition, we discuss another modeling technique, signal detection theory, and apply the technique to understanding risk propensity, a bias that investors and fund managers always have when making investment decisions.

MULTINOMIAL MODELS FOR RETAIL INVESTOR GROWTH

In general, a multinomial choice experiment (Kanninen 2002) starts with constructions of a matrix with cells constructed with matching levels of independent (input) and dependent (output) variables. Latent variables and their relationships to the choice (decision) process are then assumed (hypothesized) based on empirical findings as to forming equations for each cell. Then the hypothetical cell equations are used to estimate the expected cell frequencies that are further used to fit the empirical data (cell frequencies) collected in lab experiments. In other words, statistical tests are performed to measure the distance between expected and observed cell frequencies. The hypothetical latent variables and their relationships may be refined to vary the cell equations to fit the empirical cell data.

Theoretically, multinomial modeling is a statistically based technique that involves estimating hypothetical parameters that represent the probabilities of unobservable events (Riefer and Batchelder 1988; Batchelder and Riefer 1990). It uses the multinomial distribution to analyze models based on binary trees. It has been applied to study implicit memory processes that could serve as a more general model for the process-dissociation procedure (Buchner, Erdfelder, and Vaterrodt 1995). Besides psychological studies, in marketing literature, multinomial modeling is becoming popular (Ashok, Dillon, and Yuan 2002; Kanninen 2002).

Technically, maximum-likelihood estimation is employed to estimate the parameters (or latent variables) of a multinomial model (Riefer and Batchelder 1988). The parameters are estimated at an equilibrium point where the maximization of the multinomial likelihood function is reached. Steps to obtain maximum-likelihood estimates (MLEs) are as follows:

1. Generate the likelihood function for the model. The likelihood function (denoted by L) of a sample is the value of the joint probability distribution or the joint probability density of independent random variables, that is, $L = f(x_1, x_2 \ldots, x_n) = f(x_1)f(x_2) \ldots f(x_n)$.

2. A log likelihood transformation to the likelihood function is performed.

3. For multiple-parameter cases, partial derivatives are found for the likelihood function with respect to each parameter. After setting each partial derivative equal to zero, the equations are solved to obtain the MLE for each parameter.

4. The goodness of fit of the model is determined. These four steps can be implemented using a multinomial binary tree (MBT) program developed by Hu (1991).

This section uses the multinomial modeling technique (Batchelder 1998) to decompose the brand-switching matrix of the RLZ model and produces conditional probabilities for alternative decision outcomes (Rust, Lemon, and Zeithaml 2004; Rust, Lemon, and Narayandas 2005). It then links the probabilities with Bayesian theorem and creates a new customer growth function on consumer choice (i.e., the customer retention rate). The growth function offers novel insights on customer growth from behavioral choice modeling perspective comparing to mainstream time-based adoption models (Bass 1969, 2004; Gupta, Lehmann, and Stuart 2004). These insights include three predictions that are corroborated with a peak analysis. The market share (k) of a brand determines the shape of the growth function. For small and medium brands, the relationship between customer growth and consumer choice follows an inverted-U curve. The peak of the growth curve may not exist if the market share of the brand is too large.

Introduction

The customer growth of a brand focuses on increasing the number and the value of customers of the brand that relate to the bottom line of a firm's financial performance (Gupta, Lehmann, and Stuart 2004). The mainstream adoption models have made tremendous contributions in marketing and management science and have offered insights to the growth and the value of customers over time (Bass 1969, 2004). This chapter uses an alternative consumer choice modeling perspective to study customer growth compared to the mainstream time-based approach.

Customer retention (retaining repeat customers) and acquisition (acquiring really new customers) are two key roles of marketing because both contribute to increasing the numbers (i.e., the size) of the customers of a brand (A). Brand A will be used in this discussion to indicate the brand of primary interest with which customers are retained and acquired. The number of the customers of brand A (N_A) is the building block of customer lifetime value (CLV) and customer equity (CE). Recently, several researchers have developed various means to assess the CLV and CE (e.g., Rust, Lemon, and Zeithaml 2004; Gupta, Lehmann, and Stuart 2004; Rust, Lemon, and Narayandas 2005).

This discussion uses a novel (to marketing research) multinomial processing tree (MPT) modeling technique (Batchelder 1998; Batchelder and Riefer 1990; Ye and van Raaij, submitted) to decompose the brand-switching matrix of the CLV equation of the RLZ model and create a new growth function (Rust, Lemon, and Zeithaml 2004; Rust, Lemon, and Narayandas 2005). The multinomial modeling method is new and ideal for behavioral choice modeling because it may describe and validate the quantitative models with consumer decision paths to alternative outcomes. The chapter attempts to explore two unknown areas: (1) How do we use behavioral modeling technique to decompose the brand-switching matrix of the RLZ model so that a new customer growth function can be created? (2) How do we predict and corroborate the patterns of customer growth with the new growth function?

Therefore we have two sections to follow: (1) develop the new customer growth function on the basis of decomposing the brand-switching matrix of the RLZ model; (2) derive and corroborate three predictions on customer growth over consumer choice from the new growth function.

Developing the New Growth Function
Step-by-Step

At first, this chapter uses the MPT modeling technique to decompose the consumer choice (i.e., the brand-switching matrix of the CLV equation) of the RLZ model (Rust, Lemon, and Zeithaml 2004). According to the RLZ model, the number of customers of brand A (N_A) contributes to both the CLV equation and the customer equity equation of the RLZ model.

The RLZ model uses the retention rate to represent the inertia driver to construct customer lifetime value. In the brand-switching matrix (Rust, Lemon, and Narayandas 2005, p. 143), the retention rate is used to calculate the number of customers that are retained in a longitudinal spectrum. For example, customers who switched away and then switched back to the brand are included in the retained number of customers. The multinomial processing tree modeling (Batchelder 1998; Batchelder and Riefer 1990; Ye and van Raaij, submitted) is natural to decompose the brand-switching matrix into visual scenarios that capture various possibilities of customer switching.

Building on the RLZ model and the MPT modeling, the conditional probabilities of alternative decision outcomes are produced. Then Bayesian theorem links these probabilities so that the growth rate becomes a function of the retention rate and market share (k, the percentage of brand A's customers over all the customers). Sections 1 to 4 describe a step-by-step process to develop the new growth function.

Understand the CLV Equation and the CE Equation of the RLZ Model   In the CLV equation, the RLZ model uses a brand-switching matrix to estimate the probabilities for repeat purchases that represent the retention rates of brand A (Rust, Lemon, and Narayandas 2005). In the CE equation, the number of customers is multiplied by the mean of CLV to produce the CE.

$$\text{CLV} = \sum (1 + d_j)^{-t/f} v_j \pi_j B_{jt} \qquad (8.1)$$

Equation 8.1 is part of the RLZ model. B_{jt} is the probability of customer Anna (a customer who has purchased brand j before) buying brand j in a repeat purchase at time t (i.e., retention rates). According to the principle of probability, the retention rate (denoted as θ_1 in this discussion) is the probability of a customer's repeat purchase and thus is the percentage of the number of customers who repeat the purchase of the total number of customers who purchased the brand before. d_j is the discount rate. v_j is the average purchase volume, and π_j is the average contribution per unit. Equation 8.1 is also part of the RLZ model in which CE_A represents the customer equity for brand j.

$$\text{CE}_A = \text{mean}(\text{CLV}) \times N_A \qquad (8.2)$$

Let N_A be the customer size of brand j (Rust, Lemon, and Narayandas 2005, p. 145). In this analysis, j is one of the brands (i.e., brand A) of a firm

TABLE 8.1 Conditional Probabilities for the Brand-Switching Matrix

		To:	A	B
From	A		$P(A\|A)$	$P(B\|A)$
	B		$P(A\|B)$	$P(B\|B)$

that may own one or several brands. The customer growth in this discussion refers to increasing the number of customers of brand A as opposed to the total number of customers of the firm. When the firm competes as a corporate brand (e.g., especially in the wireless provider sector), brand A becomes the name of the firm.

For a customer to choose a brand, he has two options to choose from, brand A or non-A brands. In this example, all the non-A brands are denoted as brand B. Thus, $P(A) + P(B) = 1$. $P(A)$ is the probability of the customer choosing brand A and $P(B)$ is the probability of choosing B, given that the customer has no previous purchase of brand A or B.

The brand-switching matrix of the RLZ model (Rust, Lemon, and Narayandas 2005) is represented as a set of conditional probabilities (see Table 8.1). $P(A|A)$ indicates the probability of a customer choosing A, given that A has been consumed in the previous purchase. $P(B|A)$ indicates the probability of choosing B, given that A has been consumed in the previous purchase. $P(A|B)$ indicates the probability of choosing A, given that B has been consumed in the previous purchase. $P(B|B)$ indicates the probability of choosing B, given that B has been consumed in the previous purchase. Equation 8.3 shows the relationship of distributing the numbers of customers of the market in a longitudinal spectrum that includes time t and $t + 1$. The total number of customers in the market is assumed unchanged in these two close times in our analysis.

$$N_A + N_B = N'_A + N'_B \qquad (8.3)$$

Thus Equation 8.3 shows the relationship between the distributions of customer numbers over two close times. If N_A is the number of A's customers and N_B is the number of B's customers at t, then $N_{A'}$ is the number of A's customers and $N_{B'}$ is the number of B's customers at $t + 1$.

Use the MPT Model to Decompose the Brand-Switching Matrix
The multinomial processing tree modeling has been used in psychological science for a decade but is novel to marketing research (Batchelder 1998; Batchelder and Riefer 1990; Ye and van Raaij, submitted). It is a rigorous tool for categorical analysis, especially for modeling and estimating

unobservable latent variables (parameters) of observable outcomes. The parameters in the switching matrix of the RLZ model are latent variables underlying the observable probabilities for a customer to be retained or acquired. Thus it is natural to use the MPT modeling to decompose the brand-switching matrix.

Figure 8.1 shows an MPT model that is developed for the brand-switching matrix of the RLZ model. It describes the possible outcomes for

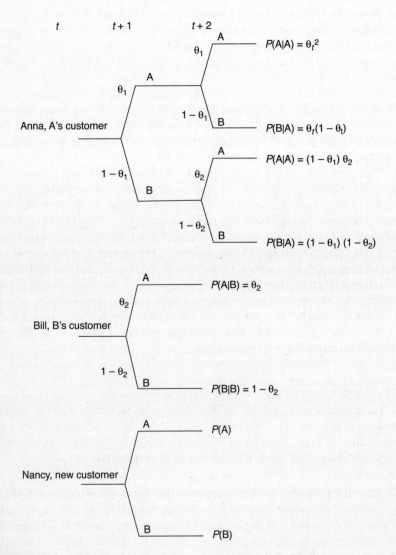

FIGURE 8.1 The MPT Tree for Producing Conditional Probabilities

three types of customers who consume (purchase) brand A or B. Anna represents customers who have previously consumed brand A. Bill represents customers who have previously consumed non-A brand (B). Nancy represents really new customers who have previously consumed neither brand A nor brand B. These three types of customers cover all the customer scenarios in the brand-switching matrix.

Note: θ_1 is the retention rate, that is, the probability of brand A's customer staying with brand A. θ_2 is the probability of a customer switching to brand A given the customer consumed brand B before. t, $t+1$, $t+2$ are times. The outcomes of the alternative decision paths are represented as the conditional probabilities of the brand-switching matrix (see Table 8.1), denoted as $P(A|A)$, $P(B|A)$, $P(B|B)$, and $P(A|B)$. $P(A|A)$ is the probability of brand A's customers eventually choosing brand A; $P(B|A)$ is the probability of brand A's customers eventually switching to brand B; $P(B|B)$ is the probability of brand B's customers eventually choosing brand B; $P(|B)$ is the probability of brand B's customers eventually choosing brand A.

Further analysis will use the notations that are organized here. A's retention rate is denoted as θ_1, that is, the probability of A's repeat customer staying with A ($\theta_1 \leq 1$ as it is a probability). If the customer purchases B before, then the probability of his switching to A is denoted as θ_2. Figure 8.1 shows the positions of θ_1 and θ_2 in the MPT tree. It also describes the paths to the conditional probabilities of alternative decision outcomes.

According to the brand-switching matrix of the RLZ model (Rust, Lemon, and Narayandas 2005, p. 143), there are two possibilities of Anna being brand A's customer after two instances of consumption choice. One possibility is that Anna chooses brand A for the first ($t+1$) and the second time ($t+2$), the likelihood of which is θ_1^2. The other possibility is that Anna first chooses B at $t+1$ and then chooses A at $t+2$, the probability of which is $(1-\theta_1)\theta_2$. If Anna chooses brand B the first time, she would act as Bill (non-A customers) to choose A the next time. Thus, after two instances of choosing, the conditional probability of Anna eventually choosing A is $P(A|A) = \theta_1^2 + (1-\theta_1)\theta_2$.

Using a similar rationale, the probability of Anna eventually choosing B after two instances of choosing includes two possible outcomes, that is, $P(B|A) = \theta_1(1-\theta_1) + (1-\theta_1)(1-\theta_2)$. That is, one outcome is that Anna chooses brand A first with the likelihood of θ_1 and then chooses B with the likelihood of $(1-\theta_1)$. The other outcome is that Anna chooses brand B first with the likelihood of $(1-\theta_1)$ followed by the likelihood $(1-\theta_2)$ of choosing B the second time. θ_2 represents the probability of Bill switching to brand A, thus the conditional probability $P(A|B) = \theta_2$. For Nancy, who has not consumed brand A or B before, $P(A)$ is the probability of Nancy choosing A and $P(B)$ is the probability of her choosing B.

Develop the New Growth Function with Bayesian Theorem
Building on the MPT tree of the switching matrix (Figure 8.1), the conditional probabilities for possible decision outcomes are produced. Then Bayesian theory is employed to link these conditional probabilities (Papoulis 1984). Thus a new growth function may be developed based on multinomial modeling and Bayesian theorem. In the new growth function, θ_1 is the retention rate, and λ is the growth rate of brand A that equals $(N'_A - N_A)/N_A$. λ indicates the percentage of the changed number of customers $(N'_A - N_A)$ over the original number of customers (N_A).

Bayesian theorem (see Equation 8.4) describes an inverse relationship between conditional probabilities, $P(A|B)$ and $P(B|A)$, adjusted by prior probabilities $P(A)$ and $P(B)$.

$$P(A|B) = \frac{P(B|A)P(A)}{P(B)} \tag{8.4}$$

Two assumptions are used for the derivation of the growth function. In Assumption 1, A's retention rate θ_1 holds stable across very short (the closest two) time intervals, namely, θ_1 holds for $t + 1$ and $t + 2$. The new growth function does not need to assume θ_1 steady in the long run. However, the RLZ model and the GLS time-growth function (Gupta, Lehmann, and Stuart 2004) have assumed that θ_1 holds stable not only in short time intervals but also in the long run.

In Assumption 2, a new customer, Nancy, who has not purchased brand A or B before (at $t - 1$), has a 50 percent chance of choosing A or not-A (B), namely, $P(A) = P(B) = 0.50$. Assumption 2 can be supported with empirical data in that a new customer has an equal chance of choosing two alternative brands.

Building on Assumption 2 and Bayesian theorem, it is derived that $P(A|B) = P(B|A)$. That is, the probability of Anna switching to brand B equals the probability of Bill switching to brand A.

The MPT tree on brand-switching matrix provides equations for $P(A|B)$ and $P(B|A)$, namely, $P(A|B) = \theta_2$, and $P(B|A) = \theta_1(1 - \theta_1) + (1 - \theta_1)(1 - \theta_2)$.

Thus, $\theta_2 = \theta_1(1 - \theta_1) + (1 - \theta_1)(1 - \theta_2)$, and we have Equation 8.5.

$$\theta_2 = (1 - \theta_1^2)/(2 - \theta_1) \tag{8.5}$$

Equation 8.6 uses U to indicate the number of all the customers for the product category that includes brand A and B. The whole market, that is, the total number of customers (U) for A and B will not change in these two instances, which last a very short time (t to $t + 1$).

$$U = N_A + N_B = N'_A + N'_B \tag{8.6}$$

Therefore, the market share of A, represented with k, is the percentage of A's number of customers of the whole market (U), that is, $k = N_A / U$, and $N_A = k U$ and $N_B = (1 - k) U$. The ratio of $N_A / N_B = k / (1 - k)$.

At time $t + 1$, the number of customers (N_A') includes the number of customers retained in A from time t, plus the number of customers switched from brand B at t. Thus, we have $N_A' = \theta_1 N_A + \theta_2 N_B$.

Let λ be A's customer growth rate, namely, $\lambda = (N_A' - N_A) / N_A$. After substituting N_A' with $\theta_1 N_A + \theta_2 N_B$, we get $\lambda = N_A' / N_A - 1 = (\theta_1 N_A + \theta_2 N_B) / N_A - 1$. With Equation 8.5, θ_2 is substituted with θ_1, then we get

$$\lambda = \theta_1 + \theta_2 N_B / N_A - 1$$
$$= \theta_1 + \theta_2 (1 - k)/k - 1$$
$$= \theta_1 + (1/k - 1)\theta_2 - 1$$
$$= (1/k - 1)\left(1 - \theta_1^2\right)/(2 - \theta_1) - (1 - \theta_1)$$

Equation 8.7, labeled as the new growth function, is the final form of the function that describes the relationship between the growth rate (λ) and the retention rate (θ_1) and market share (k). Note the retention rate is a consumer choice indicator, representing the opposite of the churn rate, which is the percentage of customers switching away from brand A. Equation 8.8 describes the function for the ratio of A's number of customers at $t + 1$ (N_A') over A's number of customers at t (N_A).

$$\lambda = (N_A' - N_A)/N_A = (1 - \theta_1) \left[(1/k - 1)(1 + \theta_1)/(2 - \theta_1) - 1\right] \quad (8.7)$$
$$N_A'/N_A = 1 + \lambda = (1 - \theta_1)[(1/k - 1)(1 + \theta_1)/(2 - \theta_1) - 1] + 1 \quad (8.8)$$

Use MATLAB to Draw the Growth Function   MATLAB is a software program that has been frequently used in engineering and computing (Hanselman and Littlefield 2001). Figure 8.2 displays the MATLAB drawing for the new growth function (i.e., Equation 8.7) that describes the relationship between the growth rate of A's customer over A's retention rates. The dependent variable is ($N_A' - N_A$) / N_A, and the independent variable is A's retention rate (θ_1). The shape of the function curve fluctuates with the market share (k) of brand A in the whole market (i.e., the total number of customers for brand A and B).

Figure 8.2 shows three sample growth curves between the growth rates and the retention rates for brand A. The shapes of the three curves are distinguished from the market shares of the brand. If the k of brand A is 0.20, the inverted-U curve indicates the behavior of a brand with a small market share, as opposed to the curves with k being 0.50 (a medium market share of brand A) and 0.80 (a large market share of brand A). Note that the

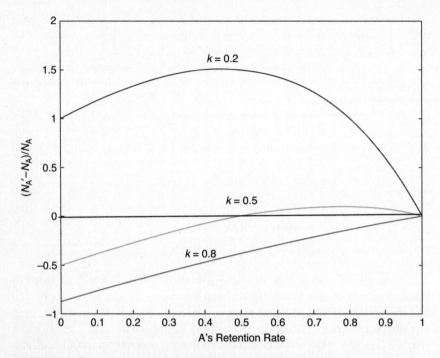

FIGURE 8.2 MATLAB Drawing of the Growth Function

peak points of the growth rates are not produced with the same retention rate for the different sample curves.

Note: $(N_A' - N_A) / N_A$ indicates the growth rate, namely λ. k is the market share of brand A (i.e., the percentage of brand A's customer size in the total market size that includes both brand A and B). Brand A's retention rate is denoted as θ_1 in the text.

Develop Predictions and Implications of the Growth Function

Different brands of a product or different products may have dissimilar numbers of customers. The market share of a brand is represented with k, namely, the percentage of the number of brand A's customers of the total number of customers for the product that comprises several brands (i.e., the total market size). The value of the market share of brand A determines the shape of the growth curves and the availability of the peak points of the curves. Based on the MATLAB drawing (see Figure 8.2), we may conceive a few observations that are organized in Table 8.2.

Note: k is the market share of brand A (i.e., the percentage of brand A's customer size in the total market size that includes both brand A and B). P_1, P_2, and P_3 are the three predictions derived for the growth function.

TABLE 8.2 Observations of the Growth Function

Brand Market Share	Example of Brands	Peak Growth Points	Predictions on the Retention-Growth Association
Small	Creative MP3 player (an iPod competitor), e.g., $k = 0.2$	Peak occurs within the range of 0.4–0.6 retention rate	Positive association before the peak; negative association after the peak (P_1)
Medium	Cingular (a Verizon competitor), e.g., $k = 0.5$	Curve skews to the right. Peak occurs within the range of 0.7–0.8 retention rate (P_2)	Positive association before the peak but negative association after the peak
Large	AT&T (pre-1984), e.g., $k = 0.8$	No peak (P_3)	Negative growth rate for most retention rates but with positive associations

Some of these observations (see Table 8.2) on the growth function (Figure 8.2) are formulated as three predictions, namely P_1, P_2, and P_3.

P_1: If the market share of a brand is small (e.g., Alltel Wireless), then the relationship between customer growth and choice follows a normal inverted-U curve; that is, the growth curve increases with smaller retention rates but decreases with larger retention rates.

P_2: If the market share of a brand is medium (e.g., Verizon Wireless), then the relationship between customer growth and choice follows a skewed inverted-U curve; that is, the growth curve shifts to the right. The growth peak occurs within the range of 0.70–0.80 retention rates.

P_3: If the market share of a brand is too large (e.g., the old AT&T in 1980s), there may not be a peak growth point.

Corroborate the Three Predictions with Peak Analysis Table 8.2 describes the range of the retention rates in which the peaks of the growth function may occur for small and medium brands. Can we figure out the values of the parameters (e.g., the retention rates and the market share) for the peak growth points? Can we support the three predictions with a peak analysis?

Estimate Retention Rate (θ_1) and Market Share (k) at the Peak Growth Rate The growth function (Equation 8.7) is derived from the

MPT tree (Figure 8.1) that decomposes the switching matrix of the RLZ model (Table 8.1). At the peak growth point, the partial derivative of the function on the retention rate θ_1 should equal zero. The partial derivative on θ_1 is taken on the retention-growth function, that is, Equation 8.7, as follows.

Since, $\partial(NA' - NA/NA)/\partial\theta_1 = \partial(\lambda)/\partial\theta_1 = 0$,

$$\Rightarrow \partial(\lambda)/\partial\theta_1 = \partial\{(1 - \theta_1)[(1/k - 1)(1 + \theta_1)/(2 - \theta_1) - 1]\}/\partial\theta_1 = 0$$

$$\Rightarrow 1 + (1/k - 1)\left[(2 - \theta_1)(-2\theta_1) + 1 - \theta_1^2\right]/(2 - \theta_1)^2 = 0$$

$$\Rightarrow (1 - 1/k)\left[-2\theta_1(2 - \theta_1) + 1 - \theta_1^2\right] = (2 - \theta_1)^2$$

$$\Rightarrow (1 - 1/k)\left(\theta_1^2 - 4\theta_1 + 1\right) = 4 + \theta_1^2 - 4\theta_1^2$$

$$\Rightarrow \theta_1^2 - 4\theta_1 + 3k + 1 = 0$$

After solving the equation, we get

$$\theta1 = 2 \pm \ sqrt\,(3)\ sqrt\,(1 - k) = 2 \pm 1.73\ sqrt\,(1 - k), \text{ or} \qquad (8.9)$$

$$k = 1 - (\theta_1 - 2)^2/3 \qquad (8.9')$$

Note that θ_1 is brand A's retention rate. k (i.e., NA/U) is brand A's customer market share. Using Equation 8.9, we may calculate the retention rates for the three sample market share values that are shown in Figure 8.2 and Table 8.2. The condition $\theta_1 \leq 1$ has to be satisfied by the solutions because brand A's customers cannot exceed the size of the market for the product category.

$$k = 0.2 \Rightarrow \theta_1 = 2 \pm 1.73\ sqrt\,(0.8) = 2 \pm 1.54 = 0.46$$

Thus P_1 is corroborated because the peak growth point occurs with medium retention rates (i.e., a normal inverted-U curve). Note that the other solution is 3.54. As it is greater than 1, it is not meaningful.

$$k = 0.5 \Rightarrow \theta_1 = 2 \pm 1.73\ sqrt\,(0.5) = 2 \pm 1.22 = 0.78$$

Thus P_2 is corroborated because the peak growth point occurs with a skewed retention rate (i.e., the peak of the inverted-U curve shifts to the right). Note that the other solution for $k = 0.5$ is $3.22 > 1$, so it is not meaningful.

$$k = 0.8 \Rightarrow \theta_1 = 2 \pm 1.73\ sqrt\,(0.2) = 2 \pm 0.77 = 1.23 > 1$$

Note that the other solution for $k = 0.8$ is $2.77 > 1$, so neither solution for $k = 0.8$ is meaningful. When k is too large (e.g., k equals 0.80), neither of the solution values satisfies the $\theta_1 \leq 1$ condition. So there is no peak point for the growth function for $k = 0.80$. Thus P_3 is corroborated with the peak analysis.

Conclusion

The peak analysis on the shape of the growth function corroborates the three predictions (i.e., P_1, P_2, and P_3) that are derived from the observations of Table 8.2.

Implications to Decisions

We discuss theoretical and managerial implications.

Theoretical Implications The mainstream time-based adoption models have made profound contributions to theory and practice in marketing and management science. There are hundreds of articles in marketing and management science that extend or refine the quantitative adoption models (Bass 2004).

The focus of the mainstream adoption models is the adoption of new technology or new products (especially consumer durables like TVs and DVD players). Normally a new technology or a new product has a small market share (k) in its introduction stage. This fits in the new growth function that is illustrated by the one for $k = 0.20$ (see Figure 8.2). Before the peak of the curve, the customer growth rate positively associates with the repeat-purchase (retention) rate. After the peak, the growth rate negatively associates with the retention rate.

The growth function (i.e., Equation 8.7) offers new insights on customer growth from an alternative choice-modeling perspective to the S-shape time-based adoption models (Bass 1969, 2004; Gupta, Lehmann, and Stuart 2004). The alternative choice modeling perspective uses market shares (k) and retention rates (θ_1) to predict customer growth, compared to using time t in the mainstream time-based adoption models. These new insights are organized in Table 8.2; they include answers to (1) What is the impact of the market share to the customer growth of a brand? and (2) Does the growth peak of the brand always exist?

The market share of a brand determines the shape of the growth curve for the brand. With a medium market share (e.g., $k = 0.5$), the relationship between growth and retention follows a normal inverted-U curve. If the market share becomes too large (e.g., $k = 0.8$), the peak of customer growth for the brand may not exist (see P_3). The peak analysis corroborates these findings.

Implications to Managerial Decisions In addition to knowing the timing of the peak growth point from mainstream adoption models, this new growth function advises marketing managers with new insights on a brand's customer growth. These insights are described in the three predictions that are corroborated with the peak analysis. With the knowledge of the market shares, a reasonably accurate MATLAB drawing on a brand's growth curves may illustrate the elements of decisions for the managers (see Figure 8.2). The managers may conceive effective decisions and predictions based on the relationships such as the one between the retention rates and the customer growth under various conditions. For example, the managers may predict that after an existing peak growth point, it is expected that the customer growth will slow down while the retention rate will go up, given that the brand's market share is small.

Future Work The customer growth defined in this chapter focuses on increasing the numbers of customers for a specific brand of a firm, where U indicates the number of all the customers (i.e., market size) for the product category that the brand belongs to. For the purposes of simplicity and the initial introduction of the new growth function, U is assumed to be a constant over the short time period of interest (t to $t + 1$). In reality, it is possible that U may change within this short time period. Thus, the future work may incorporate the change of U over time. For example, $U_2 = U_1 + \Delta U$, where U_1 indicates the overall market size at time 1, U_2 indicates the market size at time 2, and ΔU indicates the changes of the market size from time 1 to time 2.

Summary

Customer retention rate (θ_1) is the percentage of customers who stay with a previously consumed brand in a repeat consumption. It represents a consumer choice parameter and is the driver of brand inertia in the brand-switching matrix of the RLZ customer equity model. Building on the RLZ model, this chapter uses the multinomial processing tree modeling (see Figure 8.1) to decompose the brand-switching matrix and produce conditional probabilities for alternative decision outcomes. It then links the probabilities with Bayesian theorem. After that, it derives that the customer growth rate (λ) is a function of the retention rate and the market share (i.e., the new growth function, see Equation 8.7 and Figure 8.2). Three predictions are derived on the shape of the growth function, with corroborations from the peak analysis. The growth function offers insights to unknown areas of customer growth from an alternative behavioral choice modeling perspective compared to the mainstream time-based adoption models.

DERIVING IMPLICIT UTILITY FUNCTIONS

In this section, several basic elements for building a theoretical framework for an implicit utility function are introduced. These include empirical evidence from economics, psychology, finance, capital gains and losses, implicit economic cognition, and implicit cognition research.[1]

As implicit processes operate in investment behavior, it is postulated that irrationality may exist with investor ratings in the stock market. A ratings bias caused by "implicit prejudice" (Greenwald and Banaji 1995) may have occurred during the1997–99 period when the high-tech stock prices were pushed to an unreasonably high level. The stock market run-up could not be explained by the financial data (e.g., corporate earnings) (Thaler 1993; Shiller 2000a) or empirical research (Lei, Noussair, and Plott 2001).

In a similar fashion, some market crash phenomena cannot be interpreted with rational economic data either. For example, incidents such as the terrorist attacks of September 11, 2001, may induce significant declines in stock prices without any relation to the soundness of corporate financial data (Thaler 1993; Shiller 2000a). It is believed that these incidents stimulate overtly implicit investor processes that cannot be consciously or rationally controlled and as a result can exert negative market influences.

From an economic perspective, stock gains and losses may be represented by the rate of return with regard to stock prices. A stock gain leads to a positive wealth change; that is, the ending price is higher than the beginning price. A stock loss leads to a negative wealth change in which the ending price is lower than the beginning price. Following the definition of the arithmetic rate of return (Goetzmann 1996), the stock rate of return (gains and losses) may be operationally defined as the magnitude of the price fluctuation from the beginning price, denoted as r.

The rate of return may be perceived as a rational economic index attributed to the financial investors' upgrading or downgrading of stock evaluations and decisions. This occurs as a conscious, or explicit, rational evaluative process. However, the rate of return may affect investor ratings even without the investor's awareness. Unconscious mental processes of the investor's evaluations and decisions may be provoked by the rate of return, thus implicitly contributing to the final rating outcome.

At the conceptual level, investor ratings may consist of explicit or conscious processes of precise technical/fundamental analyses and rational estimates of corporate financials, as well as implicit components of preference and utility. The implicit mental processes contribute to the irrationality of financial decision-making behavior. This is in sharp contrast to the rationality hypothesis that assumes that one is consciously making decisions and maximizing utility (Fama 1970; Fama and French 1992; Rabin 1998).

In economics and behavioral finance, implicit processes may be understood as mechanisms of overconfidence, anchoring and adjustment, and investor self-control and self-awareness. Full awareness is often absent in these choice processes (O'Donoghue and Banin in press). Studies have consistently revealed that people are unaware of their overconfidence and biased self-attribution (tendency to attribute success to self and failure to others) in making decisions, including investment decisions (Daniel, Hirshleifer, and Subrahmanyam 1998).

An additional factor is hindsight bias. The hindsight bias posits that stock estimates are influenced by the outcome of a prior investment. This may occur automatically without investors' awareness (Arkes 1991). Implicit mental processes may be reflected in a statement such as "I can't recall the fundamentals of that stock but it has consistently made money for me in the past."

Implicit processes of investor judgments of stocks are viewed as unobservable and involuntary mental processes without awareness or consciousness. Research on implicit processes in general can be categorized into four stages based on its development history (Fazio, Sanbonmatsu, Powell, and Kardes 1986; Greenwald and Banaji 1995; Greenwald et al. 2002; Janiszewski and Meyvis 2001). The first stage is the phenomenon stage, represented by the mere-exposure effect (Zajonc 1968) where affective response to a subliminal stimulus is found without recognizing the stimulus. The second stage is the conceptual exploration stage, represented by the interests in the priming effect in areas such as memory research (Schacter 1987; Roediger 1990), attitude research (Fazio, Sanbonmatsu, Powell, and Kardes 1986), implicit social cognition (Greenwald and Banaji 1995), and marketing (Ye and van Raaij 1997; Ye 2000). Priming is interpreted as the different processing of a stimulus due to its prior encounters. The third stage is the computational models of experimental effects, such as the process dissociation procedure (Jacoby 1991) where automatic and conscious recollection is dissociated by the level of processing manipulations and where conscious, automatic, and affective components are represented in a multinomial model fitted for the observed frequency data (Ye 2000). The fourth stage is neuroscience stage where the brain region of implicit activations may be located (Schacter and Badgaiyan 2001).

The multinomial decision process (MDP) model provides an equation that describes the process of preference formation. It is a statistical technique that involves estimating hypothetical parameters that represent the probabilities of unobservable events (Batchelder and Riefer 1990). The model is based on the literature pertaining to the congruence between the implicit component (familiarity) and liking (Zajonc 1968; Zajonc and Markus 1982) and the dissociation between explicit and implicit processes

TABLE 8.3 Observed Frequencies of the MDP Model

	R&L	R&~L	~R&L	~R&~L
AS	N_{11}	N_{12}	N_{13}	N_{14}
UAS	N_{21}	N_{22}	N_{23}	N_{24}
NS	N_{31}	N_{32}	N_{33}	N_{34}

$N = \Sigma\ N_{ij},\ i = 1,2,3;\ j = 1,2,3,4$
AS = attended old stimuli
UAS = unattended old stimuli
NS = new stimuli

relative to the level of cognitive development (Jacoby 1998). Subsequent analyses resulted in several iterations of the equation to ensure a good data fit.

The MDP model was developed with data collected from recognition and liking judgment responses of subjects involved in laboratory experiments. To measure the mere exposure effect, subjects were exposed to pairs of neutral and unfamiliar options such as brand names (van Raaij 1989; Ye and van Raaij 1997; Ye 2000; Ye and van Raaij 2003). Subjects were instructed to attend to half of these options and ignore the other half. The priming effect was measured by querying the subjects to ascertain (1) whether the brands had been "seen before" from the brands that they had not been exposed to, and (2) whether they had positive (liking) or negative (disliking) feelings about the brands. The subjects were isolated and the brands were judged separately to control for possible bias effects.

The independent variable is the stimulus (i.e., attended [*AS*], unattended [*UAS*], new stimuli [*NS*]), a within-subjects factor. Dependent variables are the recognition and liking judgments. The judgment can be categorized as one of four outcomes: (1) recognized (R) and liked (L), (2) recognized (R) and not liked (~L), (3) not recognized (~R) and liked (L), and (4) not recognized (~R) and not liked (~L). Therefore, the data were collected as cell frequencies in a 3×4 matrix (Table 8.3) with the rows representing the three levels of the independent variable and the columns denoted as the four categories of the dependent variable.

	old/new	like/dislike
R&L	old	like
R&~L	old	dislike
~R&L	new	like
~R&~L	new	dislike

For example, R&L means that the stimulus is recognized as "old" and responded to as "liked."

The Equations of the MDP Model

The parameter of the implicit processes (i) presented in the multinomial decision process model may be estimated by the observed frequency data (Ye 2000, 2002; Ye and van Raaij 2002). The model captures the information processing of an object (e.g., stock), with explicit, implicit, and affective components. It depicts the detailed mental processing for the evaluated stimulus and the decision outcome. There are four different mental processes, or parameters, and judgment is rendered after the processing has been completed. The mental processes are categorized as implicit, explicit, affective, and guessing. The general interpretations of these parameters are as follows:

Implicit (unconscious) component, that is, implicit memory and affect, denoted by i.

Explicit (conscious) component, namely, explicit memory, denoted by e_2 (attention-conscious component) and e_4 (inattention-conscious component).

Affective component, that is, explicit affect, denoted by a_2.

Guessing component, denoted by g_1 and g_2.

Note that parameters i, e_2, e_4, a_2, g_1, and g_2 denote both processes (or components) and probabilities. The equations of the MDP model are shown in Table 8.4. The equations are developed from tree diagrams depicting the parameters that are present in the options of information processing conditions of Table 1a (Ye 2000, 2002; Ye and van Raaij 2002).

Estimates of the parameter (i) of the implicit processes (Ye 2000), denoted as Σ i, may be estimated with observed frequency data as follows:

$$\sum i = \frac{(N_{11} + N_{13}) - (N_{31} + N_{33})}{N_{32} + N_{34}}$$

Where the N_{ij} represents observed frequencies in a 3×4 matrix (see Table 8.3).

TABLE 8.4 Formulas of the MDP Model

	R&L	R&~L	~R&L	~R&~L
AS	$i + (1 - i) e_2 a_2$ $+ (1 - i)(1 - e_2)$ $a_2 g_1$	$(1 - i)e_2(1 - a_2)$ $+ (1 - i)(1 - e_2)$ $(1 - a_2) g_2$	$(1 - i)(1 - e_2)$ $a_2(1 - g_1)$	$(1 - i)(1 - e_2)$ $(1 - a_2)(1 - g_2)$
UAS	$i + (1 - i) e_4 a_2$ $+ (1 - i)(1 - e_4)$ $a_2 g_1$	$(1 - i)e_4(1 - a_2)$ $+ (1 - i)(1 - e_4)$ $(1 - a_2)g_2$	$(1 - i)(1 - e_4)$ $a_2(1 - g_1)$	$(1 - i)(1 - e_4)$ $(1 - a_2)(1 - g_2)$
NS	$a_2 g_1$	$(1 - a_2)g_2$	$a_2(1 - g_1)$	$(1 - a_2)(1 - g_2)$

Transforming Investor Rating Data into Observed Frequencies

Individual ratings and evaluations are used frequently and constitute a common measurement approach in behavioral survey studies. A typical rating practice used by investors is to base buy/sell recommendations on a five-point Likert scale of 1 to 5. These recommendations reflect investor preference and likeability ratings of specific stocks. With the MDP model, the rating data are transformed to observed frequencies so that the implicit, affective, and explicit components may be estimated. It is stated that investor ratings reflect an array of potential responses including the prospects of implicit processes. The classical self-reported or explicit measures of behavior contain implicit or automatic influences. The implicit components can be separated from the other components with an algorithm derived from the MDP model.

The transformation from likeability ratings to observed frequencies is described later. The rating data are conditional probabilities from the likeability scale such as P(Liking|old&attended), that is, the past likeability rating of the attended attributes of an object (stock); and P(Liking|new), that is, the current likeability rating of the new attributes of an object (stock). In the case of stock ratings, P(Liking|old&attended) and P(Liking|new) may be investor ratings of stocks at the end and the beginning and of the period of interest. Therefore, the algorithm to estimate the implicit component of brokers' likeability ratings can be calculated as follows:

$$
\text{aggregate implicit process} = \sum i
$$

$$
= \frac{|\, P(\text{Liking}|\text{old\&attended}) - P(\text{Liking}|\text{new})\,|}{1 - P(\text{Liking}|\text{new})}
$$

Aggregate implicit processes refer to the value of implicit or unconscious mental processes estimated with a priori and a posteriori ratings relative to the period of beginning and ending prices. It may be provoked by the rate of return of a stock as represented by fluctuation in price. This leads to an issue that the aggregate implicit processes may not be comparable across stocks because different levels of stimulus strength (i.e., degree of price fluctuation) may provoke various statistically uncontrollable implicit processes. In order to control the covariance of the price fluctuation, the value of the aggregate implicit processes is standardized with the rate of return (r) in order to obtain unitized implicit processes (i), whereas

$$
\text{unitized implicit processes } (i) = \frac{\text{aggregate implicit process}}{\text{rate of return}} = \frac{\sum i}{r}
$$

The direction of stock price fluctuation, such as gains or losses, may be indicated by the positive and negative wealth change. Thus, the implicit processes are estimated with the absolute value from the above equation. The unitized implicit processes will be used as a measure of implicit processes to test specific propositions. This is required for establishing an implicit utility function, that is, the asymmetric value function associated with prospect theory's implicit processes.

The Implicit Utility Function

Utility functions can be defined as arbitrary sets of consequences with various attributes that might affect preferences. The utility function for wealth is a mathematical function with wealth being the independent variable (Bell and Fishburn 2000). The most important and widely used class of utility functions is known as the Hyperbolic Absolute Risk Aversion (HARA). This family of utility functions includes linear, exponential, logarithmic, and power functions. An implicit utility function also belongs to the HARA class with its property of risk aversion. The equation of the implicit utility function derived from the MDP model (Ye 2000, 2002; Ye and van Raaij 2002) is cell N_{23} of Table 1b; whereas:

Implicit utility (value) function $= f(i, e_4) = (1 - i)(1 - e_4)a_2(1 - g_1)$

The implicit utility function is a mix of implicit, explicit, affective, and guessing components. Given the homogeneity of the latter two components, implicit and explicit components react differently to gains and losses. The explicit component reacts symmetrically to gains and losses, whereas the implicit component reacts asymmetrically according to prospect theory. Hence, the asymmetry to loss aversion is a function of variances across the implicit component.

Three Propositions

A mathematical exploration of an implicit utility function is presented later. The objective of the exploration is to establish the implicit utility function as a value function of prospect theory (Kahneman and Tversky 1979; Tversky and Kahneman 1992).

A value function of prospect theory is (1) defined on derivations from the reference point; (2) generally concave for gains and convex for losses; and (3) steeper for losses than for gains (Kahneman and Tversky 1979). A value function that satisfies these properties is displayed in Figure 8.3.

The implicit utility function possesses the three properties of the value function in order to maintain the integrity of risk aversion and the

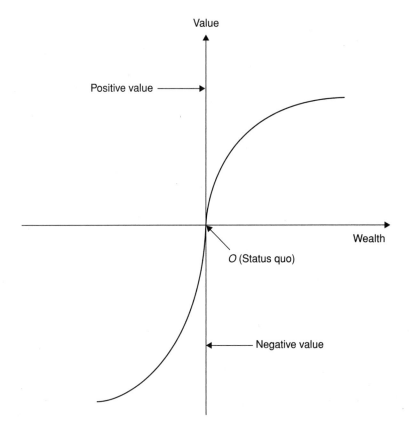

FIGURE 8.3 Values of Losses and Gains

diminishing sensitivity described in prospect theory. Risk aversion suggests that people are more sensitive to the risk of losses than of gains. The diminishing sensitivity suggests that the first derivative of the value function decreases as the wealth change increases, that is, less sensitivity to wealth per unit is elicited as one experiences an increasing wealth change.

To summarize, the research is based on the following three propositions:

P_1: An inverted relation is postulated to exist between wealth change (gains or losses) and unitized implicit processes, whereas $i = b/w$. The more gains (losses) of wealth, the fewer implicit processes are provoked, where w stands for wealth and b is a positive constant.

A statistically significant regression coefficient of the unitized implicit processes (i) and gains (losses), estimated with the above

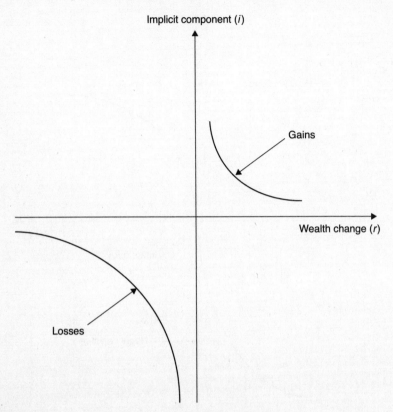

FIGURE 8.4   Implicit Components of Losses and Gains

algorithm, is expected after an inverted data transformation of the rate of return (representing gains and losses). Figure 8.3 illustrates the asymmetrical graphed function. The O point on the vertical axis indicates that no implicit process is activated. A negative i denotes a deactivation of the implicit process, analogous to the disutility for losses.

P_2: It is postulated that there are more implicit processes provoked for losses than for gains, namely, $b' > b > 0$, where b' is the constant for losses and b is the constant for gains. Figure 8.4 illustrates the asymmetrical graphed function relative to gains and losses (the gains curve is closer to the original point than the losses curve).

P_3: A logarithmic relationship is postulated to exist between wealth (gain) and explicit processes (utility), analogous to the relation between wealth and classical utility, $w/x < 0$; that is, the greater the wealth gain, the more explicit processes are provoked.

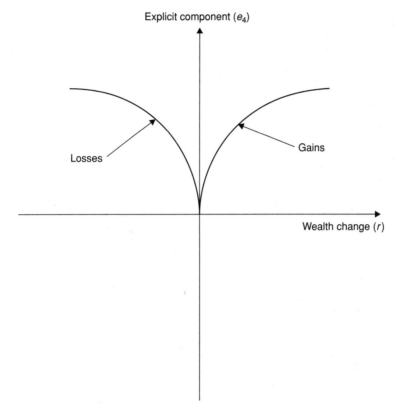

FIGURE 8.5 Explicit Components of Losses and Gains

A correlation of wealth change and explicit processes is expected after a logarithmic data transformation of the value for gains or losses. The logarithmic relation between wealth change and explicit utility is a classical and widely used utility function of the HARA class.[2] Figure 8.5 illustrates the symmetrical graphed function (the number of explicit processes is activated identically with the same number of gains or losses).

Summary

The MDP model's implicit utility function is depicted as a mix of implicit and explicit processes. It is assumed that the implicit component reacts asymmetrically to gains and losses, whereas the explicit component reacts symmetrically to gains and losses. Hence, the implicit utility function serves as the foundation to explain the asymmetry of the value function and loss aversion.

TRANSFORMING LIKEABILITY RATING DATA INTO OBSERVED FREQUENCIES

Given individual ratings of likeability for the three aspects (attended, unattended, and new) of a brand (see Table 8.4), we obtain:

$P(\text{Liking}|\text{attended}) = $ liking rating of attended attributes $= P(\text{R\&L}) +$

$P(\sim\text{R\&L}) = N_{11} + N_{13}$

$P(\text{Liking}|\text{new}) = $ liking rating of new attributes $= P(\text{R\&L}) +$

$P(\sim\text{R\&L}) = N_{31} + N_{33}$

$P(\text{No liking}|\text{new}) = 1 - P(\text{Liking}|\text{new}) = N_{32} + N_{34}$

Hence, the equation of estimating implicit mental processes (i) is:

$$\sum i = \frac{(N_{11} + N_{13}) - (N_{31} + N_{33})}{N_{32} + N_{34}}$$

$$= \frac{|\ P(\text{Liking}|\text{old\&attended}) - P(\text{Liking}|\text{new})\ |}{1 - P(\text{Liking}|\text{new})}$$

What are the three propositions of the implicit utility function?

The Implicit Utility Function

The function is derived from the equations of the MDP model (see Table 8.4).

Implicit utility (value) function $= P(\text{liking}) = P(\sim\text{R\&L}|\text{UAS})$

$$= (1 - i)(1 - e_4)a_2(1 - g_1)$$

whereas i operates in the equation for preference, choice, and decision making.

Properties of a Value Function

This is the value function of prospect theory (Tversky and Kahneman 1992, p. 303):

$P''(w) <= 0, w >= 0$, concave above a reference point.

$P''(w) >= 0, w <= 0$, convex below a reference point.

$P'(w) < P'(-w), w >= 0$, steeper for losses than for gains.

Where w stands for wealth. $w >= 0$ stands for gains; $w <= 0$ stands for losses. The value function is asymmetrical.

Property I of Implicit Processes (*i*)

We discuss the background, proposition, analogy, and proof of Property I of the implicit utility function.

Background   Groves and Thompson's (1970) dual-process theory was the accepted theory for interpreting affective responses of the mere-exposure effect. The theory states that the response to stimuli can be classified as sensitization and habituation. Sensitization is a response that builds up during initial exposure to a stimulus but declines with later exposure. Habituation process is a neutral-specific response that increases at a marginally decreasing rate with each additional exposure. The two responses are analogous to the utility function where a diminishing marginal utility results from a logarithmic relationship between wealth and utility (Bernouli 1738). Therefore, it is assumed a logarithmic relationship exists between habituation and exposure (denoted as x), namely, habituation = $c\log_e(x) = cln(x)$, where c is a positive constant. It is also assumed that an inverted relationship between sensitization and exposure; that is, sensitization = b/x, where b is a positive constant. Note that the exposure stimulus may be wealth change (w).

Linking w and x   We propose that w and x are linked. This is derived from the affect and repetition (x) relationship (aka the mere-exposure effect) (Zajonc 1968) and the affect and wealth change (w) relationship (aka the utility or value functions) (Bernouli 1738; Kahneman and Tversky 1979, 2000), with the assumption that the stimuli in both relationships are monetary gains and losses. For example, a logarithmic relationship exists between wealth change (w) and value (experienced affect) in a value function. Similarly, a positive relationship exists between affect and repetition (x). Hence, with affect in both relationships, we establish the link between w and x.

Analogy   Implicit processes (i) are analogous to sensitization; explicit processes are analogous to habituation, whereas, $i = b/x$; $e_4 = cln(x)$; x: exposure, $x > 0$; $b > 0$; $c > 0$.

Proof   Therefore, $e_4 = cln(x) = cln(b/i) = c(ln(b) - ln(i)) = -cln(i) + cln(b)$.

$$P(\text{liking}) = P(x) = (1 - i)(1 - e_4)a_2(1 - g_1) = a_2(1 - g_1)(1 - i)(1 + cln(i)$$
$$-cln(b))$$

Where $x = 0$, $i = 0$, $e_4 = 0$, $P(\text{Liking}) = a_2(1 - g_1) = $ status quo

The first derivative (with i) of $P(\text{liking}) = P'(\text{liking})$

$$= a_2(1 - g_1)[(1 - i)(1 + c\,ln\,(i) - c\,ln\,(b))]'$$

$$= a_2(1 - g_1)(c/i - c\,ln\,(i) + ln\,(b) - c - 1) \qquad (8.10)$$

The second derivative (with i) of $P(\text{liking}) = P''(\text{liking})$

$$= a_2(1 - g_1)(-ci^{-2} - ci^{-1}) = (-c)a_2(1 - g_1)(i^{-2} + i^{-1})$$

As $-c < 0$, $a_2 \geq 0$, $(1 - g_1) \geq 0$, $i > 0$, so $P''(\text{liking}) \leq 0$. (8.11)

Conclusion   Property I of the implicit utility function is proven: $P''(i) \leq 0$, $w \geq 0$, concave above reference point. Note that the exposure stimulus may be wealth change (w). This is consistent with the features of prospect theory's value function.

Property II of the Implicit Utility Function

We discuss the objective and propositions of Property II of the implicit utility function.

Objective $P''(w) > = 0$, $w > = 0$, convex below reference point.

Propositions

P_1: Assuming the inverted relationship between wealth (gains) and implicit processes, analogous to the relation between exposure and implicit processes (sensitization) (Groves and Thompson 1970);

P_2: Assuming the logarithmic relationship between wealth (gain) and explicit processes (Bernouli's utility; Bernouli 1738), analogous to the relation between exposure and explicit processes, $w/x > 0$;

Axiom 1: With losses of wealth, implicit processes is the inverted absolute value of wealth weighted by a constant (b'), namely, $i = b'/|w|$; where w stands for losses and is smaller than zero, $w > 0$; and

P_3: $b' > b > 0$, where b' is the constant for losses and b is the constant for gains. P_3 postulates that there are more implicit processes provoked for losses than for gains. P_3 will be used for the proof of feature III of the implicit utility function.

Axiom 2: With losses of wealth, explicit processes is the absolute logarithmic value of wealth weighted by a constant (c), namely,

$e_4 = cln|w|$ (Bernouli 1738), where w stands for losses and is smaller than zero, $w < 0$.

The first derivative (with i) of P(liking) $= P'$(liking)

$$= a_2(1 - g_1)(-ci^{-2} - ci^{-1}) = (-c)a_2(1 - g_1)(i^{-2} + i^{-1})$$

Axiom 3: the value of affective component is negative toward losses of wealth, namely,

$$a_2 = -|a_2| < 0$$

$$\text{As} - c < 0, a_2 \leq 0, (1 - g_1) \geq 0, i > 0, \text{ so } P''(\text{liking}) \geq 0$$

Conclusion   We proved Property II of the implicit utility function with losses, $w < 0$, namely $P''(i) \geq 0, w \leq 0$, convex below reference point. This is consistent with the features of a value function of prospect theory.

Property III of the Implicit Utility Function

We discuss the objective and proof of Property III of the implicit utility function.

Objective $P'(w) < P'(-w), w \geq = 0$, steeper for losses than for gains.

Proof   Equation of the first derivative:

$$P'(w) = a_2(1 - g_1)(c/i - c \, ln(i) + ln(b) - c - 1)$$

$$P'(-w) = a_2(1 - g_1)(c/i - c \, ln(i) + ln(b') - c - 1)$$

As $b' > b > 0$ (see $P3$), then $ln(b') > ln(b)$, hence $P'(-w) > P'(w)$, $w \geq = 0$.

Conclusion   The implicit utility function is steeper for losses than for gains.

SIGNAL DETECTION THEORY

Signal detection theory (SDT) evolved from the development of communications and radar equipment in the first half of the last century. It moved to psychology (Green and Swets 1966), initially as part of sensation and perception, in the '50s and '60s as an attempt to understand some of the features of human behavior when detecting very faint stimuli (e.g., buying or selling signals) from other stimuli (noise) that were not being explained

Signal

	Present	Absent
Yes	hit	false alarm
No	miss	correct rejection

Response

FIGURE 8.6 2 × 2 Matrix of Signal Detection Theory

by traditional theories of thresholds (Snodgrass and Corwin 1988; Yonelinas 1994, 1999; DeCarlo 2002). However, besides the methodology introduction, little about SDT has been reported in investment research.

A typical SDT paradigm usually encompasses a detection task. With the detection task, a mix of stimuli contains signals and noise. Signals are stimuli to be detected. Noise is background, not to be detected. For example, in a recognition task, signals are exposed items in a study phase, whereas noise consists of new items never exposed before. The detection task of a test phase is to find the signals in a mix of signals and noise. When a signal is responded to by Ss as a "signal," it is called a "hit"; otherwise it is a "miss." When noise (distracters, or signal not present) is responded to by Ss as a "signal," it is called a "false alarm"; otherwise it is a "correct rejection" (see Figure 8.6).

In signal detection theory, the sensitivity and bias of an operator's reactions are measured. Sensitivity is specified by the signal-to-noise ratio. More specifically, the sensitivity of strength is the standardized mean difference of strength between signal and noise distributions (Figure 8.6). If the sensitivity is high (i.e., the signal is strong relative to the noise), the operator is effective in detecting the presence of signals.

On the other hand, operator's response propensity (bias) is distinct from its sensitivity. It specifies how certain one must be before one is willing to say "yes, a signal is present." In other words, the bias is the cutoff criterion to report a signal (e.g., response bias in Figure 8.7). The response propensity can change even though the sensitivity remains the same. For example, a radiologist may decide to accept weaker indications of abnormality of X-rays to refer patients for treatment.

Note these:

- X_c and $X_{c'}$ are cutoff points of preference strength, separating reported positivity and negativity on the continuum of strength.

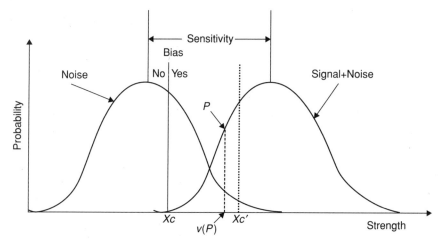

FIGURE 8.7 Signal Detection Distributions

- Nonparametric SDT is used in the current study. According to Snodgrass and Corwin (1988), normal distributions are not required in this case, although Figure 8.7 uses normal-like distributions for display. The actual distribution of the data may not necessarily be normal.

Three nonparametric SDT experiments are reported to test the four hypotheses on the effect of attention on the four new components. We first introduce nonparametric SDT, followed by the generic method used in all of the three experiments.

Nonparametric SDT

SDT was introduced to the marketing and consumer research community in the late twentieth century (Tashchian, White, and Pak 1988; Cradit, Tashchian, and Hofacker 1994). In our brand name experiments, the preference bias indicator is the response propensity (bias) index (B'') of a nonparametric SDT (Grier 1971; Snodgrass and Corwin 1988).

Nonparametric SDT analysis is used here rather than parametric SDT. In this way, a normal distribution is not required for the data (Snodgrass and Corwin 1988). Therefore, with a liberal restriction on data distribution, nonparametric signal-detection analysis can calculate the sensitivity (A') and response (preference and recognition) propensity (B''). The response bias and the sensitivity are computed with nonparametric formulas.[3] The hit rate (H) is defined as the conditional probability of responding "yes" to a signal (e.g., attended or unattended "old" brands) in recognition and likeability judgment tasks. The false alarm rate (FA) is defined as the conditional probability of responding "yes" to noise (e.g., new brands).

Response propensity, B'', represents one's response propensity when one says "yes" to a brand name in a recognition or likeability judgment task of the test phase. A high B'' indicates a more conservative decision criterion, whereas a low B'' means a more liberal decision criterion (Snodgrass and Corwin 1988). As we know, B'' is affected by one's motivation to respond. A high motivation for doing a good job (more hits) is accompanied by a liberal decision criterion B''. A low motivation is accompanied by a conservative decision criterion.

These are nonparametric formulas. In parametric SDT, sensitivity d' is the separation (mean difference) of the two distributions over spread (variance).

ASSESSING A FUND'S PERFORMANCE WITH SDT

A fund's performance is largely determined by a portfolio manager's ability to make correct choices in asset allocation, market timing, and security selections. In general, the Sharpe ratio (returns over risks) is the standard measure of a portfolio manager's performance of operating funds.

However, the Sharpe ratio does not consider a portfolio manager's absolute ability to tell the difference between a right option (signal) and a wrong option (noise) and his/her bias to select the right option. In psychophysics research, this has been discussed as a major issue for non-SDT techniques. Hence, this gives rise to the adoption of SDT in choice and assessment.

We argue that a portfolio manager's performance should be viewed from two aspects, d' and β. As SDT has suggested, d' is the absolute ability to distinguish signal and noise trials, and β is the response propensity. In this context, a signal trial refers to a correct option (e.g., securities) that leads to portfolio gains, while a noise trial refers to an incorrect option that leads to portfolio losses.

Computer algos of SDT have been developed (see Chapter 14) to calculate the d' and β for mutual funds or ETF funds. These algos may be implemented with nice user interfaces to assess all types of funds so that the performances of portfolio managers may be assessed in detail with SDT, as opposed to a single Sharpe ratio.

ASSESSING VALUE AT RISK WITH RISK PROPENSITY OF SDT FOR PORTFOLIO MANAGERS

There are at least three types of assessments of value at risk (VaR): historical simulation, Monte Carlo simulation, and the parametric approach. Here we discuss the parametric approach to introduce a new notion called the risk propensity framework for assessing VaR.

For a parametric approach, let us assume a normal distribution of portfolio losses with standard deviation *sigma* million dollars. VaR is defined as a threshold value for the probability (100 percent confidence) of loss of a portfolio. For example, with 95 percent confidence, we can say that losses would not exceed VaR = $(-1.645) \times sigma$. If *sigma* is $1 million, then the VaR is $–1.645 million. In other words, the portfolio manager is 95 percent confident that the portfolio loss would not exceed $1.645 million.

In the parametric approach to assessing VaR, the risk levels (e.g., 5 percent) or the confidence levels (e.g., 95 percent) are generic and are set arbitrarily. For portfolio managers, the level of risk that he or she is willing to take varies from person to person. A generic risk level for assessing VaR may not be applicable to specific portfolio managers. How to determine the risk level of a portfolio manager? We propose to use the risk propensity of the SDT. This new VaR framework is called the risk propensity framework for assessing VaR. Table 8.5 compares four types of frameworks for assessing VaR.

Engaging Figure 8.7 of SDT, the risk propensity is indicated as X_c, a Z score along with the cutoff line for the signal and noise distributions. The probability associated with the Z score may be calculated by a computer algo (see Chapter 14), called CND(). With the probability and standard deviation, a customized VaR may be calculated for a portfolio manager.

TABLE 8.5 Comparing VaR Frameworks

VaR Frameworks	Characteristics	Comments
Monte Carlo	Simulation for future data with random variables	
Historical	Straight use of historical data	
Parametric	Arbitrary and generic confidence (risk) levels	Reference VaR for all portfolio managers
Risk propensity	Determine the risk level for a portfolio manager; VaR is a function of risk levels	Customized VaR for specific portfolio managers

How to calculate the cutoff score for risk propensity? We may use the hit and false alarm rates from the historical data for a portfolio manager. With the hit and false alarm rates, the SDT formula may be employed to compute risk propensity, β for the parametric approach or B'' for the non-parametric approach.

DEFINING RISK PROPENSITY SURFACE

Naturally, a portfolio manager's confidence level may be assessed by the risk propensity indicator (β) of signal detection theory. In other words, investor confidence as risk propensity may be measured with the SDT formula. We may develop a theoretical relationship between risk propensity (β), implied volatility (σ), and strike price (X), illustrated as the risk propensity surface against volatility and price. Derived from the volatility smile with the Black-Scholes model and the SDT formula for risk propensity, one may predict that (1) risk propensity increases as volatility increases, given stable price: $\sigma \downarrow \rightarrow \beta \uparrow$ |stable X; (2) risk propensity increases as strike price increases, given stable volatility: $X \uparrow \rightarrow \beta \uparrow$ |stable σ; (3) the strike price increases as volatility increases, given stable risk propensity: $\sigma \uparrow \rightarrow X \uparrow$ |stable β and $X > X_{on}$; (4) the risk propensity surface may explain the volatility smile. The strategy derived from the risk

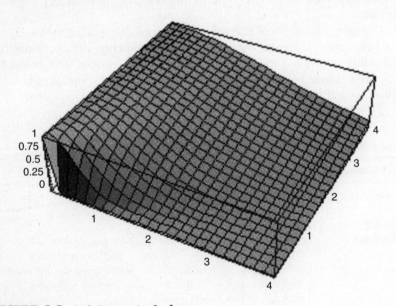

FIGURE 8.8　Risk Propensity Surfaces

propensity surface may lead to the creation of new financial instruments that consider both behavioral (risk propensity as investor confidence) and quantitative (volatility) ingredients. Figure 8.8 visualizes a risk propensity surface for a simplified version of the formula.

CONCLUSION

In this chapter, we extended the use of the multinomial modeling technique to understanding the growth mechanism of retail investors for a stock or a fund. This includes more understanding of the investor's unconscious mind. In addition, another modeling technique, signal detection theory, is discussed, which is used to assess the value at risk, risk propensity, and performance of a fund or a fund manager.

CHAPTER 9

Behavioral Economics Models on Fund Switching and Reference Prices

T here are various factors that may affect an investor to choose a fund or stock as investment vehicles. For example, economic factors such as the risk, return, and cost of the investment vehicles may affect the selection or switch of the investment vehicles. From a behavioral economics perspective, we look at psychological factors such as the endowment effect, inertia, and the anchoring effect, which may also affect the choice of investment vehicles. In this chapter, we discuss the psychological factors behind investors' fund switching behaviors. The findings on the psychological factors may be programmed into high-frequency computer algos for seeking alpha, risk management, or regulatory monitoring.

WHAT IS *VisualFunds* FOR FUND SWITCHING?

Investment management needs institutional and retail investors to put in their capital in financial instruments such as mutual funds and exchange-traded funds (ETFs). Investors may choose to switch between these instruments by comparing their risks, returns, and expense ratios. Figure 9.1 shows the automated comparisons between two funds with a proprietary tool called *VisualFunds*, which may be accessed at http://www.yeswici .com.

For the horizontal dimension, the risk scores are displayed for two funds. For the vertical dimension, the expense ratios are displayed. The size of the bubbles indicates the returns of the funds.

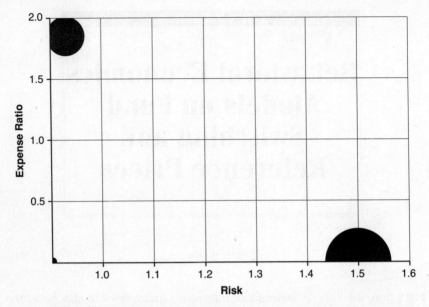

Mouse over balloon for detail; balloon size represents return; ticker with negative return does not display

A novel visual tool with real-time data for ETF and mutual funds

FIGURE 9.1 *VisualFunds* Compares Two Funds

In addition to the financial criteria for an investor to evaluate whether to switch funds, some behavioral factors also matter. One of these behavioral factors is the endowment effect, or the psychological attachment to the funds that an investor already owns.

BEHAVIORAL FACTORS THAT AFFECT FUND SWITCHING

There is more to fund switching than just financial factors. Psychological factors also play an important role. In this chapter, psychophysics laws have been used to model the endowment effect in fund switching. Inertia equity is a new assessment for the value of the endowment effect that jointly assesses the willingness to accept (*WTA*) and willingness to pay (*WTP*) in fund switching, although generally the *WTA* and *WTP* of the effect are assessed separately. We find that the relationship between the inertia equity and reference prices (i.e., the logarithmic model) can be transformed to Stevens' law, a basic principle of psychophysics. The logarithmic model describes that the (log of) inertia equity is a constant portion of the (log of) reference prices. Empirical data show that the new model is superior to alternative psychophysics laws in explaining variances.

A fund name is a brand. A brand is a name, logo, design, or other indicator for a product such as a fund, a kind of derivative, and so forth. When it comes to investment management with mutual funds and ETF funds, a fund name becomes a brand name. In the following text, we use "brand" and "fund" interchangeably in the context of investment management.

Brand switching (van Heerde, Gupta, and Wittink 2003) from competition factors (Shankar and Bolton 2004) has accounted for a large portion of a firm's revenue loss. For example, about 15 percent of Cingular's revenue (some $2 billion of the major U.S. wireless carriers) is lost every year due to customer churning. The present research offers an incrementally new concept called "inertia equity" to link the consumer variable "inertia" to the financial variable "equity."

Modeling brand switching usually takes an aggregate approach that uses sales or household scanner-panel data (Rust, Lemon, and Zeithaml 2004; van Heerde, Gupta, and Wittink 2003; Shankar and Bolton 2004). Less used are behavioral approaches based on behavioral choice theory (Kahneman and Tversky 1979, 2000; Thaler 1980; Simonson and Drolet 2004) and the psychophysics of pricing (Monroe 1971, 2003; Nunes and Park 2003) using experimental data. The present research employs a behavioral approach to conceptualize and model brand switching. Specifically, consumers' assessment of the minimum price reduction to switch brands ("inertia equity") is related to comparing the value of the presently used brand to the value of a similar new brand. This assessment may be biased by the market price of the present brand, or even an arbitrary price (e.g., the last two digits of a social security number). These biased assessments follow a general rule that is mathematically transformable to an advanced psychophysics law.

Endowment Effect

As a manifestation of loss aversion (losses loom larger than identical gains; Kahneman and Tversky 1979), the endowment effect postulates that a consumer's willingness to pay to buy an item is smaller than the willingness to accept to sell the item (Thaler 1980) due to the ownership of the item or loss aversion.

The endowment effect has been extensively demonstrated in the literature (for a review, see Kahneman and Tversky 2000). According to Kahneman, Knetsch, and Thaler (1991, p. 205), "After more than a decade of research on this topic we have become convinced that the status quo bias, endowment effect, and aversion to losses are both robust and important." However, factors that may influence the measures (the *WTA* and *WTP*) of the endowment effect remain to be understood. One of the factors is the anchoring effect. The effect shows that random numbers can anchor the *WTA* and *WTP* judgments. In addition, anchoring the assessment relevant to the *WTA* is still underinvestigated (Ariely, Loewenstein, and Prelec 2003; Simonson and Drolet 2004).

Anchoring Effects

Anchoring effects refer to the biased estimate toward a reference point (anchor), even if the anchor is arbitrary. For example, Tversky and Kahneman (1974) asked their participants to estimate the percentage of African countries in the United Nations by giving them an arbitrary anchor, say 65 or 10. Consistently, the percentage that the participants estimated has been biased toward the arbitrary anchor. For example, the participants estimated a median of 45 percent if anchored with 65, and a median of 25 percent if anchored with 10. Starting with the (irrelevant) anchor value, participants adjusted their estimate, but not enough to get the correct value.

The values of the arbitrary anchor are different from one participant to another. For example, Simonson and Drolet (2004) have used the last two digits of participants' social security numbers (i.e., coded as the *SSN* digits) to anchor (bias) *WTA* and *WTP* judgments. The *WTA* value is assessed by asking a question, namely, "what is the lowest price for which you would be willing to sell an item (e.g., a toaster)?" The *WTP* value is assessed by asking another question, namely, "what is the highest price you would be willing to pay for the item (e.g., the toaster)?" For different participants, the *SSN* digits are unlikely to be identical. So the anchor is arbitrary. It has been found that the arbitrary anchor can influence the *WTA* and *WTP* judgments. With larger *SSN* digits (> 50), participants' estimates are higher on their willingness to pay for or sell the item. With smaller *SSN* digits (< 50), participants give lower *WTA* and *WTP* values.

The anchoring effect is present with relevant anchors as well. The values of the relevant anchor are identical for many participants. For example, a consumer may perceive the market price of the brand that they have typically used in the past as a relevant anchor price (e.g., the price of the old brand). The relevant anchor prices have been set with pricing strategies such as the cost-plus pricing method or based on market demand (Monroe 2003). It is identical for many participants as opposed to the arbitrary anchor prices (e.g., *SSN* digits) that differ between participants.

In previous studies, it has been found that consumers follow a general version of Weber's law (Monroe 1971, 2003) in estimating the lowest price reduction that induces them to switch brands. Weber's law states that the just noticeable difference of the price change of a single brand or product increases as the magnitude of the base price (i.e., the anchor price) increases (Nunes and Park 2003). Similarly, the higher the anchor price, the larger the price reduction will be. The threshold price reduction is anchored to the relevant anchor price. In other words, the anchoring effect also occurs with relevant anchors.

Anchoring the Value of the Endowment Effect

The value of the endowment effect refers to the value of the difference between *WTA* and *WTP*. The endowment effect results from loss aversion (Kahneman and Tversky 2000). A similar notion is pioneered by Hardie, Johnson, and Fader (1993). Loss aversion also results in the status quo bias (the tendency to stay at the status quo rather than change; Samuelson and Zeckhauser 1988) because the loss, as a consequence of the change, looms larger than the gain. The status quo bias is the mental force of inertia in brand switching (the reluctance to change or the momentum to stay with the present brand). The inertia can be assessed by inertia equity that is defined as the minimum price reduction to induce brand switching. Hence, conceptually the value of the endowment effect can be assessed by inertia equity (see H_1). Empirical evidence supports this notion (see study 1).

Simonson and Drolet (2004) found that an arbitrary anchor (i.e., the last two digits of participants' social security numbers) affects the elements of the endowment effect, namely the *WTA* and *WTP* judgments. In other words, using estimates of *WTP* and *WTA* judgments as separate dependent variables, the anchoring effect is present both with *WTP* and *WTA* judgments. If we construct a new dependent variable for the endowment effect, namely, the difference of *WTA* and *WTP*, will the arbitrary anchoring effect also occur with the value of (*WTA* – *WTP*)?

It has not yet been investigated how the anchoring effect is related to the endowment effect (study 1). Both the anchoring effect and the endowment effect are robust, studied separately. The influence of anchoring on the value of the endowment effect (*WTA* – *WTP*) is still unexplored, although in recent research, arbitrary anchors may impact the individual terms (*WTA* or *WTP*) of the endowment effect. Understanding the anchoring of the value of the endowment effect is as important because it affects the outcome of consumer choice and decision making.

In contrast to the separate assessments of *WTA* and *WTP*, the assessment of the value of the endowment effect is the joint effect of the willingness to sell an item and the willingness to pay for an item. In other words, it assesses the value of the difference between *WTA* and *WTP*. The prediction of *WTA* > *WTP* is equivalent to (*WTA* – *WTP*) > 0. In general, for the separate assessment of the endowment effect, the values of the *WTA* and *WTP* judgments are measured separately and then compared (Thaler 1985), using the ratio of *WTA/WTP* (Kahneman, Knetsch, and Thaler 1991). For our new assessment of the endowment effect, the *WTA* and *WTP* will be compared jointly, using an arithmetic difference rather than a ratio.

In brand switching (van Heerde, Gupta, and Wittink 2003), we consider the cases in which customers switch from a present brand (*A*) to a similar new brand (*B*) induced by a price reduction. In these cases, customers jointly compare the *WTA* (willingness to give up an old brand) and *WTP* (willingness to pay to acquire a similar new brand) and assess the value of (*WTA* – *WTP*) with inertia equity. Other determinants of brand switching such as convenience, personalization, variety seeking, and quality (Rust, Lemon, and Zeithaml 2004), are controlled in these cases. As competitor (price) factors account for the most variance in pricing strategy (Shankar and Bolton 2004), we focus on competitor's price reduction to overcome inertia (loss aversion) of brand switching in the present research.

For example, in a brand-switching case for wireless carriers, say a customer of Cingular (now AT&T) is induced to switch to Verizon for the identical service offering with a price reduction. The value of (*WTA* – *WTP*) is then inferred from the price reduction that just induces the customer to switch brands. Since it has been found that the separate *WTP* and *WTA* judgments are susceptible to the influence of an arbitrary anchor (i.e., anchored by the *SSN* digits), we predict that the value of (*WTA* – *WTP*), namely the value of the endowment effect in brand switching, is also influenced by the arbitrary anchoring effect.

Although brand switching in customer equity has been modeled from an aggregate (macro) perspective (Guadagni and Little 1983; Rust, Lemon, and Zeithaml 2004), little research has been done to link the endowment effect to customer equity and customer retention. Theoretically this linkage is important because a rich body of literature in consumer choice can thus be employed to investigate customer equity in a systematic manner (e.g., relevant to the switching matrix of Rust, Lemon, and Zeithaml 2004). Customer equity is a central concept in modern marketing management of customer retention.

Questions of Interest

If the arbitrary anchoring effect can affect the value of the endowment effect, what are the boundaries of the anchoring effect? In other words, under what conditions will the arbitrary anchoring effect be suppressed? We address this question in study 2. In this study we observed the behavior of choosing an anchor from a set of anchor prices for subsequent anchoring.

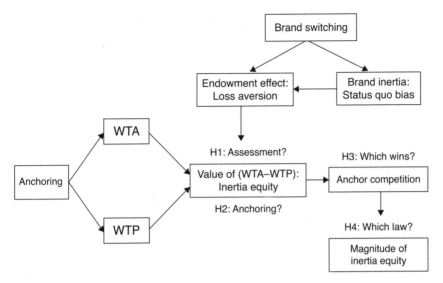

FIGURE 9.2   Conceptual Framework

The anchor competition behavior for consumers' willingness to pay has recently been introduced (Nunes and Boatwright 2004). However, still unexplored is the anchor competition for anchoring the value of (*WTA − WTP*). Understanding this mechanism for the value of (*WTA − WTP*) is as important as exploring the mechanism for the *WTP* because we can predict consumers' choice outcome by knowing which anchor is responsible for anchoring their judgments.

If both arbitrary and relevant anchor prices may affect inertia equity, are they behaving according to a general principle? The literature offers no answers. We will examine the relationship of inertia equity and both anchor prices with various transformations in study 3. Figure 9.2 depicts the relationships that provide a road map for analytically deriving constructs and hypotheses and empirically testing these hypotheses.

THEORY AND PREDICTIONS

The theoretical foundation of assessing the value of the endowment effect can be related to the value function postulated by prospect theory (Kahneman and Tversky 1979, 2000). The inertia value describes the value difference between the *WTA* and *WTP*. Inertia equity (the minimum price reduction to induce brand switching) then measures the endowment effect in brand switching.

Following the theoretical analysis, three predictions can be derived. We test that inertia equity is consistent with the prediction of the endowment effect. We also predict that the arbitrary anchor will influence the value of the endowment effect, but that the relevant anchor price will suppress the arbitrary anchor price and take control of the subsequent anchoring.

Endowment Effects as Inertia Equity to Model Brand Switching

We conceptualize that inertia equity can assess the value of the endowment effect. Both the endowment effect and the status quo bias are manifestations of loss aversion (Kahneman and Tversky 2000). Loss aversion states that losses loom larger than equivalent gains (Kahneman and Tversky 1979, 2000). We conduct a theoretical analysis and make predictions on the assessment of the value of the endowment effect using a typical asymmetric value function (see Figure 9.3) postulated by prospect theory to interpret loss aversion (Kahneman and Tversky 1979).

In a value function of Figure 9.3, OB is the gains curve and OA is the losses curve. According to the principle of loss aversion, the absolute value (utility) of gains ($v(B)$ or *WTP*) is smaller than the absolute value (disutility) of losses ($v(A)$ or *WTA*) for an identical monetary change ($X(A)$), namely $v(A) > v(B)$. $v(A)$ is the *psychologically richer* (Thaler 1985) value of losses, namely, the willingness to accept to lose an item. $v(B)$ is the value of gains, namely, the willingness to pay to acquire an identical new item. The separate assessment of the endowment effect is stated as *WTA* > *WTP*, or $v(A) > v(B)$.

It is not arbitrary to associate *WTA* to the value of losses and *WTP* to the value of gains. While introducing the endowment effect, Thaler (1980) states that "... removing a good from the endowment creates a loss while adding the same good (to the endowment that does not possess the good) generates a gain." The willingness to accept to give up an item indicates the value of the "removal of the good from the endowment." Thus it equals the value of losses due to removing the item from the owned items. On the other hand, the willingness to pay for an item measures the gain of adding the item to the endowment.

If we draw the gains curve in the section of losses, we have OB' and $v(B')$, $v(B') = v(B)$. The arithmetic difference between the *WTA* and *WTP* value is then $v(A) - v(B')$. (*WTA* – *WTP*) is the *inertia value* because *inertia* indicates that consumers are more reluctant to change the status quo or to lose an owned item (*WTA*), as opposed to gaining a new item (*WTP*).

The inertia value illustrates the nature of the endowment effect in brand switching, defined as the difference between the *WTA* and *WTP*. The

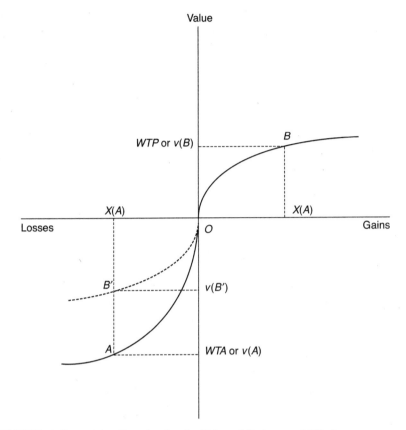

FIGURE 9.3   Value Function for the Value of Endowment Effect

difference results from the attachment to the old object that develops due to the experience of the ownership of the object. The inertia value is the source of the inertia equity, referring to the difference between the price that just induces a customer to switch to a new brand, and the price of the brand the customer has typically been paying in the past (i.e., the anchor price). The price reduction, equivalent to the amount of the inertia equity, generates a *psychologically richer* value that just equalizes the *inertia* or the *status quo bias* that is a vital driver to keep a customer from switching brands (with other drivers like quality and convenience controlled). As a result, the customer switches brands at the price reduction that is equivalent to the inertia equity.

The inertia equity is the unique price reduction that induces a customer to switch brands. It entails a threshold price change, namely the just noticeable price reduction for the customer to initiate brand-switching actions. In the experimental settings of the prior and the current studies, we assume that brand switching only occurs because of the price reduction. All other factors (e.g., convenience, quality, and variety seeking) are assumed to be identical for the old and new brand.

Inertia equity is a new measure of the endowment effect. Thus it should support the prediction of the endowment effect in a systematic manner. The prediction is $(WTA - WTP) > 0$. This can be formulated as hypothesis H_1:

> H_1: Inertia equity $(WTA - WTP)$, consistent with the prediction of the endowment effect, is positive: $(WTA - WTP) > 0$.

Brand inertia refers to the reluctance of a customer to change the brand she has typically been using in the past. It can be traced to Guadagni and Little (1983), and has been used as a vital driver for customer equity. Customer equity is defined as the total of the discounted (expected) lifetime values summed over all of the firm's current and potential customers (Rust, Lemon, and Zeithaml 2004). As a result, inertia equity is a vital component of customer equity.

From a micro perspective, inertia equity is represented as the monetary change (e.g., $X(A)$ on the horizontal axis in Figure 9.3). Its source is the inertia value, namely, the value of $(WTA - WTP)$. A congruent (e.g., loglinear) relationship is assumed between inertia value (i.e., the magnitude of the attachment of the endowment effect) and inertia equity. As a result, the inertia equity can assess the value of the endowment effect from an analytical perspective.

Two More Predictions

Simonson and Drolet (2004) found that separate WTA and WTP judgments are affected by an arbitrary price anchor. We use inertia equity to assess the value of the endowment effect, namely, the value of $(WTA - WTP)$. On the basis of simple equation arithmetic, the value of $(WTA - WTP)$ should also be affected by the arbitrary price anchor on the separate WTA and WTP judgments.

As the arbitrary price anchor (i.e., the SSN digits) affects the WTA judgment, we assume a linear relationship between the expected WTA judgment (coded as $Exp\,(WTA)$) and the arbitrary price anchor (say, x), namely:

$$Exp(WTA) = c_1 + a\,x \qquad (9.1)$$

where c_1 and a are constants, x stands for the arbitrary price anchor. The difference between the $Exp\,(WTA)$ and the observed WTA value is the statistical error.

Similarly, the arbitrary price anchor affects the *WTP* judgment. We also assume a linear relationship between the expected *WTP* judgment (coded as *Exp* (*WTP*)) and x,

$$Exp(WTP) = c_2 + b\,x \tag{9.2}$$

where c_2 and b are constants, and x stands for the arbitrary price anchor. The difference between the *Exp* (*WTP*) and the observed *WTP* value is the statistical error.

The value of the endowment effect (coded as *Exp* (*y*)) is equivalent to the expected value of (*WTA* – *WTP*). After replacing the expected *WTA* and *WTP* with Equations 9.1 and 9.2, we obtain

$$Exp(y) = (c_1 - c_2) + (a - b)\,x \tag{9.3}$$

where *Exp* (*y*) stands for the expected value of the endowment effect of brand switching that is assessed by the inertia equity. The difference between the *Exp*(*y*) and the observed (*WTA* – *WTP*) is the statistical error.

With linear Equation 9.3 we observe that the value of (*WTA* – *WTP*) (*y*) is a function of the arbitrary price anchor (*x*) given that the *WTA* and *WTP* judgments and the arbitrary anchor (*x*) are related. This derived prediction is formulated as hypothesis H_2.

H_2: The arbitrary anchor (the last two digits of *SSN*) affects the value of the endowment effect in brand switching, and thus affects inertia equity.

In a separate analysis with similar data (this can be obtained from the authors), we found that the arbitrary anchoring occurs on the *WTA* while not on the *WTP* in brand switching. We may note that the endowment effect is mainly an effect on *WTA* rather than on *WTP*. This can be observed from the data of the experiment by Kahneman, Knetsch, and Thaler (1991). Represented in Equations 9.1 and 9.2, we then have $a > 0$ and $b = 0$. Inserting them into Equation 9.3, we obtain:

$$Exp(y) = (c_1 - c_2) + a\,x \tag{9.4}$$

Consistent with the prior derivation, H_2 can be derived from Equation 9.4 as well.

If H_2 holds true, the next question will be: Is the arbitrary anchor the only determinant of the inertia equity? In other words, in a situation with dual anchors (e.g., a relevant and an arbitrary anchor), what will be the role of the arbitrary anchor?

On the basis of the assumption that consumers tend to use the anchor with the easiest accessibility in memory, we predict that the arbitrary anchoring effect on the value of ($WTA - WTP$) will be suppressed by the relevant anchor (e.g., a market price presented later than the SSN digits). This is described in hypothesis H_3.

H_3: The relevant anchor suppresses the arbitrary anchor and takes control of the subsequent anchoring on inertia equity.

Hypothesis H_3 postulates that the arbitrary anchoring effect will not occur if the relevant anchor is present. In other words, when a consumer is exposed to a relevant anchor (anchor prices such as $30 and $90) that appears later than the arbitrary anchor (i.e., such as the SSN digits), the impact of the relevant anchoring price will persist, while the impact of the arbitrary anchor on inertia equity will be suppressed.

Hypothesis H_3 is relevant to consumers' assessment of their willingness to pay anchored by multiple cues (Nunes and Boatwright 2004). An alternative hypothesis to H_3 is that the arbitrary anchoring effect on inertia equity may persist when the relevant anchor is present.

However, we believe that this alternative hypothesis may not hold true on inertia equity. Most consumers will use the anchor with the easiest accessibility in memory (Chapman and Johnson 1999; Mussweiler and Strack 2001). An anchor presented later has an easier accessibility in memory than an earlier presented anchor (see the order effect in Nunes and Boatwright 2004). In the present research, the relevant anchor is chosen because it is presented later (in the second question) than the arbitrary anchor (in the first question). We propose an account on anchor competition to explain H_3, which focuses on the process of choosing an anchor from a choice set (with an arbitrary and relevant anchor) rather than the mechanism of the subsequent anchoring process (given that the anchor is chosen). The mechanism of the anchoring process is well documented in the literature (Chapman and Johnson 1999; Mussweiler and Strack 2001).

Anchor Competition Accounts for Inertia Equity

In a typical anchoring situation with a single anchor, the anchoring effect has been extensively demonstrated with various dependent variables (see Mussweiler and Strack 2001, for various domains of anchoring) such as the estimates for percentages of African countries in the United Nations (Tversky and Kahneman 1974), semantic and numerical anchors (Mussweiler and Strack 2001), willingness to pay in auctions (Nunes and Boatwright 2004), valuation of ordinary goods (Ariely, Loewenstein, and Prelec 2003), and willingness to accept and willingness to pay under uncertainty (Simonson and Drolet 2004). In the present study, the value of the endowment effect (i.e., the inertia equity, namely, the difference between *WTA* and *WTP*) is used as the dependent variable.

The original account for the anchoring effect with a single anchor is that people provide estimates on the basis of accessible information in mind (i.e., the anchor) and adjust their responses in a direction that seems appropriate (Tversky and Kahneman 1974; Epley and Gilovich 2001). A framework has been proposed to describe the underlying mechanism for both semantic and numerical anchors (Mussweiler and Strack 2001). In addition, two recent accounts are relevant to our research: the activation account (Chapman and Johnson 1999) and the uncertainty account (Simonson and Drolet 2004). The activation account suggests that anchors affect judgments by increasing the availability (accessibility) and construction of features that the anchor and judgments hold in common. The uncertainty account suggests that arbitrary anchors influence only consumers who are uncertain about the transaction, and the impact of the arbitrary anchor disappears when consumers become certain about the transaction.

In the anchoring situation with a choice set of two anchors (e.g., the arbitrary and relevant anchors), it is still unknown how a numerical anchor is selected from the numerical anchor set to affect subsequent judgments. The anchor competition account attempts to bridge this gap. It is developed on the basis of the activation account. It also extends part of the uncertainty account.

First, the account assumes that consumers use an anchor with easier accessibility in memory to influence the subsequent assessment of the value of (*WTA* − *WTP*), on the basis of the activation account (Chapman and Johnson 1999). In the present research, because the relevant anchor (market price) is presented later than the *SSN* digits, it has easier accessibility in memory than the arbitrary anchor. Therefore, consumers will choose the relevant anchor for subsequent anchoring. It is consistent with the notion on anchoring as a knowledge accessibility effect (Mussweiler and Strack 2001).

If the relevant anchor is not available, consumers will use the arbitrary anchor in judgments. If both the relevant and the arbitrary anchor are present, the arbitrary anchor will not be used and hence will not influence the value of (*WTA* − *WTP*).

The anchor competition account underscores part of the uncertainty account in that the arbitrary anchoring effect will disappear when consumers are certain about the transaction. If we perceive the relevant anchor price as the average market value of the product or service (e.g., $30 monthly fees roughly indicates the average market price of a service program), consumers become certain about the market value of the transaction when exposed to the relevant anchor price. The induced certainty suppresses the arbitrary anchoring effect.

In the case of brand switching, the arbitrary and relevant prices are competing for the status of subsequent anchoring. According to the anchor competition account, the relevant anchor price will succeed in acquiring the reference state for the subsequent evaluation due to its easier accessibility in memory. The relevant anchor price will take control. As predicted in H_3, the relevant anchor price will affect the value of the endowment effect. At the same time, it will suppress the effect of the arbitrary anchor.

STUDY 1: ARBITRARY ANCHORING ON INERTIA EQUITY

In H_1, we hypothesized that inertia equity is systematically consistent with the prediction of the endowment effect. We predicted in H_2 that the arbitrary anchor (i.e., the last two digits of participants' social security numbers) affects inertia equity. The inertia equity assesses the value of the endowment effect in brand switching. Because prior studies have found that an arbitrary anchoring effect is present on separate *WTP* and *WTA* judgments, we predict it will be present on inertia equity as well. We will test these hypotheses in study 1.

Participants

Twenty-one undergraduate students of an introductory marketing class from an east-coast university in the United States participated in the study. All students were aware of the monthly fees of service plans of wireless cellular and many of them were cell phone users.

Design

Inertia equity is the dependent variable and the arbitrary anchor is a between-subject factor. The students were randomly assigned to one of the two conditions depending on the value of their *SSN* digits. They were presented with questions and then prompted to provide estimates of the questions about switching brands to competitive wireless firms.

Similar to Simonson and Drolet's (2004) study, participants were first asked to enter the last two digits of their social security numbers (*SSN*). They then assumed that the last two digits of their *SSN* were a price in dollars. Then the question was "Would you be willing to pay this price for your wireless service on a monthly basis?" They circled Yes or No as an answer.

Then the participants moved to the second question, namely, "Let A and B be two similar wireless firms with equal offerings in everything except for price. Assume that you are A's customer paying for a monthly service fee of X. Firm B offers you a price reduction to win you over. Assuming that you decide to switch to firm B at a threshold (minimum) price reduction, what would be the minimum price reduction from firm B to induce you to switch?" Other factors that might impact brand switching (e.g., transaction cost) except for price were assumed to be constant. For example, the mobile phone numbers were assumed to be portable.

Adopted from prior research (Ariely, Loewenstein, and Prelec 2003; Simonson and Drolet 2004), the level of the arbitrary anchor was categorized as "high" if the *SSN* digits were greater than 50. It was categorized as "low" if the digits were smaller than 50.

Results

A simple effect analysis was performed with the inertia equity as the dependent variable. The independent variable was the arbitrary anchor with two levels ("high" versus "low").

The main effect of the arbitrary anchor was significant ($F(1, 19) = 6.12$, $p < .03$). The mean M is 16.33 (1.66) for the "high" level of *SSN* digits, and $M = 8.67$ (2.62) for the "low" level of *SSN* digits (standard errors are in parentheses). Both means are larger than zero ($p < .01$). A t-test for all participants shows that the mean of the total is 14.14, significantly larger than zero ($t(20) = 9.01, p < .001$).

Discussion and Analysis

As predicted by the endowment effect, $WTA - WTP > 0$. This prediction (H_1) is supported with the data to assess the value of the effect. That is, the inertia equity is significantly larger than zero.

In order to provide empirical evidence for H_1, the inertia equity that is postulated as a direct measure of the value of ($WTA - WTP$) should be related to the difference between the two elements of the endowment effect that are assessed separately. In other words, the inertia equity should be related to the dollar difference between WTA and WTP.

Derived from the scales used by Simonson and Drolet (2004), the separate WTA and WTP values were collected in dollar amounts. Following the question asked on the inertia equity, the scale to assess the WTP was executed, namely, "Assume that you want to switch to firm B; what is the highest price you would be willing to pay for B?" The scale to assess WTA dollars was also executed, namely, "Suppose that you can sell the service plan of firm A to others; what is the lowest price you would be willing to sell it for?"

In summary, in addition to estimating the values of the inertia equity, a total of 75 students ($n = 75$) were also asked to estimate the *WTA* and *WTP* dollars separately. The difference between the individual *WTA* and *WTP* dollars was calculated and then related to the inertia equity that assessed the value of the endowment effect. A simple regression was performed between the inertia equity and the difference of separate *WTA* and *WTP* dollars. We found that the relationship was significant ($F(1, 72) = 6.85, p < .02$).

The analytical derivation for using inertia equity to assess the value of the endowment effect is validated empirically from one aspect. The empirical findings of study 1 underscore the validation. It demonstrates that the value of inertia equity offers consistent support for the prediction of the endowment effect (H_1) in that the value of ($WTA - WTP$) is always larger than zero, hence $WTA > WTP$.

Conclusion

We found that inertia equity significantly relates to the difference between the *WTA* and the *WTP* dollars assessed separately. This validation is underscored by empirical data that show inertia equity is systematically consistent with the prediction of the endowment effect (H_1). The value of inertia equity is larger than zero in various conditions.

We have also obtained a main effect of an arbitrary anchor on inertia equity. In other words, the arbitrary anchoring effect occurs on the inertia equity, as predicted by H_2. The larger the value of the arbitrary anchor (i.e., the *SSN* digits), the larger the inertia equity will be. The inertia equity is anchored on the reference set by the arbitrary anchor.

STUDY 2: ANCHOR COMPETITION

H_3 predicts that the arbitrary anchoring effect on the value of the endowment effect will be suppressed by the relevant anchor. Because of the easier accessibility of the relevant anchor in memory (Srull and Wyer 1989; Chapman and Johnson 1999; Mussweiler and Strack 2001), consumers will use the relevant anchor as the reference state to assist evaluations, rather than relying on the arbitrary anchor. We will test this hypothesis in study 2.

Participants

Sixty-two undergraduate students of a marketing class from an east-coast university in the United States participated in the study. All students were aware of the monthly fees of the service plans for wireless cellular and many of them were cell phone users.

Design

The base design is a factorial design with inertia equity as the dependent variable and the levels of anchors and the *SSN* digits as between-subject factors. The students were randomly assigned to the conditions. They were presented with questions and then prompted to provide estimates of the questions pertinent to switching brands to competitor wireless firms.

In the condition of the "low" level of the anchors, similar to Simonson and Drolet's (2004) studies, participants were first asked to enter the last two digits of their social security numbers (*SSN*). They assumed that the last two digits of their *SSN* were a price in dollars. Then the question was "would you be willing to pay this price for your wireless service on a monthly basis?" They circled Yes or No as the answer.

The participants then moved to the second question, namely, "Let A and B be two similar wireless firms with equal offerings in everything except for price. Assume that you are A's customer, paying for a monthly service fee of $30. Firm B offers you a price reduction to win you over. Assuming that you decide to switch to firm B at a threshold (minimum) price reduction, what would be the minimum price reduction from firm B to induce you to switch?"

In the condition of the "high" level of the anchors, the wording was the same as the "low" condition except for an anchoring price of $90 instead of $30 in the second question.

In the condition of the "arbitrary" level of the anchors, the wording was the same as the "low" condition except that the unknown price of X replaced $30 in the second question.

Similar to study 1, participants were automatically divided into two groups based on the values of their *SSN* digits. If the value was greater than 50, they were assigned to the "high" *SSN* group. If the value was smaller than 50, they were assigned to the "low" *SSN* group.

Results

A 2 (*SSN* digits: low vs. high) × 3 (anchors: arbitrary vs. $30 vs. $90) analysis of variance (ANOVA) was performed with inertia equity as the dependent variable. Independent variables were the arbitrary anchor (> 50, < 50) and the relevant price anchor (arbitrary, $30, $90).

With inertia equity as the dependent variable, the main effect of the anchors (arbitrary vs. $30 vs. $90) was significant ($F(2, 56) = 15.34, p < .01$), effect size (partial eta squared) = .35. The main effect of the *SSN* digits was

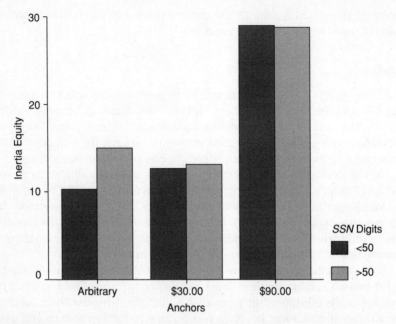

FIGURE 9.4   Suppressing the Arbitrary Anchoring Effect

not significant ($F(1, 56) = .40$, $p > .52$), effect size (partial eta squared) = .007. The interaction between the *SSN* digits and the anchors was not significant ($F(2, 56) = .32$, $p > .72$), effect size (partial eta squared) = .01. In Figure 9.4, the effects of the relevant and "arbitrary" anchors are compared.

Discussion and Analysis

In study 1, the relevant anchors are not present. In study 2, the anchor prices are coded as different levels of an independent variable, namely, as relevant anchors with values of $30 and $90, along with the "arbitrary" anchor. As a result, the relevant anchors suppressed the effect of the arbitrary anchor. It gives rise to the relevant anchoring effect that suggests that inertia equity increases as the magnitude of the anchoring price increases, which is supported by further analysis of the main effect of the anchors. A test for the contrast between the $90 and $30 condition shows that the means of the two conditions are significantly different ($p < .001$). The mean of the $90 condition ($M = 28.76$) is larger than that of the $30 condition ($M = 12.86$). The means come from the merged data on *SSN* digits because the effect of the *SSN* digits is not significant.

Conclusion

H_3 is supported with empirical data. The arbitrary anchoring effect (demonstrated in study 1) is suppressed due to the availability of the relevant anchor. In addition, the relevant anchoring effect shows that inertia equity increases as the magnitude of the anchoring price increases. When consumers are presented with relevant and arbitrary anchors, the arbitrary anchoring effect is suppressed by the relevant anchor. This is because consumers select the relevant anchor with its easier accessibility in memory as the reference to assist subsequent judgments.

STUDY 3: DOUBLE LOG LAW

H_2 and H_3 state that inertia equity is anchored by numerical cues. The cues are either arbitrary or relevant anchor prices. The arbitrary anchor varies from one participant to another and sometimes seems unrealistic to wireless users (e.g., if the *SSN* digits are 02, the anchor price is $2). The relevant anchor is more realistic and is identical for many participants (either $30 or $90 in study 2). In study 1, the arbitrary anchor affects inertia equity, while in study 2 the relevant anchor affects inertia equity. However, both arbitrary and relevant anchor prices are numerical anchors such that the anchoring mechanism may be the same (Mussweiler and Strack 2001). Hence our next question is: Are these biased assessments (inertia equity) following a general principle? We intend to find a common law for the arbitrary and relevant prices to anchor inertia equity in study 3.

Background

The relationship between inertia equity (a threshold price reduction) and continuous anchor prices in brand switching is not yet conceptualized and studied. We trace the relationship to the basic psychophysics laws that describe the relationship between a threshold magnitude change and the magnitude of the initial stimulus. Then we propose a new relationship that can explain more variance than the present psychophysics laws.

Weber's law suggests that we look at the ratio between the magnitude of the biased assessment (inertia equity) and the initial anchor value, coded as *inertia ratio*. The results of studies 1 and 2 suggest that the magnitude of inertia equity increases as the anchor price increases. In study 1, the magnitude of inertia equity is larger when the value of the *SSN* digits is larger (> 50). In study 2, the magnitude of inertia equity is larger when the relevant anchor price is larger ($90 > $30). So the result is consistent with a general version of Weber's law. However, with limited levels of anchor prices ($20, $60, and $120), we did not find in prior research that inertia equity is a constant portion of the anchor prices, as suggested by the strong version of Weber's law.

Then we attempt to investigate the transformations of the inertia ratio, inspired by a similar solution from the literature on the psychophysics of pricing. In the 1970s, in response to a challenge to Weber's law in price (Kamen and Toman 1970), a logarithmic transformation (Weber-Fechner law) was proposed (Monroe 1971). So we examine two options to transform the inertia ratio. In option 1, a natural logarithmic transformation for the inertia ratio is used, that is, ln(inertia equity / anchor price). In option 2, a ratio of the natural logarithmic transformations for both inertia equity and anchor prices is used, that is, ln(inertia equity) / ln(anchor price). The result shows that option 1 offers little information, but option 2 provides interesting results. That is, we cannot reject the null hypothesis in that the logarithmic inertia equity is a constant portion of logarithmic anchoring price. The data for the tests can be obtained from the authors.

Hypothesis

Although the result of option 2 provides limited information to establish a case, it guides us to extend a hypothesis formulated as H_4.

H_4: The logarithmic inertia equity is a constant proportion of the logarithmic anchor prices.

In H_4, the anchor prices are the prices that are actually used for anchoring, like the arbitrary anchors in study 1 and the relevant anchors in study 2. The arbitrary anchors in study 2 were not used for anchoring. So those will not be regarded as the anchor prices that will be used as data points in study 3.

Hypothesis H_4 can also be formulated as Equation 9.5:

$$Exp(ln(y)) = m \ ln(x) \qquad (9.5)$$

Where y is inertia equity, m is a constant, x stands for the anchor prices. The difference between the $Exp(ln(y))$ and the observed inertia equity is the statistical error. $ln(y)$ is coded as *log inertia equity*.

Although Equation 9.5 uses logarithmic transformations for both inertia equity and anchor prices, the equation is not identical to the ones suggested in Fechner's law that extend Weber's law in describing mental responses to a physical stimulus like sound and taste (Atkinson, Herrnstein, Lindzey, and Luce 1988). We will test these laws as alternative models to Equation 9.5.

Data

A total of 129 data points were collected from experiments that include studies 1 and 2, in which participants were asked to estimate a minimum price reduction for them to switch to another wireless service program. The data points are all independent estimates. They are anchored either by the magnitude of the *SSN* digits (continuous with a range from 01 to 99), or by the prechosen anchor prices by the experimenters including $20, $30, $60, $90, and $120. So the anchor prices were continuous in the collection of data. The actual anchor prices were used in the collection. For example, anchor prices like the arbitrary anchors in study 2 were replaced by the relevant anchor prices that actually affected the anchoring.

Results

A standard linear regression was performed between the (log of) inertia equity and the (log of) anchor prices. We found that the relationship is significant ($F(1, 124) = 84.24$, $p < .001$), $r^2 = .40$, $m = .72$.

To examine the fit of Equation 9.5 to the subset of arbitrary anchor prices, another regression was performed between the (log of) inertia equity and the (log of) arbitrary anchor prices. This relationship is significant ($F(1, 21) = 5.71$, $p < .05$). Similarly, the test for the relevant anchor prices to fit Equation 9.5 is also significant ($F(1, 101) = 81.58$, $p < .01$). Hence, both arbitrary and relevant prices anchor inertia equity in a similar way.

The model is validated with another data set from a slightly varied context to assess the inertia equity to switch restaurants. Forty-one data points were collected and used to test the predictive validity. The expected log inertia equity was first estimated based on the model ($m = .72$) and anchor prices, and was then correlated with the observed log inertia equity. We found that $r = .67$ ($p < .001$) for the expected and observed log inertia equity.

Alternative Models

The selection of the alternative models is based on the conceptual relevance to a perceived threshold of monetary change, because inertia equity is the perceived threshold price reduction that induces brand switching. So the three psychophysics laws (Weber's, Fechner's, and Stevens' law) serve as alternative models to Equation 9.5 as they have been employed to model mental response to threshold changes of stimulus magnitude. We use the variance accounted for (r^2) to judge the strength of the relationship (Tabachinick and Fidell 1996) between inertia equity and anchor prices that use the transformations offered by these laws.

The strong version of Weber's law assumes that inertia equity is a constant portion of anchor prices (can be described as Equation 9.4). A simple regression was performed to examine this statement. We found that the relationship was significant ($F(1, 127) = 54.65$, $p < .001$), $r^2 = .30$. It appears that Weber's law holds true with continuous anchor prices. This underscores Equation 9.4 and extends prior findings with categorical anchor prices. However, the variance accounted for is 10 percent lower than that by Equation 9.5. An F test for the difference of variance (10 percent) shows that the difference is significant ($F(1, 126) = 21$, $p < .01$, F-critical (.01 level) $= 6.85$). So Equation 9.5 describes a stronger association between the two variables.

Fechner's law states that the mental response is a logarithmic function of physical stimulus. Applied to our context, a simple regression is performed between inertia equity and the (log of) anchor prices. We found similar result as with Weber's law. The relationship was significant ($F(1, 127) = 54.45$, $p < .001$), $r^2 = .29$. So Equation 9.5 describes a stronger association (11 percent more variance, $p < .01$) between inertia equity and anchor prices than Fechner's law.

Stevens' power law states that the mental response is a power function of the physical stimulus. Applied to our context (the mental response is indicated by inertia equity), we have:

$$Exp(y) = k\, x^m \tag{9.6}$$

where $Exp(y)$ = expected inertia equity, k = constant, x = anchor prices, and m = exponent for a particular sensation (varies from .33 to 3.5 for various physical stimuli such as loudness, smell, and electric shock). Table 9.1 lists the exponents for 12 types of physical stimuli (Stevens 1961).

Twelve regressions were performed between the inertia equity and the (power values of the) anchor prices with the various exponents. The variances explained (r^2) for each exponent and the variance explained with Equation 9.5 are listed in Table 9.1 for comparison.

The results listed in Table 9.1 show that the exponents of Stevens' power law on average explain about 10 percent less variance than Equation 9.5.

If we take logarithmic values of both sides in Equation 9.6, Equation 9.6 becomes similar to Equation 9.5. This suggests that Equation 9.5 is transformable to Stevens' power law. Mathematically, this makes a lot of sense. However, statistically and empirically, Equation 9.6 has inflated the unexplained variance as opposed to Equation 9.5. We take the present data (129 anchor prices) and transform them to power values with the observed exponent for inertia equity ($m = .72$). Then a simple regression is performed between the inertia equity (y) and the power values. We find that they are

TABLE 9.1   Exponents of Stevens' Law and Their Association to Inertia Equity

Continuum	Exponent	Stimulus	Variance Explained
Loudness	.6	Both ears	.30
Brightness	.33	5° target—dark	.30
Lightness	1.2	Grey paper	.29
Smell	.55	Coffee odors	.30
Taste	1.3	Salt	.29
Temperature	1.0	Cold—on arm	.30
Temperature	1.6	Warm—on arm	.29
Vibration	.95	60 Hz—on finger	.30
Duration	1.1	White noise	.30
Finger span	1.3	Thickness of wood	.29
Heaviness	1.45	Lifted weights	.29
Electric shock	3.5	60 Hz—through finger	.21
Money	.72	anchor prices	.40—Equation 9.5

Note: The variance differences between .40 and the other explained variances are significant ($p < .01$).

correlated ($F(1, 127) = 55.34$, $p < .01$), $r^2 = .30$. However, the unexplained variance of the power transformation is inflated. The inflated unexplained variance (10 percent) is significant ($p < .01$), as opposed to the strength between the two log values ($r^2 = .40$).

A simple explanation for this is that the nonuniform residuals (heteroskedasticity) of the initial data become uniform due to the log transformations, while the power transformations still keep the nonuniform residuals. As a result, the unexplained variance is inflated for power transformations as opposed to that of the log transformations (Tabachinick and Fidell 1996).

Conclusion

Both arbitrary and relevant prices follow the same rule to anchor inertia equity. When compared to various psychophysics laws such as Weber's, Fechner's, and Stevens' law, the (log of) inertia equity and the (log of) anchor prices offer a description for a stronger relationship between the inertia equity and anchor prices. We code the relationship described in Equation 9.5 as the double log law because two natural logarithmic values (for inertia equity and for anchor prices) have been taken to form the equation. The double log law is mathematically transformable into Stevens' law.

Weber-Fechner's laws have been used to describe relative prices in marketing literature (Monroe 2003; Nunes and Park 2003). The merit has to be acknowledged because the construct of the relative prices is well accepted conceptually. Empirically, however, Stevens' law has replaced Weber-Fechner's law in psychophysics (Stevens 1961; Atkinson, Herrnstein, Lindzey, and Luce 1988). Unexplored is Stevens' law in marketing and consumer research. The present research offers the double log law (mathematically transformable to Stevens' law) to fill the gap. In the meantime, the double log law describes a closer relationship between inertia equity and anchor prices as opposed to other psychophysics laws including Weber-Fechner's. Exploring Stevens' law or its transformed laws in consumer research is important because it can provide more precise predictions for inertia equity of brand switching in consumer judgment and choice.

General Discussion

We discuss the implications of the studies from theoretical and managerial perspectives. The theoretical implications have four aspects. First, inertia equity is a new and meaningful measure of the value of the endowment effect that psychologically conceptualizes and models brand switching. It underscores and extends the findings from the separate assessments of *WTA* and *WTP*. Second, we conclude that the arbitrary anchoring effect on the endowment effect is robust, because it has occurred regardless of whether the elements are assessed jointly or separately. Third, we discuss the boundaries of the arbitrary anchoring effect in the dual-anchors situation, in which the anchor competition behavior on anchoring inertia equity is observed and explained. Fourth, we discuss the implications of the double log law. The marketing implications are relevant to inertia equity that is instrumental to customer acquisition policies in competition.

Inertia Equity to Assess the Endowment Effect As brand-switching behavior has been underconceptualized with the endowment effect, inertia equity becomes a new concept to assess the value of the endowment effect to model brand switching. Inertia equity offers a new measure of the value of the endowment effect. It is also consistent with the predictions of the endowment effect in a systematic manner. In the meantime, it offers more meaningful insight to understand customer equity with the endowment effect.

The endowment effect predicts that the willingness to accept to lose an item is normally larger than the willingness to pay for the item, due to the ownership of the item (Thaler 1980; Kahneman, Knetsch, and Thaler 1991). In the present research, the prediction of the endowment effect is consistently supported. Inertia equity is larger than zero in a systematic manner (see Figures 9.3 and 9.4 and the results of study 1). Therefore, the assessment of the value of the endowment effect (i.e., inertia equity) is systematically consistent with the prediction of the endowment effect.

More importantly, separate assessments of *WTA* and *WTP* seem to have little relationship with customer equity. However, if we jointly assess them and measure the value of the endowment effect with inertia equity, it links consumer choice (e.g., on endowment effect, inertia, or status quo bias) to customer equity that bridges a marketing construct ("customer") and a financial construct ("equity") (Ambler et al. 2002). This seems important to brand switching and marketing management because a rich body of literature on individual consumer choice (at a micro level) can be employed to study customer equity (at a macro level) in a systematic manner.

From a macro perspective, inertia equity is a vital part of customer equity that plays a compelling role in offering marketing strategies to customer acquisition and retention practices. As a result, the endowment effect in brand switching, assessed by inertia equity, becomes more meaningful to marketing management. As the "brand inertia" can account for a large portion of the variance of the customer equity (Rust, Lemon, and Zeithaml 2004), the endowment effect in brand switching assessed by inertia equity tends to provide more meaningful insights to understand customer equity from a micro (consumer choice) perspective.

To summarize, using inertia equity to assess the endowment effect is systematically consistent with the prediction of the endowment effect (H_1). It also links the endowment effect to customer equity.

Nature of the Endowment Effect in Brand Switching   The endowment effect seems to occur due to customer self-attachment to a product or service that develops as a result of owning the product or service. This attachment is revealed when assessing the value difference between losing the old brand and gaining the new brand. When a customer signs up with a wireless service provider (e.g., Verizon) and starts to own its cell phones and service, he develops a personal attachment (e.g., possession or belongings) to the provider as well (e.g., I own Verizon's cell phone and have access to its services).

With empirical data it can be demonstrated that self-attachment of the endowment effect functions in switching wireless service providers. When respondents are asked to estimate others' (e.g., a regular wireless customer) inertia equity to switch wireless providers, the magnitude of the inertia equity is significantly reduced as opposed to the magnitude of assessing their own inertia equity. This suggests that the self-attachment contributes to the inertia equity for self-owned items that include the service providers.

Although we attempted to minimize the potential transaction cost (e.g., the new policy for the portability of the phone numbers has been conveyed to the participants), further research may investigate whether there is a part of the magnitude of the price reduction (now ascribed to inertia or the ownership bias) that does not really belong to inertia equity. If there is any, it is supposed to be controlled for in the present research.

Robustness of the Arbitrary Anchoring Effect   We identified a gap between anchoring effects and the endowment effect. The gap suggests that little is known about the anchoring effect on the value of ($WTA - WTP$), although knowledge is accumulated on anchoring WTA and WTP separately.

Derived analytically from the arbitrary anchoring effect on separate WTA and WTP judgments, the arbitrary anchoring effect on inertia equity has been demonstrated empirically. The inertia equity assesses the value of ($WTA - WTP$). Consumers are anchored by the value of the last two digits of their social security numbers. This underscores the findings from the separate assessments of the endowment effect. It also demonstrates the robustness of the arbitrary anchoring effect on the individual elements or the value of the endowment effect.

We have analytically derived the arbitrary anchoring effect on inertia equity based on the findings on anchoring the separate elements (WTA and WTP) of the endowment effect (see H_2). The analytical derivation is supported with empirical data. That is, the SSN digits anchored inertia equity, namely, the value of ($WTA - WTP$). This also suggests that the arbitrary anchoring effect on the elements or the value of the endowment effect is robust, regardless of the assessment manners (separately or jointly) for the WTA and WTP judgments.

To summarize, the arbitrary anchoring on the value of the endowment effect (i.e., inertia equity) is derived analytically (H_2) and supported empirically.

Boundaries of the Arbitrary Anchoring Effect   The boundaries of anchoring effects on inertia equity that are relevant to the WTA judgment address the conditions under which the effect will be suppressed. The boundary due to the relevant anchors for judgments relevant to the WTA has been underinvestigated. We find that the arbitrary anchor is suppressed by the presence of the relevant anchor that takes control of the subsequent anchoring.

Extended from previous work, several important issues are addressed in the present research. The first is the assessment of the value of the endowment effect (i.e., inertia equity) in brand switching. The second is the arbitrary anchoring on the inertia equity and the suppression of the arbitrary anchor, namely, the boundaries of the arbitrary anchoring effect due to the relevant anchor. The third is the model that best describes the relationship between inertia equity and anchor prices (this will be discussed in the next section).

As we find in study 2, the boundary condition for the arbitrary anchoring effect in brand switching is the presence of the relevant anchor. The relevant anchor price suppresses the arbitrary anchor price and takes control of the subsequent anchoring. This indicates the boundary to the arbitrary anchoring effect on inertia equity.

The boundary of the arbitrary anchoring effect on inertia equity can be explained by the anchor competition account. The account extends our knowledge on numerical anchor competition for anchoring the value of $(WTA - WTP)$, on the basis of the findings on anchoring a proportion of the value, namely, the WTP dollars (Nunes and Boatwright 2004). It assumes that the anchor with easier accessibility in memory (Chapman and Johnson 1999) will be used to assist in the judgments. When both the arbitrary and the relevant anchor are present, consumers tend to choose the relevant anchor that has been presented more recently. As a result, the influence of the arbitrary anchor is suppressed.

To summarize, in the anchoring situation with dual price anchors, the relevant anchor suppresses the arbitrary anchor and takes control of subsequent anchoring on the inertia equity (H_3).

Anchor Prices and the Double Log Law With the double log law, the two types of anchor prices (the relevant and arbitrary) are consolidated since both are numerical anchors as opposed to semantic anchors (Mussweiler and Strack 2001). We find that both arbitrary and relevant prices can be used in the same law to model the anchoring effect on inertia equity, namely, the double log law. Being in charge of the anchoring, the two anchor prices affect the assessment of inertia equity in an identical way. When the data are integrated to examine the statistical relationship with continuous anchor prices, the double log law offers a description of a stronger relationship between inertia equity and anchor prices than various psychophysics laws.

Psychophysics laws have three meanings. First, the present psychophysics laws describe well the relationship between threshold mental responses and physical stimuli such as sound and taste. However, they may not be the best to describe consumers' response to monetary changes in brand switching. We found that consumers' response to monetary changes can be best described with the double log law, which accounts for more variance than other psychophysics laws.

Second, the double log law is a new equation that not only offers superior prediction power, but also bridges the gap in marketing literature.

To describe the relationship between inertia equity and continuous anchor prices, there have been few models that are transformable to Stevens' law (which is advanced but unexplored in marketing and consumer behavior literature). The double log law fills the gap.

Third, theoretically the double log law may be useful and important to model customer equity and brand switching. Models that describe brand switching and customer equity at the macro level (van Heerde, Gupta, and Wittink 2003; Rust, Lemon, and Zeithaml 2004) may employ the double log law to connect price perceptions and switching behavior. Although the models relevant to brand switching may have incorporated relative prices conceptually, an empirical and more precise relationship between inertia and anchor prices may be employable. The relationship is best described in the double log law.

With the bridge established between the endowment effect and brand switching, more findings in behavioral choice literature (e.g., the value function of loss aversion and endowment effect) may be integrated in modeling brand switching and customer equity.

With these findings, it is difficult not to think about the link between price anchoring effect and the mechanism of relative prices. The present research describes the relationship between initial prices and inertia equity but does not answer why this happens. Further research should investigate the two mechanisms (anchoring and relative prices) that seem to follow similar laws.

Investment Implications

The findings of the present research can be instrumental for practitioners to win investors from their competitors. These investors may be fund switchers who account for a large portion of the sales increase due to promotions (Monroe 2003; van Heerde, Gupta, and Wittink 2003).

Inertia equity is a threshold price reduction to induce brand switching. In practice, the meaning of the "threshold" can be instrumental. For example, suppose the inertia equity ("threshold") is $30 for Cingular to win over Verizon's customers with identical service offerings. If Cingular's marketers do not know the inertia equity, they may cut the price by $15 or $45 to acquire Verizon's customers. Both overshooting (wasting $15 to succeed in customer acquisition) and undershooting (wasting $15 to fail in the acquisition) at the inertia equity result in inefficient use of company resources. The inefficient use of resources may be amplified by millions of customers who attempt to switch brands.

In summary, properly utilizing the meaning of inertia equity will help managers and marketers to design effective marketing mixes, and in particular pricing strategy, that may ultimately enhance the financial return on the marketing investment.

Further Research

Further research may enhance the approach to assess inertia equity by improving the methodology and using new technology. Efforts are underway to extend the assessment of the inertia equity with confidence ratings. Participants will be asked to rate their level of confidence for the judgment on whether the monetary threshold of inertia has been reached. A methodology called signal detection theory (Green and Swets 1966; Yonelinas 1994) can be employed to analyze the confidence rating data. This new approach has been automated with e-commerce technology that collects participants' responses from the Web.

CONCLUSION

As a new measurement of the endowment effect in brand switching, inertia equity assesses the value of $(WTA - WTP)$ with a threshold price reduction for a customer to switch brands. It relates to the calculated difference of the separate assessments of the WTA and WTP, and is consistent with the prediction of the endowment effect in a systematic manner (H_1). Using inertia equity to assess the value of the endowment effect, it is found that the arbitrary anchor affects inertia equity in brand switching (H_2). We also find that the relevant anchor suppresses the arbitrary anchor and takes control of the subsequent anchoring (H_3). Both findings underscore and/or extend previous work. As a result, the endowment effect is linked to customer equity through inertia equity, and the new relationship between anchoring effects and inertia equity is discovered. A new model, the double log law, further describes the relationship for both kinds of anchor prices (H_4). Empirical evidence shows that the new model is superior to other psychophysics laws in explaining variance.

To conclude, in an important departure from the literature on modeling brand and fund switching, the present research uses behavioral approaches that include behavioral choice theory and psychophysics of pricing. It uses inertia equity to assess the value of the endowment effect that is systematically consistent with the predictions. It also bridges the gap between the anchoring and the endowment effect, and uses the endowment effect to conceptualize and model brand and fund switching. More importantly, the present research offers valuable insights on two new topics: the anchor competition for anchoring inertia equity and Stevens' law in investment research. With careful designs, these findings may be programmed into computer algos for high-frequency trading operations.

A Unique Model of Sentiment Asset Pricing Engine for Portfolio Management

P art II established the theoretical foundation of behavioral economics models for investment research. Part III develops a unique set of computer algos, called the Sentiment Asset Pricing Engine (SAPE), to automate the process of building behavioral strategies for high-frequency trading.

By the end of 2009, high-frequency trading had swept Wall Street and accounted for over 60 percent of U.S. equity trading volume. Why did the academic world keep relatively silent on this? Maybe it happened so quickly that the academic world did not have time to respond? Or high-frequency trading has touched the fundamental aspects of finance and financial theories that need more examination to develop a paradigm shift?

Paul Samuelson of MIT created a paradigm shift in economics by introducing mathematical analysis to economics. Harry Markowitz and William Sharpe created a paradigm shift in financial economics by adopting linear regression analysis from statistics. Black and Scholes created a paradigm shift in finance by developing an option pricing model with nonlinear analysis. With these examples, we find that introducing new technologies (disciplines, methodologies, or analytics) to financial economics may create a profound impact on the field.

I argue that the advent of high-frequency trading may create the next paradigm shift in financial economics by introducing the principles of computer science (e.g., scientific computing requires certainty in financial modeling) and computer algos to transform financial theories. Incorporating some existing issues in financial theories such as (1) the assumption of not considering behavioral factors in financial decisions, and (2) the assumption of estimating expected returns with historical data, I would like to propose a new framework called Sentiment Asset Pricing (SAP) model with computer algos to address the well-known issues.

As we know, the foundation of traditional financial theories is linear analysis and as a result we have modern portfolio theory and capital asset pricing theory. It is well accepted that the assumption of utility maximization may not hold true in the real world as traders and portfolio managers are humans who may not maximize utility all the time. The solution to relax this assumption is the adoption of behavioral economics that considers human emotion and sentiment in trading and investment decisions.

Another assumption in traditional financial theories is the use of historical returns to estimate future expected returns of a portfolio. As we all know, history may not always predict the future. It is understandable that decades ago we did not have advanced information technology to acquire real-time future-related data. As a result, we had to use historical data to estimate expected returns of a portfolio. Now we have automatic access to a massive data set that relates to future estimates with the option data. Can we develop a new model to estimate the future expected returns with data from future estimates as opposed to using historical data?

The sentiment asset pricing engine relaxes the two assumptions by incorporating behavioral economics models and the future option data with computer algos. In other words, we introduce new disciplines (psychological modeling and computer science) to financial economics. The SAPE algos are suited for high-frequency trading operations.

This section covers the development of the SAPE theory, and the application of the theory to portfolio management. The following diagram describes the drivers of SAPE with the building blocks of the Black-Scholes model (for future data), behavioral economics models (for sentiment), computer science (for high-frequency trading), and modern portfolio theory (for expected return). The implications of SAPE on portfolio management (portfolio construction) and derivatives (new revenue model for high-frequency trading) are also outlined.

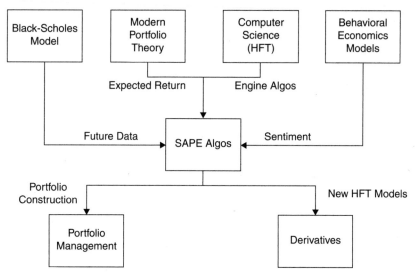

SAPE and Its Relationship to Portfolio Management

CHAPTER 10

A Sentiment Asset Pricing Model

I n this chapter we attempt to answer these questions: What is SAPE? How does SAPE link behavioral economics to financial economics? Why SAPE? Who are the primary users of SAPE? What does SAPE look like? Is it easy to install SAPE as software? What are the extensions of SAPE?

WHAT IS THE SENTIMENT ASSET PRICING ENGINE?

The sentiment asset pricing engine (SAPE) is a unique set of computer algos that are built on the capital asset pricing model (CAPM), the Black-Scholes option pricing model, and the ARCH (autoregressive conditional heteroskedasticity) model, by adding a human factor, namely traders' sentiment. Though the traditional models have considered important elements like risk and returns, future-dated option pricing, and volatility clustering, traders' sentiment can also affect stock prices. As the traditional models did not consider human factors, SAPE fills the gap of the traditional models by adding traders' sentiments into the equation. SAPE estimates future prices of assets by aggregating traders' real-time sentiments.

Compared to traditional financial models that provide theories and formulas, SAPE provides an end-to-end solution to portfolio management, including a new theory on behavioral investing, a new formula on estimating future prices of individual assets, and a new computer system for real-time future asset pricing, asset allocation, and market timing.

The SAPE model contains a set of mathematical formulas that aggregate professional traders' psychological sentiments to estimate individual assets' future-dated prices. The SAPE engine, namely the SAPE computer algos, is a collection of computer programs that implement the SAPE model. Based on the user interface, the engine has two forms: Web- or mobile-based computer programs. The core of the engine estimates future prices for 10,000+ equity or ETF assets, which is shared by the two UI (user interface) platforms.

The theoretical foundations of SAPE in financial economics may be traced to the two Nobel models: the Black-Scholes model for option pricing and the modern portfolio theory. We have introduced the Black-Scholes model in previous chapters. Here we just review the basic formulas. The Black-Scholes formula calculates the price of a call option to be:

$$C = SN(d_1) - Xe^{-rT}N(d_2)$$

where: C = price of the call option
           S = price of the underlying stock
           X = option exercise price
           r = risk-free interest rate
           T = current time until expiration
           $N()$ = area under the normal curve
           $d_1 = [ln(S/X) + (r + \sigma^2/2) T] / \sigma T^{1/2}$ $d_2 = d_1 - \sigma T^{1/2}$
           Put-call parity requires that:

$$P = C - S + Xe^{-rT}$$

Then the price of a put option is:

$$P = Xe^{rT}N(-d_2) - SN(-d_1)$$

Delayed for about 20 minutes compared to real-time data, the near real-time option data of an underlying asset for a future expiration date are publicly available. SAPE uses the basic formula of the Black-Scholes model to derive the future prices of an underlying asset from the near real-time option data. Let's denote the future price of an underlying asset as P_f.

Given an individual underlying asset, the traders' sentiment may be collected real-time for the options of the asset. Let's denote the sentiment value as *Senti*. Therefore, using the denotations of the parameters of the Black-Scholes model, the SAPE formula may be:

$$P_f = f(Senti, C \text{ or } P, S, X, r, T)$$

Given the detail of the formula is a part of proprietary computer algos for high-frequency trading, the formula and the algos are not published here. However, readers may go to a web site: http://sap.yeswici.com, to look at a live demo of SAPE formulas in action.

Based on the SAPE formula, the future prices and returns of an individual asset of a portfolio may be estimated. This addresses a longtime issue in modern portfolio theory (MPT; Markowitz 1952). The MPT uses historical data of individual assets in a portfolio to estimate a portfolio's expected returns, which are supposed to be the future returns of the portfolio. As history may not be the consistent proxy for the future, the MPT predictions built on the historical expected returns are not consistently reliable. For example, it is claimed that MPT might be part of a disastrous incident with Long Term Capital Management (LTCM) in 1998.

CONTRIBUTIONS OF SAPE

We discuss the theoretical contributions of SAPE at first, followed by the practical contributions.

Behavioral economics, especially behavioral finance (Shiller 2000a) has been established as a respectable subfield in finance after more than 20 years of work by Robert Shiller, Richard Thaler, and many others. Studying investor sentiment may contribute to two aspects of the connections between behavioral finance and financial economics, namely, the macro and micro aspects.

From the macro aspect, the CME group's volatility index (VIX) has indicated the market sentiment. VIX is sometimes called the fear index of the market. Figure 10.1 shows a chart that was created in part by SAPE

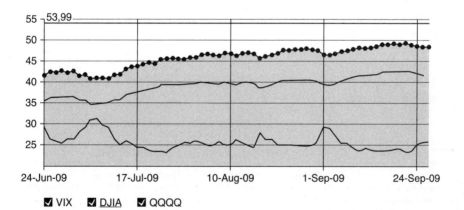

☑ VIX   ☑ DJIA   ☑ QQQQ

FIGURE 10.1 VIX over Time
Source: Yeswici.com.

algos to illustrate the relationship between VIX, the Dow Jones Industrial Average Index (DJI), and an ETF fund named QQQQ (PowerShares Exchange-Traded Fund). In separate calculations, we found that VIX and the future DJI index are highly correlated. A proprietary computer algo has been developed to forecast the market index performance with the previous day's VIX values.

From the micro aspect, SAPE algos may aggregate and compute many traders' sentiment on individual assets, stocks, or ETF funds. Building the option pricing formula of the Black-Scholes model, we may compute the future asset prices with future option prices and the spot price of the asset. Then the traders' sentiment may be added to the equation to compute the final future asset prices.

VIX and SAPE connect behavioral finance with financial economics by adding the sentiment factor, which is a behavioral element. Another human behavioral factor is the principle of loss aversion. In theory, loss aversion should be considered in asset pricing because measuring the loss and gain of future asset prices matters. In Part Two, we discussed the findings on loss aversion in option pricing. Loss aversion is a classical behavioral finance theme. Option pricing is a classical financial economics theme. Hence, finding loss aversion in option pricing connects the two disciplines.

Therefore, we conclude that theoretically SAPE extends the Black-Scholes model with a human behavioral factor, traders' sentiment, which is not considered by traditional financial models. SAPE, as the micro sentiment, along with the macro sentiment VIX and loss aversion for option pricing, has linked behavioral economics with financial economics.

To elaborate the contributions of SAPE, Table 10.1 illustrates the unique features of the SAPE model compared to legacy asset pricing models (APM). The features of future-dated and sentiment are transparent. Real-time means that the data feeds for SAPE algos may be real-time, while traditional APMs use historical data on an ad-hoc basis. Empirical means that the testing of the SAPE algos may use statistical testing methods such as *ANOVA*. Actionable means that the recommendations of the SAPE algos (e.g., for SAPE funds) may be used directly in building actively managed funds.

TABLE 10.1   Comparing SAPE with Legacy Asset Pricing Models

	Future-Dated	Sentiment	Real-Time	Empirical	Actionable
SAPE model	Yes	Yes	Yes	Yes	Yes
Legacy APMs	No	No	No	Somewhat	No

We may also find that the practical contribution of SAPE for actively managed funds is significant. As we will prove in the next chapter that SAPE effectiveness exists with several case studies, we may build actively managed funds (mutual, ETF, or hedge funds) that may repeatedly beat the market. The value of SAPE may be assessed in a way similar to the stock picking (advisory) fees of mutual funds. For example, Fidelity Magellan took in $3.7 billion fees during a 10-year period, 1999 to 2008.

Another practical contribution of SAPE is to build behavioral trading strategies for high-frequency trading operations. We may look at a technical architecture that connects SAPE algos and high-frequency trading operations.

Here is a simple architecture (see Figure 10.2) for high-frequency trading operations that includes the SAPE algos to replace manual algo executions by MATLAB or other tools. The SAPE algos may run as a Unix service (daemon) that is running all the time. Based on the algo calculations with

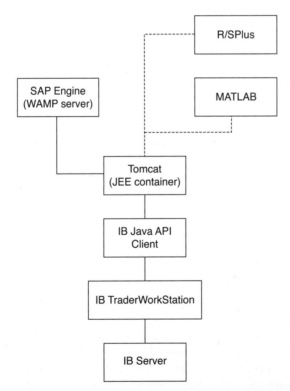

FIGURE 10.2 High-Frequency Trading Architecture with SAPE

the SAPE model, it generates signals with real-time data feeds. Once the signals become valuable, the SAPE algos may trigger the order executions by sending the orders to investment banks' servers that may execute the orders. The order execution may be interfaced with investment banks' API client through a Web server (e.g., Tomcat) with J2EE (Java 2 Enterprise Edition) containers.

Therefore, SAPE algos may become part of a high-frequency trading system.

TESTING THE EFFECTIVENESS OF SAPE ALGOS

When the SAPE algos were initially developed, I was fortunate to have comments from several money managers. A portfolio manager who runs a small fund of $20 million asked how to justify the effectiveness of the SAPE algos. This is similar to testing the validity of a statistical model. Hence, let's do some statistical testing to find out the answer to that question.

Based on the SAPE algos, I developed a TopTickEngine that takes in 500 tickers of the Standard & Poor index. For each of the 500 components, the SAPE algos are called to estimate the future returns of the ticker. These future returns are then collected and ranked from the largest to the smallest to form a list. A SAPE T5 fund would hold the top 5 components of the ranked 500 ticker returns. A SAPE T30 fund would hold the top 30 components of the ranked 500 ticker returns. A SAPE L5 fund would hold the bottom 5 components of the list, which may be used for a hedging strategy with T5 in long positions and L5 in short positions.

I then compare the SAPE funds to market indices such as the DJI index performance with historical, intraday, and real-time data. Due to the nature of the SAPE algos, the holdings of the SAPE funds are time sensitive. In theory, the holdings are valid for a few weeks before the option contracts expire around the middle of the month.

We test the performance of SAPE fund portfolios with the intraday data. In an *ANOVA* (analysis of variance) design, the SAPE factor is designed as the three levels of fund construction, namely, SAPE T5 fund, T30 fund, and the benchmark with DJI index. After collecting the intraday data, the one factor *ANOVA* on the SAPE effect is revealed, $F(2,99) = 82.88$, $p < .001$. The statistical testing suggests that the SAPE has produced the significantly better performance for SAPE funds over the benchmark.

For testing the SAPE effectiveness with daily data, a case study has been conducted that will be reported in the next chapter on portfolio management. For the testing with real-time data, a Web demo site has

been created that may show the evidence. This is available at http://www
.yeswici.com or upon request to info@yeswici.com.

PRIMARY USERS OF SAPE

SAPE algos are designed to improve traditional portfolio management theories such as the CAPM and the MPT, by estimating the future returns
of individual assets of a portfolio. Therefore, the primary users of SAPE
algos are money managers who actively manage the portfolios for financial institutions or wealthy individuals with the intention to beat market
performance.

The secondary users of SAPE algos are institutions or individuals who
would like to engage in high-frequency trading operations who need to
have a unique quality strategy. The unique feature of the SAPE strategy
over other strategies is its theoretical foundation with behavioral finance.
The advent of behavioral finance has produced a tide to add human factors
to asset pricing and portfolio management. SAPE algos have done this in
theory, materialized this with computer programs, and are ready to use for
high-frequency trading practice.

THREE IMPLEMENTATIONS OF SAPE

So far, SAPE has been implemented in three forms: (1) SAPE on the Web;
(2) SAPE on mobile; and (3) SAPE algos as API.

Figure 10.3 shows a screen shot of a sample ticker with the Web SAPE.
With login into a Web site, SAPE can create a longitudinal chart for a given
ticker. The longitudinal chart uses the horizontal dimension to show future
dates. The vertical dimension shows the future prices of the ticker for the
future dates. For example, the screen shot shows that the SAPE estimation was performed on October 26, 2009 (2009-10-26), with a spot (present)
price of $4.25 for the ticker. There were a total of 5,916,588 trials from
the traders on estimating the future prices on October 26, 2009. The future
dates are 2009–11, 2009–12, 2010–01, 2010–03, 2010–06, and 2011–01. As the
results of traders' estimations based on their sentiment, the future prices
of the given ticker are illustrated in the chart.

The ticker may represent a stock or an ETF fund as far as the ticker is
optionable. Hence, there are thousands of tickers that may be entered as
data input at the bottom. After changing the ticker, clicking on the submit
button would produce a different chart for the changed ticker.

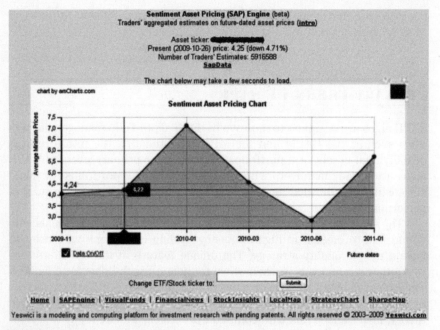

FIGURE 10.3 Web SAPE Forecasts a Ticker over Time
Source: Yeswici.com using free software by amCharts.

The mobile version of SAPE uses the Android mobile platform that has been used in Android smart phones through wireless providers such as Verizon and Sprint. Figure 10.4 shows that the SAPE app of the Android phone displays the future prices for many tickers. The trader# shows the number of traders' estimates with their sentiments. The SAPE estimation was conducted in August 2009. The future prices are for the next month (September 2009).

An Android phone user may download and add the SAPE app from the Android market to his or her smart phone. After double-clicking the SAPE app, the screen will ask the user to enter tickers. After entering a ticker, the future prices will show up for the ticker. More tickers may be added to form a portfolio of assets with the future prices estimated by SAPE.

The third form of SAPE implementation is the APIs (application programming interfaces) that are computer algos for high-frequency trading or other types of automation. These APIs may be accessed through service-oriented architecture (SOA) that uses HTTP services to obtain the SAPE estimation. The SAPE algos are designed on a SOA infrastructure so that the interoperability with different platforms and programs languages will be efficient and seamless.

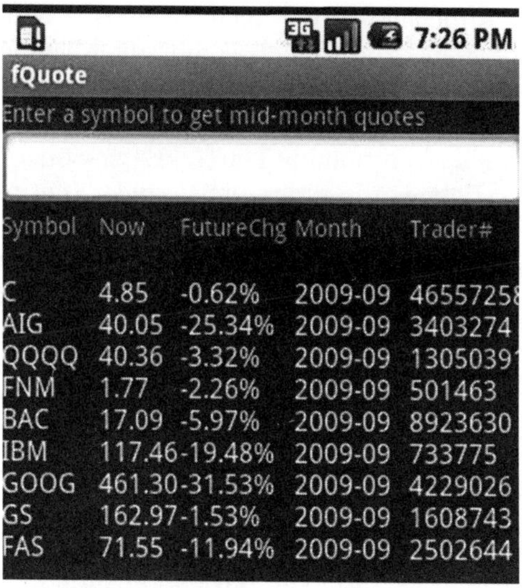

FIGURE 10.4 Mobile SAPE Forecasting over Time

With the SOA design, SAPE APIs are easy to use for high-frequency trading systems. A knowledgeable software architect or developer may integrate SAPE algos with HTTP services as the signal engine. This is much easier than hard-wiring a third-party application that may not be compatible in platforms (e.g., LINUX vs. Windows) or programming languages (e.g., Java vs. PHP).

The Web version of SAPE is portable Internet software. The size of the software is about 1 gigabyte. It is built on a WAMP (Windows, Apache, MySQL, and PHP) server. The installation of the SAPE engine may take less than half an hour. It may run as a local application for individual portfolio managers or as an Intranet/Internet application for enterprise users.

The mobile version of SAPE is hosted on Android market. Thus a mobile user may find SAPE in the Android market and download it onto her local mobile devices to use. It needs only a few clicks to access Mobile SAPE.

SAPE EXTENSIONS: TopTickEngine, FundEngine, PortfolioEngine, AND TestEngine

Building on the SAPE algos, there are a few extensions to suit different needs. These include TopTickEngine, FundEngine, PortfolioEngine, and TestingEngine. All are Web based and may be extended as mobile apps.

TopTickEngine focuses on the need for market entrance strategy. It ranks hundreds of stocks and ETFs based on their estimated future-dated returns with the SAPE algos to provide stock-picking recommendations. Based on TopTickEngine, portfolio managers may create and operate actively managed funds when running TopTickEngine on a regular basis.

FundEngine estimates the future-dated prices (net asset value, NAV) of mutual funds with the SAPE algos. Given the tickers of a mutual fund, FundEngine may estimate the future NAV of the fund after computing and aggregating the future prices of the individual assets of the mutual fund. This is especially useful for mutual fund managers who need to use a reference NAV price for the fund to make important decisions. This would also be useful for employees who choose mutual funds as part of their retirement portfolio. Knowing a mutual fund's reference price for the future would enable wise decisions on better returns of their hard-earned retirement funds.

PortfolioEngine estimates the future-dated prices of the portfolios of investment holdings. It assesses the risks and health of the portfolios. In addition to suggesting hedging measures to minimize the risk, PortfolioEngine also signals the timing of an exit strategy.

TestEngine automates the performance assessment of the SAPE-based program-trading strategy over time. This is helpful to test the strategy ideas created by the SAPE algos at the lab stage before the strategy is mature for real execution.

SUMMARY ON SAPE

This section on SAPE is very important in the sense that it connects many chapters of the book. It explains the concept and contributions of SAPE algos; its foundations; and its unique feature of adding sentiment as human factor to investment and portfolio management. The section discussed the connections of behavioral finance (economics) with investment management and the users of SAPE algos such as portfolio managers and high-frequency trading systems. Then the three forms of SAPE algos are discussed, including the Web version of SAPE, mobile SAPE, and SAPE algos as APIs for system integration over HTTP services. The ease of use and deployment of SAPE is also discussed, as SAPE has a SOA design on a WAMP server. At the end, four extensions of SAPE algos are elaborated.

ALTERNATIVE ASSESSMENT TOOLS OF MACRO INVESTOR SENTIMENT

The SAPE algos calculate traders' real-time sentiment for individual assets. This underscores and extends the existing sentiment measures for

TABLE 10.2   Comparing SAPE Algos with Shiller Sentiment Measures

Sentiment	On Individual Assets (micro)	On Market (macro)	Real-Time
SAPE algos	Yes	Yes	Yes
Shiller sentiment measures	No	Yes	No

the market as a whole by Shiller (2000b). The SAPE algos may also assess the macro sentiment for the market. As the sentiment for market index funds (e.g., QQQQ) may be computed by SAPE, the sentiment for the market may be represented by the sentiment for the market index funds. Table 10.2 illustrates the connection and difference between SAPE sentiment measures and traditional sentiment measures for the market.

Nevertheless, we have implemented the Shiller sentiment index as a computer app that is based on the similar PHP infrastructure that the SAPE engine is built on. SAPE algos run on a WAMP server, while the Shiller sentiment app runs on a Fireserv server.

In addition to assessing traders' sentiment with option data for the micro sentiment on individual assets, we could also develop online apps to assess macro investor confidence index for the market. The Web system is database-driven with a relational database management system to record, store, and retrieve data. The index is automatically calculated in real time and reported on the Web. It provides an automated, interactive, and sustained resource for constructing, reporting, and recording the index, which may be instrumental to understanding and ultimately predicting the dynamics of stock prices.

Introduction

One of the financial metrics, stock returns of the firms, is vital to evaluating the performance of senior managers. The stock returns, usually calculated with arithmetic formulas, measures the proportions of the difference between stock prices for a period over the starting price. The performance of senior managers such as CEO, CFO, and CIO may be evaluated by shareholders based on annual stock returns of the firms. Therefore, one of the objectives for senior managers is to satisfy shareholders with well-performing corporate fundamentals such as expanded revenue, reduced cost, sufficient cash flow, and so forth.

The stock returns may be determined with not only the fundamentals but also investors' confidence in deciding on buying or selling firms' stocks (Shiller 2000a). The fundamentals such as revenue (sales), expenses, and profits are traditionally treated as the components for the formation of

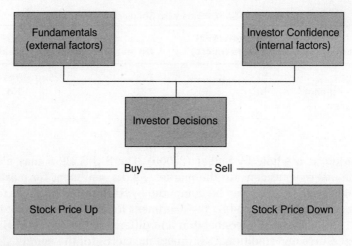

FIGURE 10.5 Investor Confidence and Stock Price

stock returns (Sharpe et al. 1999). Recent finance research has discovered that investors' buying behavior is of vital importance to stock prices. From an information-processing perspective, the fundamentals of firms are first processed by investors who are the immediate interface to stock buying/selling actions. Investors' behavioral factors such as investor confidence (part of emotion), personalities, cognitive capabilities, and so on may be as important as the corporate fundamentals as determinants of stock prices. As a result, the behavioral factors such as investor confidence have received extensive research interest in modern finance (Daniel et al. 1998). The conceptual relationship between investor confidence and stock prices may be illustrated in Figure 10.5.

In order to understand better and ultimately predict the relationship between investor confidence and stock returns, the measurement of investor confidence should be addressed first. Measuring investor confidence off-line with paper and pencil began in the late 1980s by Shiller and his associates, supported by the Cowles Foundation for Research in Economics at Yale University (Shiller 2000b). Four different time-series indicators of investor confidence were produced. The investor confidence index was computed as the average of the four indicators.

However, from the perspective of a networked economy where technology plays a vital role, challenges with the off-line measurement for investor confidence may be identified as follows: (1) the process to compute the off-line index is manual, thus not efficient and not sustainable. The questionnaires have to be mailed to participants who would complete and mail them back. Hence, the process may not provide a real-time index to the market. In addition, repetition of the survey process may not be sustainable and frequent. (2) The response data are not stored in a digital and manageable form. Therefore, it poses limited usage for data mining. For example, we cannot use structural query language (SQL) to investigate potential relationships between the indicators. (3) Survey participants were not offered a user-friendly and customized interface for convenient access at times of will. (4) The off-line index measures overall confidence in the market, not specific to selected corporate stocks. As a result, the usability of the index may be limited to academia.

As a result of these challenges that are not yet addressed, we lack an efficient, reusable, sustained, individual-stock oriented, and interactive source to build a real-time investor confidence index. Because of these challenges, the off-line investor confidence index has not been widely implemented in financial investment practice. Therefore, we need a Web system for investor confidence. The intention of the section is to develop a Web investor confidence index to address the first two (1, 2) of the four challenges.

Development Process

To develop a system for the Web Investor Confidence Index (WICI), we follow the life cycle of software development (Sommerville 1996). The four phases are requirement analysis, design and development, testing, and software release.

In the requirement analysis phase, we built a questionnaire on the Web that was used by Shiller (2000b) for an off-line survey. Four questions are presented to elicit responses in order to measure investor confidence:

1. How much of a change in percentage terms do you expect in the following (fill in one number for each):

	In 1 Month	In 3 Months	In 6 Months	In 1 Year	In 10 Years
Dow Jones Industrial	____%	____%	____%	____%	____%

2. What do you think is the probability of a catastrophic stock market crash in the U.S. in the next six months?

    Probability: ____%

3. "If the Dow dropped 3 percent tomorrow, I would guess that the day after tomorrow the Dow would:"

    1. Increase. Give percent: ____%
    2. Decrease. Give percent: ____%

   3. Stay the same.
   4. No opinion.

 4. "If the Dow dropped 25 percent over the next six months, I would guess that the succeeding six months the Dow would:"

   1. Increase. Give percent: _____%
   2. Decrease. Give percent: _____%
   3. Stay the same.
   4. No opinion.

These four questions are presented online. Participants' responses to the questions are transmitted across the Internet to a Web server where the database system is situated.

In the architecture and development phase, the three-tier Web architecture is first produced (Rayport and Jaworski 2003). The Web browser (e.g., Internet Explorer) serves as the presentation layer. The Web server (Apache) serves as the business logic layer. The third tier, the data layer, employs a database created from a database management system named MySQL. Figure 10.6 illustrates the three-tier Web architecture for the e-finance application. Database design is then followed to create tables and table relationships. These tables record the data submitted by participants from their responses to the online survey questions. With these data, additional computations occur automatically to calculate the average of the four indicators. The results, actually being the WICI index data, are then saved in the database. They are used as input to later reporting on the Web. The business logic, inclusive of saving/recording participants' responses, computing and saving WICI index, and reporting the index online, are realized with programming languages such as PHP and JAVA.

After developing the individual modules of the Web system, an integrated testing and quality assurance phase follows. Users are invited to test the usability of the system at the development environment. Defects are reported and corrected. In the final phase of the process, the online system is launched with a dedicated IP address to the Intranet. It will be launched to the Internet at a later time.

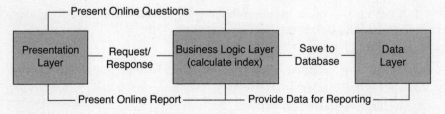

FIGURE 10.6 Three-Tier Web Architecture

Functions of the Web System

There are three modules built into the Web system. First, it automatically calculates the average of the four indicators (i.e., the WICI index) based on responses submitted from investors. The off-line index is calculated with a formula after manually keying in all the responses into a computer. Second, the system presents the WICI index online upon request. The data is up-to-date in the sense that the index is calculated and saved to the database with the latest participants' responses. The off-line index data does not have such an automated and efficient reporting process. Third, the WICI index data are saved in the database for later use with data mining technique.

Contributions

As the off-line index is the first of its kind to measure investor confidence (Shiller 2000b), the WICI is the first to collect online data for the index. In the meantime, the contributions of the Web system are threefold: (1) address the problems of the off-line index; (2) improve the construct validity and reliability of the investor confidence index, and (3) are instrumental to understanding stock prices.

The Web system for WICI addresses two of the four problems of the off-line index. First, it provides an automated process to calculate and present the WICI index. As a result, the process is streamlined and more efficient in supplying sustainable time-series data. Second, it provides a database to store and retrieve the WICI data in a digital and manageable form. This enables applications of data mining techniques such as SQL to discover potential relationships between the investor confidence index and stock prices.

The Web system provides resources to improve the construct validity and reliability of the index. By asking a number of questions online (in addition to off-line surveys) that are relevant to investor confidence, we enhance the ability to measure what we want the index to measure (construct validity). With more data collected from the Web, the impact of the erratic answers may be minimized; thus the reliability of the index may be improved.

The third aspect of the contributions is that the Web system is instrumental to understanding and ultimately predicting the dynamics of stock prices (see Figure 10.4). Inclusive of the real-time WICI index, the behavioral element relevant to stock prices can be materialized with empirical data. Sophisticated statistical techniques may be applied to search new evidence to explore the conceptual relationship between stock prices and investor confidence.

CONCLUSION

The sentiment asset pricing engine entails a unique set of computer algos that derive from the Black-Scholes model and the capital asset pricing model by employing traders' real-time sentiment, a psychological factor. This chapter discusses the creation of SAPE, the three computer implementations of SAPE, and the extensions of SAPE such as TopTickEngine. We also compare SAPE with Shiller's sentiment measures.

CHAPTER 11

SAPE for Portfolio Management— Effectiveness and Strategies

W ith the advent of behavioral finance and investor psychology (Kahneman and Tversky 1979, 2000; Thaler 1991, 1999; van Raaij 1984; Ye 2005; Shiller 2000a; Barberis, Shleifer, and Vishny 1998; Barberis and Xiong 2009), more and more people realize that investor sentiment (confidence) plays a crucial role in asset pricing. Yet one lacks sound real-time measures of investor sentiment for an individual asset that matters in the asset's price movement.

Sentiment asset pricing engine (SAPE) is a unique set of computer algos that are built on top of modern portfolio theory (MPT; Markowitz 1952), capital asset pricing model (CAPM; Sharpe 1964; French 2003), and especially the Black-Scholes option pricing model (1973), by adding a human factor in asset pricing, namely, traders' real-time sentiment. Though the traditional models have considered important elements like risk and return, future option pricing, and volatility clustering, traders' sentiment can also affect stock prices. As the traditional models did not consider human factors, SAPE fills the gap by adding traders' sentiments into the equation. SAPE estimates future prices of individual assets by aggregating traders' real-time sentiments. It provides evidence-based and actionable recommendations for practical investment decisions.

An investment portfolio contains a collection of assets such as bonds and equity that are categorized as either domestic or international, growth or safety, and so on. With a tradeoff of risk and return, portfolio management determines the choice of the assets of the portfolio, and the allocation of the financial resources on the assets for individual investors or financial institutions.

The TopTickEngine, built with the SAPE algos, is designed to transform portfolio management with quality and actionable behavioral trading strategies.

CONTRIBUTIONS OF SAPE TO PORTFOLIO MANAGEMENT

For mutual funds and exchange-traded funds (ETFs), there are two forms of portfolio management: passive and active. Passive management tracks a market index such as DJI, the Dow Jones Industrial Average. Active management involves a portfolio manager or a team of managers who attempts to beat the market returns by actively changing a fund's portfolio based on research on the individual holdings of the portfolio. Closed-end funds are generally actively managed.

In general, the three tools used for traditional portfolio management are asset allocation, market timing, and security selection. Among these tools, asset allocation is the most important (Swensen 2000, 2005). As a result of running TopTickEngine on stocks and funds, we may find the top-ranked assets based on their expected future prices and allocate financial resources to the assets that have the potential to profit most.

Market timing is not recommended for individual investors because emotions and unconscious sentiments always dominate in this situation (Swenson 2000, 2005): Individual investors tend to sell low and buy high due to the uncertainty to the future prices of assets. SAPE provides the reference of many traders' expectations and sentiments on the future prices over time. Hence uncertainty about the future is largely controlled with SAPE for individual investors. We should revisit the recommendation given the engagement of SAPE as the traders' emotions and sentiments are salient. For institutional investors and high-frequency trading systems, market timing has been in practice to beat the market indexes. SAPE should contribute to the space of market timing for institutional investors as the future reference prices over time are available for portfolio components.

SAPE is designed for active portfolio management that manages the fund portfolio using short-term forecasting of expected returns of portfolio holdings. This extends the methodology used by traditional portfolio management. For example, a commonly used and widely taught traditional methodology is the efficient portfolio frontier.

With an efficient portfolio frontier, portfolio managers pursue the mix of market portfolio where the Sharpe ratio of the portfolio is the largest among all portfolios. A market portfolio is sometimes called a tangency portfolio.

The efficient portfolio frontier is part of the modern portfolio theory that uses the historical returns of the portfolio assets as the expected returns for the portfolio. This would be challenging in the forecasting of expected returns, as history may not always predict the future. For active portfolio management, the expected returns of the portfolio should be estimated by data from the future. The future data may come from options data for underlying assets because options' premiums assess traders' judgments on future events with the future expiration dates.

SAPE uses the future data for underlying assets to estimate future returns of a portfolio, which extends the traditional portfolio management that relies on historical data for future returns.

INTRADAY EVIDENCE OF SAPE EFFECTIVENESS

The basic SAPE algos estimate individual assets' future prices by aggregating traders' real-time sentiments. The TopTickEngine uses the SAPE algos to create SAPE funds that contain assets with top future returns. The SAPE T5 fund contains 5 top-ranked assets on future returns with the algos. The SAPE T30 fund contains 30 top-ranked assets on future returns.

Here is the process to rank the assets on their future returns. TopTickEngine takes in a flat file that holds 500 tickers of S&P 500 index components. For a given date, the TopTickEngine calculates the future returns (normally until the middle of next month) for each ticker and build a list with ticker names and the future returns. The engine then sorts the list on the value of the future returns in descending order. The top 5 tickers become the components of the SAPE T5 fund. The top 30 components become the holdings of the SAPE T30 fund. And the bottom 5 tickers become the components of the SAPE L5 fund for shorting with arbitrage strategies. Here is the sample result of running TopTickEngine on Nov 29, 2009. Table 11.1 shows a total of 30 stocks that are ranked as the top 30 tickers on future expected returns among the S&P 500 components. These tickers become the holdings of the SAPE T30 fund for the weeks around early December 2009.

The SAPE fund holdings are time sensitive. They are valid in theory for about a few weeks due to the nature of the SAPE algos. These funds are actively managed with the objective to beat the market or peers with

TABLE 11.1 Result of Running TopTickEngine

Ticker	Expected Return	Ticker	Expected Return	Ticker	Expected Return
DYN	0.3528	KEY	0.0843	CPWR	0.065
MI	0.2161	DF	0.083	DNR	0.0644
Q	0.2062	IVZ	0.0806	ERTS	0.0627
CFN	0.1975	TLAB	0.0805	TSO	0.0619
FSLR	0.1902	NYT	0.0779	STT	0.0613
FIS	0.1421	GCI	0.0711	PLL	0.0598
VLO	0.1032	WFMI	0.0697	TROW	0.0576
WFR	0.0941	PLD	0.0688	ETFC	0.0551
JNS	0.0903	ZION	0.0681	EFX	0.0517
SUN	0.0877	LEN	0.0662	PTV	0.049

principles of financial anomalies that derive from the behavioral (sentiment-based) strategies.

Although the SAPE fund holdings are time sensitive in general, my finance graduate students and I also observed that the SAPE T5 fund holdings are stable for a week prior to the future mid-month.

Let us look at the effectiveness of these funds with some intraday data. Later in this chapter, we will look at several case studies to test SAPE effectiveness.

One example is on 02-Dec-09, time 14:51:07. The SAPE T30 fund has a real-time intraday return of –0.07 percent; The SAPE T5 fund has a real-time return of 0.28 percent; and the market index DJI has a return of –0.21 percent. With this data at this time, the SAPE T5 fund has outperformed the DJI index.

Other intraday evidence on the same day shows that the SAPE T30 fund return is 0.32 percent; the SAPE T5 fund return is 0.7 percent; and the DJI return is –0.01 percent. Hence, SAPE T5 fund outperforms the DJI index again.

Normally two data points are not sufficient to speak for the population. So we collect a sample of more than 30 intraday data points with returns for T5, T30, and DJI as the SAPE effectiveness factor. An analysis of variance (ANOVA) shows that the one factor ANOVA produces $F(2,99) = 82.88$, $p <.001$. This suggests that the SAPE effectiveness factor is significant in creating differences between T5, T30, and DJI. Figure 11.1 shows the mean of returns for the T5 fund, the T30 fund, and the DJI index.

We also calculate the Sharpe ratios for these data points on the three levels (T5, T30, and DJI). The result is similar to the ANOVA with returns as the dependent variable. Figure 11.2 shows the mean of Sharpe ratio of the T5 fund, the T30 fund, and the DJI index.

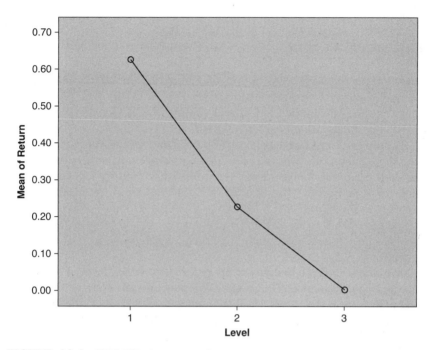

FIGURE 11.1 SAPE Effectiveness on Returns

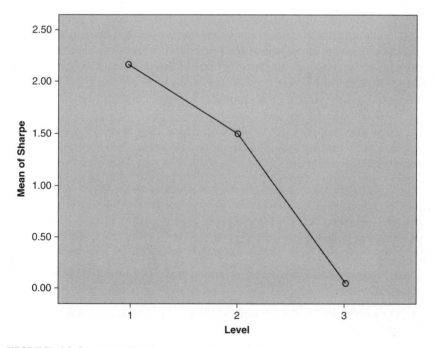

FIGURE 11.2 SAPE Effectiveness on Sharpe Ratios

TRADING STRATEGIES BASED ON THE SAPE FUNDS

Based on the above process of portfolio construction for the SAPE funds, we may develop two pure arbitrage strategies: (1) long SAPE T5 fund holdings and short market index fund; (2) long SAPE T5 fund holdings and short L5 holdings, which expands the spread.

A pure arbitrage strategy involves buying and selling assets at the same time for a given profit without risk. A risk arbitrage normally engages position holding of assets over time; thus the risk of betting incorrectly may exist for the strategy. The two SAPE strategies are pure arbitrage ones because as far as the ANOVA finding holds for SAPE effectiveness, one may always profit from the long and short combinations over time, given the commission cost is less than the revenues generated from the strategy executions.

We may develop a hedging strategy for risk management, if we do not use the two pure arbitrage strategies. We may buy put options for holding long positions in the SAPE T5 or T30 components. Thus if the long positions do not go as expected, the put options may minimize the loss when the ticker prices go down.

To summarize, SAPE is a unique set of computer algos that aggregate traders' real-time sentiment to estimate individual assets' future prices. SAPE fills the gap of the Black-Scholes model and other legacy financial models that did not consider behavioral factors in asset pricing. Compared to legacy financial models that provide theories and formulas, SAPE provides an end-to-end solution to portfolio management, including a new theory on behavioral investing, a new formula on estimating future prices of individual assets, and a new computer system for real-time future asset pricing, asset allocation, and market timing.

To further support the findings on SAPE effectiveness, the following text will present case studies with more data points and analysis. Readers may revise the strategies of the case studies to suit their own needs.

CASE STUDY 1: EXECUTION OF SAPE INVESTMENT STRATEGIES

There are three SAPE strategies provided at the beginning of the analysis:

1. Pure arbitrage strategy I: long SAPE T5 fund holdings and short market index fund.

2. Pure arbitrage strategy II: long SAPE T5 fund holdings and short L5 holdings—expand the spread.

3. Risk management with buying put options for holding long positions in the SAPE T5 fund components.

This case study is adapted from Yuqun An's original work, which attempted to test the three given SAPE strategies.

The Plan

We would like to combine the three strategies and create a new one: long for SAPE T5 holdings and buy a put option of a market index fund. We call this new strategy the extended hedging strategy. Buying the put option of the market index fund may serve as a proxy for buying the put options of the T5 components.

Identifying the Funds

For most actively managed mutual funds, the objective is to beat the market index. Successful fund managers may pick proper investment vehicles. Assisted by SAPE, we choose the T5 fund, which includes DYN, MI, Q, CFN, and FSLR.

For these stocks, the start date of the analysis is November 29, 2009. Our analysis ends on December 16, 2009. The historical prices for the five T5 components and IVV (a proxy for the DJI index) are listed in Table 11.2.

IVV (iShares S&P 500 Index (ETF) [Public, NYSE:IVV]) is chosen because it is closely correlated to the market with a beta of 1.00. Thus IVV's performance may represent the movement of the market. On the other hand, some other funds, such as IYY (iShares Dow Jones U.S. Index Fund (ETF) [Public, NYSE:IYY]) with a beta of 1.02, and BEP (S&P 500 Covered Call Fund Inc. [Public, NYSE:BEP]) with a beta of 0.71, do not correlate closely with the movement of DJI compared to IVV.

In IVV, the commission is 0.09 percent. The historical prices are listed next.

The Extended Hedging Strategy

To hedge the risk exposure of a possible declining stock price, the strategy provides the alternative to buy a put option of a market index fund, namely IVV. I recommend buying IVV put options in this case. If the stock price falls, we can sell IVV stock at a fixed price and protect the base capital. However, if the stock prices rise as expected, we only need to pay

TABLE 11.2 Historical Prices of Tickers

DYN Historical Prices

Date	Open	High	Low	Close	Volume
Dec 16, 2009	1.91	1.91	1.84	1.86	11,580,094
Dec 15, 2009	1.87	1.91	1.83	1.91	15,704,267
Dec 14, 2009	2.02	2.04	1.82	1.88	24,735,334
Dec 11, 2009	2.01	2.02	1.94	1.97	4,017,257
Dec 10, 2009	2.01	2.02	1.98	2.00	6,745,369
Dec 9, 2009	2.05	2.06	1.97	2.00	5,626,166
Dec 8, 2009	2.02	2.07	2.00	2.05	9,925,334
Dec 7, 2009	2.02	2.07	1.99	2.06	11,471,786
Dec 4, 2009	1.96	2.04	1.92	2.02	9,717,024
Dec 3, 2009	1.90	1.98	1.88	1.95	9,718,943
Dec 2, 2009	1.92	1.96	1.88	1.90	9,561,812
Dec 1, 2009	1.82	1.92	1.80	1.92	19,790,331
Nov 30, 2009	1.84	1.84	1.78	1.81	12,816,011

MI Historical Prices

Date	Open	High	Low	Close	Volume
Dec 16, 2009	5.66	5.67	5.35	5.41	8,574,176
Dec 15, 2009	5.81	5.88	5.54	5.58	10,042,010
Dec 14, 2009	5.94	5.99	5.83	5.99	4,637,524
Dec 11, 2009	5.71	5.86	5.70	5.85	4,060,786
Dec 10, 2009	5.91	5.97	5.68	5.71	5,412,060
Dec 9, 2009	5.95	6.04	5.83	5.92	8,945,407
Dec 8, 2009	5.70	5.96	5.64	5.95	10,352,053
Dec 7, 2009	5.73	5.83	5.69	5.80	7,622,110
Dec 4, 2009	5.68	5.79	5.59	5.77	9,784,248
Dec 3, 2009	5.79	5.93	5.44	5.46	8,966,448
Dec 2, 2009	5.77	5.95	5.65	5.67	13,562,343
Dec 1, 2009	5.82	5.90	5.64	5.72	7,339,181
Nov 30, 2009	5.41	5.76	5.41	5.75	13,970,222

Q Historical Prices

Date	Open	High	Low	Close	Volume
Dec 16, 2009	4.28	4.40	4.24	4.26	29,823,343
Dec 15, 2009	4.23	4.33	4.15	4.26	52,600,122
Dec 14, 2009	4.12	4.12	4.05	4.08	18,423,549
Dec 11, 2009	4.18	4.18	4.08	4.10	14,089,213
Dec 10, 2009	4.22	4.22	4.10	4.13	20,462,066
Dec 9, 2009	4.12	4.20	4.11	4.19	33,874,608
Dec 8, 2009	4.15	4.18	3.97	4.10	51,242,158

TABLE 11.2 (*Continued*)

Q Historical Prices

Date	Open	High	Low	Close	Volume
Dec 7, 2009	3.92	4.15	3.90	4.11	46,418,920
Dec 4, 2009	3.95	3.97	3.89	3.91	15,859,242
Dec 3, 2009	3.94	3.97	3.83	3.93	29,647,502
Dec 2, 2009	3.81	3.97	3.81	3.93	23,891,748
Dec 1, 2009	3.72	3.86	3.65	3.85	28,556,127
Nov 30, 2009	3.81	3.83	3.62	3.65	43,044,740

CFN Historical Prices

Date	Open	High	Low	Close	Volume
Dec 16, 2009	24.34	24.62	24.05	24.30	4,252,729
Dec 15, 2009	24.70	24.70	24.12	24.28	1,368,231
Dec 14, 2009	24.54	24.78	24.45	24.64	1,495,100
Dec 11, 2009	24.24	24.66	24.06	24.44	2,019,233
Dec 10, 2009	24.07	24.34	23.85	24.04	1,422,136
Dec 9, 2009	24.38	24.63	23.91	24.05	1,061,987
Dec 8, 2009	24.45	24.80	24.26	24.36	1,206,465
Dec 7, 2009	24.40	24.78	24.07	24.72	933,139
Dec 4, 2009	25.00	25.42	24.39	24.51	884,007
Dec 3, 2009	25.86	25.86	24.60	24.68	1,241,249
Dec 2, 2009	25.95	26.19	25.78	25.89	813,437
Dec 1, 2009	26.28	26.47	25.75	25.85	1,125,915
Nov 30, 2009	25.92	25.94	25.31	25.83	1,419,416

FSLR Historical Prices

Date	Open	High	Low	Close	Volume
Dec 16, 2009	139.70	141.50	136.51	136.74	3,800,604
Dec 15, 2009	137.98	142.66	137.54	138.99	3,216,008
Dec 14, 2009	134.84	139.98	134.11	138.65	3,495,193
Dec 11, 2009	134.65	135.46	132.65	133.10	1,610,365
Dec 10, 2009	135.00	135.88	132.55	132.94	1,750,762
Dec 9, 2009	132.79	136.20	131.52	135.36	2,169,925
Dec 8, 2009	134.22	137.30	133.51	133.54	2,331,790
Dec 7, 2009	131.20	135.94	130.69	135.18	3,331,925
Dec 4, 2009	131.69	133.44	126.30	129.62	3,731,710
Dec 3, 2009	122.95	130.27	122.19	128.12	5,305,949
Dec 2, 2009	122.50	123.15	121.16	121.71	1,104,257
Dec 1, 2009	121.09	123.86	119.11	122.02	2,125,169
Nov 30, 2009	120.79	121.99	118.06	119.11	1,600,098

(*Continued*)

TABLE 11.2   Historical Prices of Tickers (*Continued*)

IVV Historical Prices

Date	Open	High	Low	Close	Volume
Dec 16, 2009	112.18	112.49	111.65	111.90	2,842,364
Dec 15, 2009	111.85	112.29	111.37	111.69	2,537,480
Dec 14, 2009	112.25	112.36	111.73	112.23	3,200,979
Dec 11, 2009	111.47	111.73	110.98	111.47	4,259,346
Dec 10, 2009	111.06	111.48	110.83	111.00	4,291,602
Dec 9, 2009	109.93	110.53	109.37	110.35	5,393,328
Dec 8, 2009	110.44	110.60	109.45	110.02	2,816,422
Dec 7, 2009	111.29	112.65	110.85	111.19	2,330,253
Dec 4, 2009	112.23	112.73	110.39	111.36	5,508,522
Dec 3, 2009	111.90	112.55	110.65	110.76	3,256,934
Dec 2, 2009	111.66	112.38	111.28	111.70	2,847,133
Dec 1, 2009	111.26	112.02	111.10	111.58	3,674,391
Nov 30, 2009	109.85	110.50	109.37	110.30	4,405,881

Data source: Google Finance: http://www.google.com/finance?hl=en&tab=we.

the commissions. Let's assume that we bought IVV and T5 fund components on November 30, 2009, and that 1,000 shares is one unit. Figure 11.3 shows the profit function of the extended hedging strategy.

Basic Scenario of the Extended Hedging Strategy

Let us assume that we bought one unit of IVV and one unit of T5 fund in total. The T5 stock price changes are real. The commission (cost) is

$$1,000 \times \$109.85 \times 0.9\% = \$988.65$$

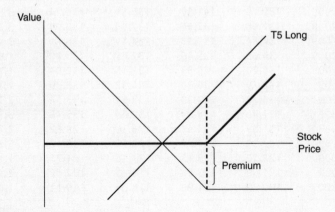

FIGURE 11.3   Profit Function of the T5 Fund

TABLE 11.3 Performance of the T5 Fund

	Price at Beginning	Price at End
DYN:	1.84	1.86
MI:	5.41	5.41
Q:	3.81	4.26
CFN:	25.92	24.30
FSLR:	120.79	136.74
Avg Price	31.55	34.51
Change		2.96

Assume this commission equals the premium we need to pay for the ETF. From November 30 to December 16, the T5 average prices rise as shown in Table 11.3.

The revenue of the portfolio is:

$$1,000 \times \$34.51 - \$988.65 = \$33,521.65$$

As the price of the T5 fund rises, considering the cost of buying the T5 fund, the profit from this portfolio with long positions in T5 components and the IVV put option is:

$$1,000 \times \$2.96 - \$988.65 = \$1,971.35$$

Scenario 1 We bought one unit of IVV and one unit of T5 fund in total. But the stock prices are uncertain. Assume the prices change is Δ. To ensure profit, we need to have:

$$1,000 \times \Delta - \$988.65 >= 0$$

$$\text{Thus } \Delta >= \$0.98865$$

This suggests that the changes in the average price of T5 must be larger than \$0.98865, or we may need to sell IVV at the put price to cover the loss.

Scenario 2 We do not buy equal units of IVV and T5 fund. Assume we bought x units of IVV put options and $k \times x$ units of T5 fund. The stock prices are uncertain, and the price change is Δ.

To ensure profit, we need to have:

$$1,000 \times k \times x \times \Delta - \$988.65 \times x >= 0$$

Solving the equation, we need to have $\Delta >= \$0.98865/k$.

This suggests that the changes in the average price of T5 must be larger than \$0.98865/k, or else we need to sell IVV to hedge the financial exposure.

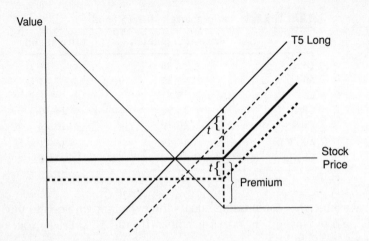

FIGURE 11.4 Profit Function of the T5 Fund with Commissions

Scenario 3: T5 Fund Needs Commission Cost Considering the cost of the T5 fund, the price change needs to increase to hedge the financial exposure. Figure 11.4 shows the profit function of the portfolio with commission costs.

The revenue of the portfolio is:

$$(1,000 \times k \times x \times \text{Average Price of T5} - t) - \$988.65 \times x$$

Considering the cost of buying the T5 fund, the profit from this portfolio with long positions in T5 components and the IVV put option is:

$$(1,000 \times k \times x \times \Delta - t) - \$988.65 \times x >= 0$$

Thus we need to have $\Delta >= \$(0.98865/k + t/1,000 \times k \times x)$

Evaluating Arbitrage and Hedging Strategies

First, let us evaluate the pure arbitrage Strategy I: long positions in SAPE T5 fund holdings and short positions in the market index fund. The basic scenario is to assume that we buy one unit of T5 and short one unit of IVV. With all the data from the market:

The market value of holding the T5 is: $1,000 \times \$34.51 = \$34,510$
The revenue from holding the T5: $1,000 \times \$2.96 = \$2,960$
The cost of shorting IVV: $1,000 \times (\$109.85 - \$111.90) = \$2,050$
The profit of Strategy I: $\$2,960 - \$2,050 = \$910$

Scenario 1:

Assume that we bought $k \times x$ units of T5 and x units of IVV. Therefore,

$$1,000 \times k \times x \times \Delta_{T5} + 1,000 \times x \times \Delta_{IVV} >= 0$$

$$\text{And thus } \Delta_{T5} >= \Delta_{IVV}/k$$

This suggests that the price change of the T5 fund must be at least (Δ_{IVV}/k), or we may not be profitable from this strategy.

The expectation of this strategy is that the price change of the T5 fund is larger than the change of the market index fund. However, there is no risk coverage if the market movement is not following expectations.

Second, let us evaluate the pure arbitrage Strategy II: long positions in SAPE T5 fund holdings and short positions in L5 holdings. The second strategy is similar to the first one. The expectation of the second strategy is that the price change of the T5 fund is larger than the change of the L5 fund. If the expectation is not met, there is no risk hedged for this strategy.

Third, let us evaluate the extended hedging strategy with risk management: We buy put options for the long positions in the T5 fund components. The extended hedging strategy is a risk management strategy. This strategy is conservative and may be profitable.

We may look at two types of hedging strategies: One is the given hedging strategy with put options on the long positions in T5 fund components, and the other is to use put options on an ETF fund, say, IVV.

The difference between the two hedging strategies is the commissions and the target of risk hedging. As IVV is a large cap ETF, the cost is low, about 0.9%. However, the T5 fund is a new fund and the cost may be a little higher. Therefore we need to expect more profit from the T5 portfolio to cover the cost.

The advantage of the third strategy is risk hedging. If we buy put options for the long positions in the T5 fund components, the risks of these long positions will be fully hedged. If the stock prices go below the break-even point, we may sell the stocks at the put strike prices. In the extended hedging strategy, we recommend buying put options on a market index fund as a proxy to hedge the risk of the long positions in the T5 components.

Table 11.4 shows the historical returns of the T5 fund components compared with the market index:

As shown, the SAPE T5 fund steadily outperforms the market.

Summary

Based on the three given SAPE strategies, we recommend taking long positions in SAPE T5 holdings and buying a put option on IVV, a market index fund. We may benefit from the low cost of the market index fund.

TABLE 11.4 Fund Returns

First Intraday Evidence	
Begin date: Nov-29–09; end date: 02-Dec-09	
The SAPE T5 fund return to-date:	2.70%
The DJI return to-date:	1.42%
Second Intraday Evidence	
Begin date: Nov-29–09; end date: 07-Dec-09	
The SAPE T5 fund return to-date:	2.44%
The DJI return to-date:	−0.22%
Third Intraday Evidence	
Begin date: Nov-29–09; end date: 17-Dec-09	
The SAPE T5 fund return to-date:	0.32%
The DJI return to-date:	−1.09%

With the real data, we have shown that the strategy produces profit. In the future, if the price change of the T5 fund remains larger than $(0.98865/k + t/1{,}000 \times k \times x)$, where t is the cost of T5 and $k \times x$ is the unit of T5 fund, we may sustain the profit from this strategy.

CASE STUDY 2: THE TRADING PROCESS WITH SAPE

This case study is adapted from the original work by PoJung Su, who analyzed the market data with the three given SAPE strategies.

About SAPE

Sentiment asset pricing engine is built on capital asset pricing models and option pricing models by adding human psychological factors. Though the traditional models considered important elements like risk and reward, traders' sentiment may also affect stock price. As the traditional models do not consider psychological factors, SAPE fill the gap by adding traders' sentiments into the equation. SAPE estimates future prices of assets by aggregating traders' real-time sentiments.

We start with the three given strategies to take advantage of SAPE:

1. Pure arbitrage Strategy I: long SAPE T5 fund holdings and short market index fund.

2. Pure arbitrage Strategy II: long SAPE T5 fund holdings and short L5 holdings—expand the spread.

3. Risk management with buying put options for holding long positions in the SAPE T5 fund components.

Basic Strategy

Theoretically, SAPE may beat the market with principles of behavioral anomalies. With the historical data analysis for a past week, we may find that Q (Qwest Communications International, Inc.), one of the T5 funds selected by TopTickEngine, has indeed outperformed the market index. Thus, we choose the pure arbitrage strategy as our main strategy by taking long positions in SAPE T5 fund components and the short position in a market index fund.

Fund Strategy

Let us assume that the strategy may use an initial fund of $1,000,000. The fund will be invested in three divisions: $300,000 will be invested in the long positions in T5 fund holdings; $300,000 will be invested in the short position in a market index fund; and $200,000 will be buying put options on the SAPE T5 fund components. Another $200,000 will be idle funds. For risk management, the hedging coverage will be 30 percent.

Trading Frequency

We have observed that the T5 fund holdings are stable for a week prior to the future mid month. Thus, our strategy would be based on two weeks' data. We will enter the market at the first trading day of the month, then, clear the portion after two weeks and again enter the market with the new selections of the T5 fund holdings.

First Fund Selection

Here are the top 30 SAPE fund holdings (tickers) recommended by Top-TickEngine on November 29, 2009: DYN MI Q CFN FSLR FIS VLO WFR JNS SUN KEY DF IVZ TLAB NYT GCI WFMI PLD ZION LEN CPWR DNR ERTS TSO STT PLL TROW ETFC EFX PTV LM BK.

Table 11.5 shows the top five fund components.

We will take long positions in the T5 holdings, which are DYN, MI, Q, CFN, and FSLR. The shares purchased are described in Table 11.4. $300,000 would be invested in short position in DIA, which is an ETF proxy of Dow Jones Industrial Average. Another $200,000 will be buying put options on the five corresponding stocks with the strike prices near the market price in the second month.

TABLE 11.5 SAPE T5 Fund Holdings

Name	Symbol	Last Price	Mkt Cap	Volume	Invested Amount	Shares Holding
Dynegy Inc.	DYN	1.91	1,615	25,375,048	$60,000	31,414
Marshall & Ilsley Corporation	MI	5.31	2,786	9,179,170	$60,000	11,299
Qwest Communications International Inc.	Q	4.25	7,338	30,312,810	$60,000	14,118
CareFusion Corporation	CFN	24.06	5,327	1,931,691	$60,000	2,494
First Solar, Inc.	FSLR	135.73	11,552	3,757,859	$60,000	442

Cost Analysis

Let us assume that the commission cost for stock trading is $12.95 per executed equity trade; and for options trading is $8.5 per contract. The transactions will include six equity trades (five stocks and one ETF) and about 180 contracts of options. Table 11.6 shows the details of the transactions.

Breakeven Analysis

According to the historical data of the two weeks' return, SAPE T5 fund has an average return of 2.43 percent. The tax on capital gain is 15 percent. The amount invested in the pure arbitrage strategy is $600,000, so the profit will be:

Profit: $600,000 \times 2.43\% \times (1-15\%) = \$12,393$
Break-even: $\$112/\$12,393 \times 14 = 0.13$

TABLE 11.6 SAPE T5 Fund Transactions

Symbol	Shares Holding	Shares to be Hedged	Option Contract (100 shares)	Commission Fees (+$8.5)
DYN	31,414	9,424	94	$14.1
MI	11,299	3,390	34	4.1
Q	14,118	4,235	42	6.3
CFN	2,494	748	7	1.05
FSLR	442	133	1	0.15
			Total	$34.2

The break-even point will be approximately one day. Assume the investment also require a certain management fee or the usage fee of TopTickEngine will cost 5 percent of the initial fund.

Initial cost: $1,000,000 \times 5\% = 50,000$

Break-even: $\$50,000 / (\$12,393 \times 2) = 2.02$

The break-even point will be approximately two months.

The annual return of the portfolio: $[(12,393 - 112) \times 24 - 50,000] / 1,000,000 = 24.47\%$

CASE STUDY 3: ADVANCED TRADING STRATEGIES WITH SAPE

This case study is adapted from Jeff Huber's original work that extends SAPE.

Based on the previous findings, the sentiment asset pricing engine has the ability to forecast individual stock prices over time. The forecasts are based on the Black-Scholes option pricing model. SAPE can be applied to all stocks that have actively traded option markets.

We will propose three trading strategies based on SAPE:

1. Large Cap Long Only
2. Large Cap Hedged
3. Long Short

The goal of having three separate strategies is to utilize SAPE's flexibility so that all types of investors can benefit from SAPE.

In this case study, please note that the dollar amounts projected in the potential assets under management (AUM) sections might be overly optimistic considering the number of holdings in each strategy. In order to achieve the projected AUM numbers, the strategies will most likely have to expand the number of stock holdings. The Large Cap Strategy could include the top 5 or 10 ideas in each sector. The Long Short Strategy could include the top 10 or 20 long ideas and top 10 or 20 short ideas.

Large Cap Long Only Strategy

The objective of this strategy is to outperform the S&P 500 with a return stream that is highly correlated to the index, a relative returns strategy. This is a common objective of many money managers, especially among mutual funds.

The sector weighting of the Large Cap Long Only Strategy will mirror the S&P 500. The strategy will select the top three stocks from each of the

S&P 500's nine sectors by using SAPE's TopTickEngine. So, the strategy will have a total of 27 stocks at all times. The TopTickEngine will run on a daily basis at 3:30 P.M. to determine if there need to be any changes in the portfolio.

Steps to Implement the Strategy

1. Separate the stocks into sector buckets:

   Consumer Discretionary
   Consumer Staples
   Energy
   Financials
   Health Care
   Industrials
   Information Technology
   Materials
   Telecommunication Services

2. Run SAPE's TopTickEngine on all the S&P 500 stocks at 3:30 P.M.

3. Generate the top 3 stocks from each sector.

4. Take the sector weights from the S&P 500 and divide the sector weight by 3 to determine the weighting of the top 3 stocks in each sector. (The 3 stocks inside each of the sectors will be equally weighted.)

   Consumer Discretionary—9.1%
   Consumer Staples—11.9%
   Energy—12.4%
   Financials—14.7%
   Health Care—12.6%
   Industrials—10.1%
   Information Technology—19.0%
   Materials—3.4%
   Telecommunication Services—3.1%

5. Repeat steps 2–4 daily.

Investment Vehicles Since this strategy has a relatively common investment mandate, it can be created as a mutual fund, ETF, or separately managed accounts (SMA). SMAs are the preferred investment vehicle for a majority of the large institutional investors. Institutional investors prefer SMAs because of their real-time transparency.

Projected Fees The Large Cap Long Only space is extremely competitive, which limits the amount of potential fees that can be charged.

We believe a 0.75 percent fee is fair, reasonable, and around the industry standard.

Potential Assets Under Management   Virtually all investors have direct exposure to U.S. Large Cap stocks, so the strategy has an extremely large potential investor base. A large investor base translates into a potentially enormous AUM for this strategy, which could exceed $50 billion.

Large Cap Hedged Strategy

The Large Cap Hedged Strategy would be an absolute return strategy. The objective would be to earn a spread between the Large Cap Long Only Strategy and the S&P 500 while having a very limited exposure to downside risk. This strategy should produce positive returns in any market environment and be a pure arbitrage play.

Implementation of the Strategy   The implementation would be the same as the Large Cap Long Only with a hedging component. The hedging component would be to short the SPDR S&P 500 ETF (ticker SPY). The value of the short SPY position would be equal to the value of all the long positions. This would create a pure arbitrage. The portfolio would be *market neutral on a dollar and beta basis*.

Investment Vehicles   The strategy can be set up as a mutual fund or as a separately managed account. We would not use in ETFs because currently there does not appear to be a market for market-neutral ETFs. Also, we would not use a hedge fund structure because we believe hedge fund investors would demand a more dynamic hedging strategy.

The current industry standard for fees for mutual funds with a hedging component is about 1.50 percent, which would be appropriate for this strategy.

Potential Assets under Management   In the past 10 years, there has been a growing demand for strategies that hedge market risk. Recently, this demand has grown stronger due to the 2008 market crisis. Based on this increasing demand, we believe the strategy could have a maximum AUM of $25 billion.

Long Short Strategy

The Long Short Strategy would be other absolute return strategy. The goal of the strategy is to maximize SAPE's ability to generate positive returns. The previously mentioned strategy constrained SAPE. The Long

Short Strategy would have the flexibility to invest in the stocks that offer the greatest return potential without any consideration given to the construction of the S&P 500.

It would be composed of the top five long ideas and the top five short ideas. The portfolio would be market neutral on a dollar basis but not a beta basis. Not being market neutral on a beta basis can create more volatility than the Large Cap Hedged Strategy. But investors will be compensated for this additional volatility with *greater returns*.

Steps to Implement the Strategy

1. Divide the capital in half for a long bucket and short bucket.
2. Run SAPE on all the S&P 500 stocks at 3:30 P.M.
3. Determine the top five long ideas.
4. Divide the amount of money in the long bucket by 5.
5. Invest an equal amount in the top five long ideas.
6. Determine the top five short ideas.
7. Divide the amount of money in the short bucket by 5.
8. Invest an equal amount in the top five short ideas.
9. Repeat steps 1–8 daily.

Investment Vehicles   The strategy can be set up as a separately managed account or hedge fund. This strategy would only be appropriate for institutional investors. Retail investors would struggle to comprehend the dynamic short component.

Projected Fees   We believe the standard hedge fund fees (2 percent management fee and 20 percent incentive fee) would apply to this strategy.

Potential Assets under Management   Clearly, limiting the investor base to institutional investors would significantly reduce the potential assets under management. We believe the strategy could have a maximum AUM of $10 billion.

Commissions and Other Trading Costs   In our view, commissions and trading costs will not have a material impact on the performance of any of the proposed strategies. Our main reasons for this view are:

- Over the past decade, commissions and trading costs have been significantly reduced.

- None of the proposed strategies will be a high-frequency trading strategy.
- SAPE strategies do not require any research from investment banks or research firms, which increase commissions and/or trading costs.

Conclusion

By having three different strategies around SAPE, the financial institution that manages SAPE could offer a product that is appropriate for any investor. In our experience, retail and institutional investors construct portfolios with various mandates. In general, the retail investor's mandate is to outperform the S&P 500. Many retail investors lack either the capital or sophistication to deviate from this mandate. The Long Cap Long Only Strategy will achieve this mandate.

Many institutional investors possess the capital and sophistication to construct portfolios that can encompass a relative return component and an absolute return component. We can envision an institutional investor using a combination of SAPE strategies such as the Long Cap Only Strategy and the Long Short Strategy.

CREATING A SUCCESSFUL FUND WITH SAPE AND HIGH-FREQUENCY TRADING

Building on SAPE effectiveness, we may design a successful hedge fund or ETF fund. We define success with this equation: success = direction × ability × passion (DAP).

A successful hedge or ETF fund needs to have the right direction (strategy), a capable portfolio manager, and the fund management team's passion for success. The strategic directions on asset allocation and market timing of the portfolio management come from the SAPE predictions and the TopTickEngine.

In general, if the overall direction is wrong, no matter how capable a person is and how passionate the person may be, success may not be achievable.

Information and knowledge about future prices are crucial to the success of managing hedge funds. SunZi, the famous military strategist in ancient China, defines success as the result of knowing yourself and your opponents completely. He says *zhi ji zhi bi, bai zhan bai sheng*, translated as: "If we know 100 percent of ourselves and 100 percent of our opponents, we will always be successful." SAPE and the TopTickEngine provide the necessary information for a successful hedge fund operation in an automated way.

Managing a Portfolio with SAPE Algos

First, we define the objective, that is, we will create and manage a hedge fund or ETF with a high-frequency strategy derived from the SAPE algos. The uniqueness of the fund is the use of the advanced high-frequency trading strategy and SAPE algos that will make it different from other funds.

Second, there are a few details to consider for the new hedge fund. For example, what is the capital? The capital includes the base and leverage. What is the target absolute return? Let's set a target at 5 percent profit per month. This is a high target for good hedge funds. What is the yearly return? We target a maximum 60 percent return yearly and a minimum target to beat the S&P index fund. How is it organized? A portfolio manager picks teams including high-frequency system developers, analysts, accountants, reporting personnel, writer, technologist, quants, P&L tracker, and so on. What is the strategy? We use SAPE algos and various derivatives for hedging risk; we may also use stat-arbitrage if possible. What is the high-frequency trading architecture with the SAPE algos? Please find answers in Figure 10.2 in Chapter 10. What is new to the portfolio management? We use SAPE algos to extend traditional portfolio management approaches such as the modern portfolio theory and the efficient portfolio frontier. Can we have an advisory board? It would be very helpful to have an advisory board. The board should include someone who has experience in portfolio management and technology.

For a sample new fund, similar to S&P/Case-Shiller home-price index and the ETFs of macromarkets.com, one may attempt to develop a national life science (including Health IT companies) index (and ETF funds) with SAPE algos.[1]

Importance of Technology to High-Frequency Strategies

According to Aldridge (2009), the most challenging and expensive element for a high-frequency trading system is the technologist or a team of technologists who program the trading ideas. This is the conclusion after analyzing many elements of a high-frequency trading system. Normally, by the end of 2009, the average pay for an experienced technologist was around a half million U.S. dollars. The technologist can design and develop a high-frequency trading system with the knowledge of capital markets and derivatives.

The concern of fund management regarding the technologists may be the knowledge transfer issue. Assuming that a technologist builds a system according to the specifications then chooses to leave the hedge fund, it would take a long time for his or her knowledge to be transferred to the next person, not to mention that the intellectual capital will leave with the technologist. A noncompete contract[2] may be part of the solution.

To summarize, one of the most important elements of creating and operating a high-frequency hedge fund is the technologists who may develop the trading ideas into computer algos. The technologists may integrate SAPE algos with existing high-frequency trading systems.

In later chapters, we focus on the technology topics such as how to create computer algos on different financial instruments (such as derivatives) as new revenue models and new computer models for high-frequency systems.

CONCLUSION

This chapter discussed the effectiveness of SAPE algos and strategies in portfolio management. With intraday data, we repeatedly found that the SAPE funds outperform the market index. The SAPE funds are created with TopTickEngine, which extends the SAPE algos. Case studies are also documented in this chapter to underscore the effectiveness of SAPE algos and strategies in asset allocation.

PART IV

New Models of High-Frequency Trading

With over 60 percent of the equity trading volume in the United States done as high-frequency trading as of the end of 2009, many existing revenue models such as "signal detection" or "liquidity rebate" are used in the equity market that produced the liquidity that many markets are eager to acquire. What will be the new revenue models for high-frequency trading operations?

Normally copying existing revenue models or strategies to new capital markets may be considered as new revenue models. Therefore, if we could identify a new capital market for high-frequency trading, we may find new revenue models based on existing ones. The new capital market may come from different asset classes such as derivatives, or from non-U.S. markets.

Reuters noticed the trends on December 2, 2009. In "High-frequency trading surges across the globe," Spicer and Kwan (2009) wrote, "The high-frequency wave, estimated to be responsible for about 60 percent of U.S. stock trading, has already washed over much of Europe and is being felt in some emerging markets, particularly in Latin America. . . . It is also making inroads in futures, options, and foreign exchange."

The new asset class for high-frequency trading may be the exchange-traded derivatives market. Derivatives contracts in exchanges may be standardized and traded electronically. For example, the futures contracts in CME Group of Chicago may be traded with high-frequency trading. At face value, as of the end of 2008, the size of the global derivatives market may be over five times the size of the global equity, bonds, and bank deposits combined (Leibenluft 2008).

Another major portion of derivatives are over-the-counter (OTC) derivatives. In the financial crisis of 2008–2009, the major reason for a frozen derivatives market is the lack of liquidity. Knowing the main benefit of having high-frequency trading is to boost the liquidity of the market, why not apply high-frequency trading to derivatives markets?

But there is a problem with OTC derivatives: They are not traded in exchanges and high-frequency trading needs exchange-traded securities to automate rapid buying and selling. Therefore, the advent of high-frequency trading may be the driver to push OTC derivatives securities to the exchanges so that the markets will increase their liquidity. As we all agree, the lack of liquidity in the OTC derivatives market has been a main cause of frozen derivatives markets.

Many signs have shown that high-frequency trading has gone global with major opportunities, especially in the emerging markets. For example, the central government of China has indicated that the financial derivatives on stock indexes may be traded in the near future. This opens a huge global market for high-frequency trading as there is no such trading in China.

In order to materialize the new revenue models in derivatives with high-frequency trading systems, developing computer algos are required for creating or maintaining the high-frequency systems. Following the introduction of the derivatives concepts, we will focus on how to create computer algos for high-frequency systems.

CHAPTER 12

Derivatives

With more and more trading going high frequency in the equities market, we argue that high-frequency trading operations will be frequently used in derivatives markets, especially the exchange-traded derivatives. Due to the regulation changes for derivatives trading, which is being discussed extensively in Congress, more and more derivatives may be standardized and will move from over-the-counter (OTC) private contracts to standard contracts traded in centralized computer platforms or exchanges, similar to the process of moving forwards contracts to futures contracts. In order to improve the transparency and liquidity of OTC derivatives, Tim Geithner, the U.S. Secretary of the Treasury, has urged the electronic trading of OTC derivatives since early 2009.

The $600 trillion face-valued derivatives market lacks liquidity, which makes most of the derivatives worthless. This is the major root cause of the financial and economic crisis during 2008–2009. One of the benefits of high-frequency trading and electronic trading is to increase the liquidity of the markets. Applied to derivatives markets (OTC or exchange-traded), the adoption of high-frequency trading would increase the liquidity of the derivatives markets, making most of the derivatives valuable.

Hence we will find new revenue models for high-frequency trading in derivatives markets. In this chapter, we will discuss the concept of derivatives; some major derivatives such as options, futures, credit default swaps (CDS), and mortgage-backed securities (MBS); and the financial models for the major derivatives such as the Black-Scholes model and ARCH (autoregressive conditional heteroskedastic) model.

WHAT IS A DERIVATIVE?

A derivative is a financial instrument with its value derived from an underlying asset. For example, a stock option is a derivative with its value derived from the right to buy or sell the underlying asset, the stock. A futures contract of oil is a derivative with its value derived from locking in the standardized future prices of the oil. A forwards contract is a derivative with its value derived from locking in the future price with private counterparties. A credit default swap is a derivative with its value derived from insuring the financial instrument against the event of credit default. A mortgage-backed security is a derivative with its value derived from mortgage deeds on residential or commercial houses.

Hence, the basic derivatives include options, forwards and futures contracts, swaps, and so on. Recent derivatives that attract a lot of attention in the news include mortgage-backed securities and credit default swaps.

Let's look at two examples of derivatives in detail: options and swaps. The first derivative I would like to talk about is options. Investors purchase an options contract for the right (with no obligation) to trade at a certain price of the underlying asset at a specific time. Similar to an option, an interest rate derivative is a contract for investors to have the right to pay or receive an underlying asset with a price at a given interest rate. The interest rate derivatives market is claimed to be the largest derivatives market in the world.

A swap is a derivative contract in which two entities exchange some benefits of one entity's financial instrument for those of the other entity's financial instrument. It is said that David Swenson, the present chief investment officer of Yale University, created the first swap contract decades ago.

Why are the derivatives markets so important? Besides the fact that the 2008–2009 financial crisis in the United States and globally was caused directly by the failure of the derivatives market, the size of the derivatives market may get people's attention right away. It was estimated recently that the size of the derivatives market (about $600 trillion globally in 2008) is more than 16 times the size of the global equity market ($37 trillion in 2008). In other words, the size of derivatives markets is much larger than the size of the underlying assets that the derivatives are derived from.

MORTGAGE-BACKED SECURITIES: LINKING MAJOR FINANCIAL INSTITUTIONS

Derivatives are important because the derivatives markets are not only much larger than the equities market, but also they link the main activities and revenue models of major financial institutions. Let us look at an example, a mortgage-backed security, a derivative security that connects major institutions.

MBSs, especially the subprime portion of the MBSs, were at center stage of the 2008 financial crisis that almost brought down the U.S. and global financial systems. Yet not many people understand the mechanisms behind MBSs.

Subprime mortgages suggest that the mortgage borrowers may not meet the standard requirements and thus they are more likely to default. A MBS starts from mortgage loans, mostly residential loans. Let us assume that 1,000 U.S. homeowners borrowed $1 million from a depository institution, normally a commercial bank. Let us also assume that each homeowner pays 6 percent interest each year for the loan, and at the end of the 10th year pays back the total of the loan. For the commercial bank, the package of the loans for the 1,000 borrowers totals $1 billion.

The commercial banks may service the loans themselves on a daily basis. They may also choose to sell all these loans to an investment bank on Wall Street for the total value of the package plus a fee. For the investment bank, the total package of the 1,000 borrowers provides a presumably steady stream of income, namely the monthly mortgage payment, which is similar to a regular income stream of a mature business such as a pharmaceutical company producing and selling prescription drugs. Therefore, the investment bank may create a new company, called a special purpose entity (SPE), using the $1 billion mortgage payment as the asset. The revenue model of the SPE is to collect the monthly mortgage payment.

The investment bank bought the total package of $1 billion loans (deeds) from the commercial bank; how does it get the money back? The specialty of investment banks is market making and underwriting of public or private offerings for new securities. In other words, the investment bank may get the money back by issuing new securities to investors. For example, an IPO (initial public offering) or private offerings to institutions of the new SPE would collect more than $1 billion that may cover the $1 billion paid to the commercial bank, fees paid to the commercial bank, and a hefty profit for the investment bank. Therefore, through holding the securities, public investors may now hold the ownership of the 1,000 borrowers' deeds. Every step of the process is done by the book. The financial

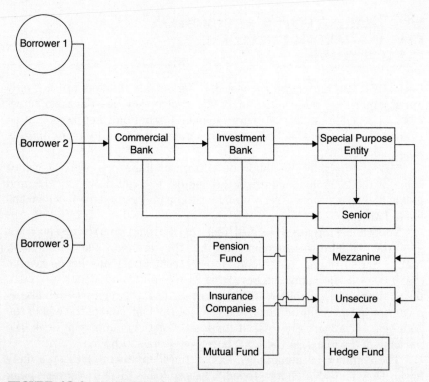

FIGURE 12.1 Mechanism of Mortgage-Backed Securities

innovation is the derived value, namely MBS, based on the underlying asset, namely the $1 billion mortgage loans and the interest.

The story does not end here. When the investment bank packages the $1 billion loans as the SPE shares for IPO, it may slice the SPE shares in several categories, called tranches. These tranches may include (1) senior shares: very secure with small returns that may be backed with insurance such as credit default swaps; (2) mezzanine[1] shares: middle-level secure shares with middle-level returns; (3) unsecure equity shares that have maximum return and risk. The SPE stock shares may be purchased by financial institutions such as mutual funds, hedge funds, insurance companies, or other commercial banks, and so on. Figure 12.1 describes the flow of the MBSs that engage the revenue models of major financial institutions.

CREDIT DEFAULT SWAPS

In the process of creating the MBS derivatives, for the senior shares of the SPE, the investment bank may increase the rating of the senior shares from a lower rating, for example, B+, to a higher grade, for example, AAA, by purchasing insurance from insurance companies like AIG. The insurance for the credit debt may be a credit default swap, which is another type of derivatives security.

Increasing the rating of a security by purchasing insurance for the security is a common financial practice because the charters of many pension funds or insurance companies may require that the funds be invested in secure or high rating securities.

Credit default swaps (CDS) link investing institutions (e.g., pension fund A), rating agencies (e.g., Moody's), insurance companies (e.g., AIG), and corporate debt issuing companies (e.g., General Motors). For example, corporation A seeks a loan of $1 billion at 10 percent interest from pension fund A. Due to the charter that pension fund A can only invest in grade A corporate bonds, corporation A with a credit rating of BB may not qualify for the loan. However, with a credit default swap, insurance companies like AIG may insure the corporate debt. According to the CDS contract, if corporation A goes under, AIG may repay the debt, and for that AIG gets a 1 percent premium on a yearly basis. As AIG is rated AAA by Moody's, the corporate A bond of $1 billion becomes a AAA bond. AIG may create many CDS contracts for other corporations' (e.g., B) bonds. Figure 12.2 visualizes the mechanism of common CDSs.

If everything goes well, this is a good business model for AIG with steady income streams from the corporate bonds. However, if a large number of the corporations were to default, AIG may not have enough reserves to repay the corporate debt. This becomes a major driver for the financial crisis in 2008–2009, especially for those CDS contracts on insuring the different classes of mortgage-backed securities.

OPTIONS AND OPTION VALUES

An options contract is an agreement for the right to buy or sell an underlying asset for a specific price at a specific future time. The right to buy or sell the underlying asset may be purchased at a price. The process to determine the price of an option is option pricing.

The elements of an option are asset spot price (S), exercise price (K), European call option price (c), European put option price (p), and expiration date (T).

Based on the expiration date T, there are two types of options: American versus European. American options can be traded anytime until the expiration dates. The naming of the options has nothing to do with where it should be traded. American options may be traded in the United States or

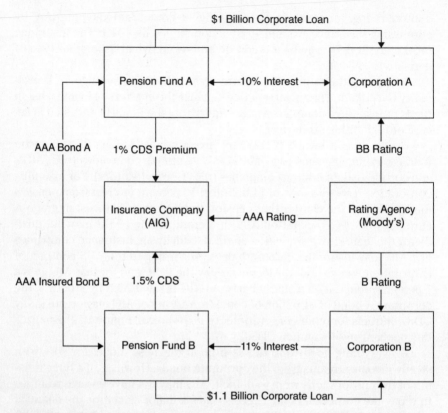

FIGURE 12.2 Mechanism of Credit Default Swaps

Europe. European options may be traded in Europe or the United States. European options may be traded only on the expiration date. Most options are American options.

Based on whether to buy or sell the underlying asset in the future, an option may be a call option if the option contract indicates that the trader would buy the underlying asset in the future at a specific price. A put option indicates that the trader will sell the underlying asset in the future at a specific price. A trader may buy the call or put options with cash, taking an immediate loss. On the other hand, he or she may write (sell) the call or put options for an immediate profit.

Options have existed for a long time. In the early eighteenth century, the concept of options appeared in Holland. Prior to the 1970s, options were traded privately between two counterparties, similar to the forwards contracts prior to the futures contracts. Private option trading has a risk if the counterparty defaults. Hence, options were standardized and traded in options exchanges (e.g., Chicago Board of Trade, CBOT, now part of Chicago Mercantile Exchange (CME) group) since the early 1970s. With the engagement of option exchanges, the default risk is eliminated.

There are three kinds of values for an option: intrinsic value, option value, and time value. For out-of-the-money options, the value of the option is worthless at the time. An option has intrinsic value if the option is in the money. When out-of-the-money, the option's intrinsic value is zero. The intrinsic value is the absolute value of the difference between the current asset price (S) and the strike price (K) of the option, floored to zero. For a call option, the intrinsic value $= \max\{0, S{-}K\}$; for a put option, the intrinsic value $= \max\{0, K{-}S\}$. When the asset price and the strike price are the same, namely, $S = K$, the option is at the money. Figure 12.3 describes the relationship between intrinsic values of a call option and the asset spot price S and strike price K.

Option pricing is of critical importance to option trading. If an option is not priced properly, an arbitrage opportunity may occur for some traders. The option value (or price) may be calculated by the Black-Scholes model or the binomial option pricing model. The difference between an option value and its intrinsic value is the time value of the option.

In Figure 12.3, a call option's value is graphed above the intrinsic value. This indicates that the time value of the call option is greater than zero at these times, that is:

$$\text{Time value} = \text{option value} - \text{intrinsic value}$$

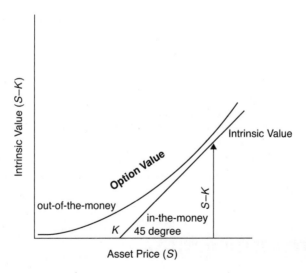

FIGURE 12.3 Values of Options

THE BENEFITS OF USING OPTIONS

There are two major drivers for engaging options in portfolio management: risk management and profit seeking. Risk management with options attempts to hedge portfolio risk with options. Profit seeking intends to profit from trading options for higher returns than for trading the underlying assets.

An example for hedging risk with options may come from managing portfolios with SAPE algos. Let's assume that the advantage for SAPE T5 fund performance over that of DJI index funds holds true for most of the time. One would take long positions in the T5 fund holdings. However, if the prices of the T5 fund holdings go down unexpectedly, how do we to minimize the risk of losing much of the capital?

A portfolio manager may purchase put options for the holdings to hedge the unexpected risk. For example, for holding ABC with spot price of $30, a put option may cost $1 for the right to sell ABC stock at $30. If one bought ABC at $30 but the spot price dives to $15 (e.g., the financial crisis in late 2008), then the portfolio would lose 50 percent for ABC on mark to market.[2] If the portfolio manager has to cut his losses for redemption, with the option of selling ABC at $30, the loss would be zero, which is far less than the 50 percent mark-to-market loss. Therefore, buying a put option has hedged the risk and paid off huge in this scenario.

Another driver for engaging options is seeking profit with less investment. For holding 1,000 shares of ABC stock at $30, the initial investment is $30 × 1,000 = $30,000. If engaging options, a trader may buy the right to own 1,000 shares of ABC stock at $30 with a much smaller initial investment. If we assume that the option price is $3 per share, then the initial investment is $3,000. If the spot price goes up to $33, then the portfolio may earn $3,000. Owning the options of ABC stocks in this case may exercise the right to purchase 1,000 shares of ABC stocks at $30 and sell them at $33. The profit is $3,000, which is identical to the profit of owning the ABC stocks directly in the first place.

Let's look at the return on investment. For owning ABC stocks directly, the return on investment is $3,000/$30,000 = 10 percent. For owning the options on the ABC stocks, the return on investment is $3,000/$3,000 = 100 percent. Therefore, options provide a means to amplify the returns on investment.

PROFITING WITH OPTIONS

With option prices (C for call option premium; P for put option premium), spot price (S), and exercise prices (K), what is the relationship between

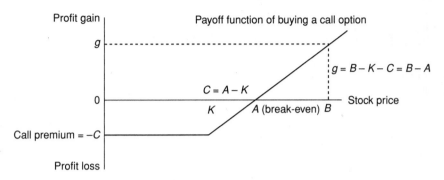

FIGURE 12.4 Payoff Function of Buying Call Options

these prices and under what conditions may a trader profit from the dynamics of the relationship? This gives rise to the payoff functions of buying call or put options. We do not recommend writing call or put options in trading as the loss could be very large.

In Figure 12.4, the payoff function of buying a call option shows that a trader would profit from buying a call option if the stock spot price goes up to cover strike price (K) plus the call premium (C). Thus the break-even point $A = K + C$. When the stock price (S) goes up to pass the break-even point A and arrives at B, then the profit of buying the call option is $g = B - A$.

In Figure 12.5, the payoff function of buying a put option shows that when the stock price (S) falls down to A where $K - S\ (A) = P$, then it reaches the break-even point of buying the put option. If the stock price falls further to B where $B < A$, then the profit $g = A - B$. A trader may exercise the put option at K by buying the stock at B and selling it at price K. The revenue is $K - B$. The profit is revenue minus the premium paid to buy the put option P. So the profit $= K - B - P = A - B$.

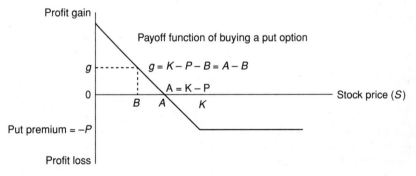

FIGURE 12.5 Payoff Function of Buying Put Options

NEW PROFITABLE FINANCIAL INSTRUMENTS BY WRITING OPTIONS

Writing an option earns the premium right away. However, in trading assets the potential loss could be very large so we do not recommend the writing-options practice for immediate cash as the risk is too high.

Nevertheless, writing options may be a very good revenue model for commodity retailing as the risk is limited. This may be a new financial instrument to increase revenue for stores and manufacturers.

Let us look at an example of writing a call option in selling personal computers (PC). Say the present spot price of a laptop is S_0. The writer of the call option may be manufacturers such as DELL or a store such as Best Buy. The writer may offer consumers a right to buy the PC at a specific price, K. To attract consumers, normally the writer should set $K < S_0$. This call option may be designed in this way: If a consumer chooses to buy a call option to get a laptop at a strike price K in the future (e.g., two months from now), and the consumer is willing to pay a premium of C for the option, what are the conditions for the writer to make a profit?

Figure 12.6 shows the payoff function for the writer to make a profit. As far as the $K + C > S_0$, the writer may be profitable for sure. The profit may be larger if the future spot price S drops, which would normally happen for laptops.

The call options contract for buying laptops in the future may create a new financial market of derivatives on goods for retail industry if the options are tradable.

Manufacturers and stores may also design a new financial instrument to increase sales with writing put options for consumers. In this case, we combine option pricing and the endowment effect of prospect theory. Let's look at designing a put option for the automobile market.

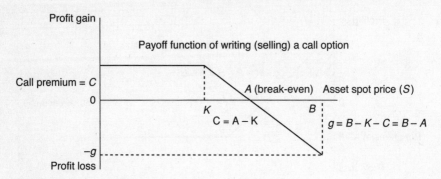

FIGURE 12.6 Payoff Function of Writing Call Options

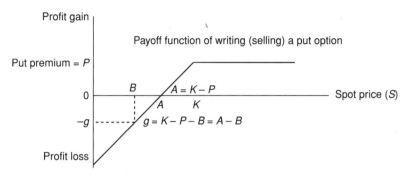

FIGURE 12.7 Payoff Function of Writing Put Options

Let's say a new car costs S_0. The dealer may write a put option for new car buyers: A new car buyer may purchase an option with price P to sell back the car in the future (e.g., two years from now) at a strike price of K. Normally $K < S_0$. What is the condition for the writer to make a profit?

$A = K - P$ is the break-even point. The value of a used car in the future may be estimated as S. If $S < A$, then the writer of the put options may not make a profit. The writer makes a profit if $S > A$. If the option is not exercised, then the profit is the put premium. For example, the dealer may find ways to make the option not be exercised, for example, producing endowment effect for consumers to feel an attachment for the car; or set the strike price far less than S_0 so that the depreciation would not reduce S to A within the option expiration date.

The new financial instrument, the put option for selling back an automobile, may create a derivative contract for the underlying asset. If the derivative contracts are tradable, then we have created a new financial market for automobiles.

THE BLACK-SCHOLES MODEL AS A SPECIAL CASE OF THE BINOMIAL MODEL

In Part II, we discussed that the Black-Scholes option pricing model is the foundation to derive loss aversion in option pricing. As a result, the Black-Scholes formula may be presented as computer algos (see Chapter 14). Here we do not duplicate the formula and algos.

If we compare the binomial model on option pricing to the Black-Scholes model, we may see that the binomial option pricing model offers a more general explanation for option pricing, including pricing bond options. In other words, the Black-Scholes model is a special case of the binomial model. The detailed discussion on this may be found in Hull (2008).

IMPLIED VOLATILITY

A typical Black-Scholes formula takes in six parameters, represented as the equation below for computing the price of a European call option:

$c = f(S, K, T, r, sigma, Y)$
c: call premium; price of the call option
S: stock spot price
K: exercise price in the future
T: duration to expiration date/250
r: riskless interest rate
sigma: greek letter for volatility
historical sigma: standard deviation of log returns
Y: yield (assuming 0)

Normally, the Black-Scholes formula assumes that the sigma is a constant so the call option price can be calculated by entering the values of the six parameters. In reality, the sigma changes over time. In the cases where the call option price for an underlying asset is known, we can compute the sigma by taking the reverse function from the Black-Scholes formula as:

$$Sigma = f^{-1}(c, S, K, T, r, Y)$$

In this case, the sigma is called implied volatility, which is derived from solving the reverse equation of the Black-Scholes formula.

With Excel, one may use the "Goal Seek" function to find the correct value of sigma that produces the given call premium. With Hypertext Preprocessor (PHP), one may figure out the value of sigma by changing sigma within a range to find the best value that fits the given call premium.

Studies have shown that there is a very good match in trend between implied volatility and historical volatility over time. As the implied volatility is computed with the Black-Scholes model, the match proves that the Black-Scholes formula has been solid in estimating option premiums.

VOLATILITY SMILE

If we also change the values of K (the strike price) in the reverse function, then we may compute the implied volatility for different strike prices. It is discovered that the shape of the curve (*sigma* on S) looks like a smiley face, with both tails up and the middle section down. In other words, the values of the implied volatility of at-the-money options are lower than that of the out-of-the-money or in-the-money options. Figure 12.8 shows

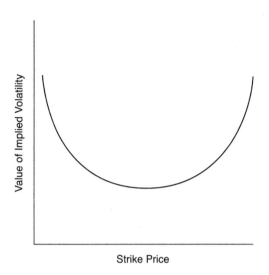

FIGURE 12.8 Volatility Smile

the volatility smile for the options of an underlying stock. The horizontal line is strike prices. The vertical line is the values of implied volatility. The shape takes a *U* curve.

The empirical support of the volatility smile has been found for post-crash (after 1987) option data. Prior to 1987, the pattern of volatility smiles was not apparent.

COMPARING VOLATILITIES OVER TIME

In the Black-Scholes model, the relationship between call or put premiums and the six parameters is given. The historical volatility (sigma) is one of the parameters. It is calculated by taking the standard deviation of the log (continuous compounding) returns of the underlying assets. Does the sigma change over time? If yes, what is the relationship between the sigma values over time?

It is found that the assumption of a constant sigma in the Black-Scholes model is questionable. In other words, the sigma does change over time for the option. Note that the time here refers to close time periods. It is related to but is not the same as the *T* (duration to expiration) of the Black-Scholes model. *T* is calculated as the number of days from the spot date to the expiration date over trading days of a year (e.g., 252 days for NYSE in 2009).

The relationship between the sigma values of close time periods is given by the ARCH (autoregressive conditional heteroskedastic) or

GARCH (generalized autoregressive conditional heteroskedastic) models. Robert Engle, a finance professor of New York University Stern Business School, won the Nobel Prize in Economics in 2003 for describing the relationship. The relationship derives from an empirical finding that the volatility values of close time periods are related; large changes in returns tend to follow large changes and small changes tend to follow small changes. This empirical pattern is called volatility clustering.

A typical ARCH formula is given as below, composed of three terms:

$$sigma_n^2 = lambda \times sigma_{n-1}^2 + (1 - lambda) \times u_{n-1}^2$$

where: $sigma\ (\sigma)_n$ = volatility of time n;
   $sigma_{n-1}$ = volatility of time $n - 1$;
   $lambda\ (\lambda)$ = weight;
    u_{n-1} = log return of time $n - 1$; e.g., daily log return

A typical GARCH(1,1) formula is given as below. (1,1) means that the model lags on only one squared return and only one variance.

$$sigma_n^2 = gamma \times V_L + alpha \times u_{n-1}^2 + beta \times sigma_{n-1}^2$$

where: V_L = long run variance of log returns;
   $gamma + alpha + beta = 1$;
     $sigma_n$ = volatility of time n;
    $sigma_{n-1}$ = volatility of time $n - 1$;
    weights = $gamma\ (\gamma),\ alpha\ (\alpha),\ beta\ (\beta)$;
     u_{n-1} = log return of time $n - 1$

In the next chapter, we will provide computer algos for the ARCH/GARCH equations, which are accessible by high-frequency trading systems through a technical design called service-oriented architecture (SOA).

FORWARDS AND FUTURES

In a nutshell, forwards and futures refer to the contracts between two counterparties who at present predetermine the prices of underlying assets in the future. Forwards contracts are private agreements between the counterparties. Futures contracts are standardized contracts that are traded on futures exchanges.

Because forwards contracts are private, the primary risk of forwards contracts is counterparty risk, namely, the risk of a counterparty defaulting on the agreement. For the futures contracts, there is very little risk in counterparty default because they are traded on an exchange, and the exchange is the counterparty that in theory will not possibly default. However, the primary risk of futures contracts is basis risk, namely, the risk due to the change in the difference between the spot price of the underlying asset and the futures price.

Depending on the underlying assets, a futures contract could be agricultural futures or financial futures. Examples of agricultural futures include goods such as rice, corn, and coffee.

There were no financial futures in the United States until the 1970s. In many other countries, the financial futures markets may not exist now. For example, the financial futures market in China did not exist in January 2010, although talks are going on that the central government of China has agreed to allow financial futures to be exchange-traded in 2010 or later.

In the United States, the biggest exchange for futures is CME (Chicago Mercantile Exchange) in Chicago, not in New York. This is because in the early days Chicago was more focused on agricultural products that gave rise to the agricultural futures.

Financial futures are the futures contracts for an underlying financial instrument such as a stock index. The stock index futures market came in 1980s. For example, one of the very first financial futures was that of the S&P 500 stock index at CME. Within a few years, there were more trades in the futures markets than the trades of the underlying assets' market, namely, the stock markets.

If one wants to trade futures, a margin account is needed to eliminate counterparty default risk. Similar to option trading, one may trade larger amounts of underlying assets by trading futures than by trading the underlying assets directly. With the same amount of capital and a sound strategy, trading futures and options may produce larger returns on investment than trading the underlying assets directly. On the other hand, the risks are normally larger for trading the derivatives.

PRICING AN INTEREST RATE SWAP WITH PROSPECT THEORY

Based on the size of the markets, swaps contracts were estimated to be over $77.6 trillion in 2006 in the United States (see Table 3.1 in Chapter 3), larger than the size of the equities market. Interest rate swaps contracts account for the largest segment of swaps markets. Other swaps contracts include currency swaps and credit swaps (i.e., credit default swaps, CDSs).[3] We discuss interest rate swaps here.

Interest rate swaps (IRS) are contracts between two counterparties who exchange the risk exposures to different types of interest rate payments such as floating-rate or fixed-rate payments. For example, company

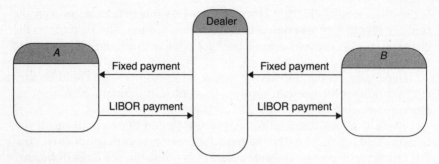

FIGURE 12.9 A Transaction of Interest Rate Swaps

A would like to change A's original floating-rate (e.g., LIBOR[4]-based) payment to a fixed-rate payment. Company A may find company B, who may exchange B's fixed-rate payment with the floating-rate payment from A. The swaps transaction may be facilitated by financial intermediaries, called swap dealers, for a fee. Figure 12.9 describes an IRS transaction.

How to price an IRS contract? We propose a new theory called the IRS value of prospect theory (PT) as a theoretical foundation for pricing IRS contracts. Figure 12.10 shows a hypothetical weighting function for valuing IRS contracts. It derives from the prospect theory (Kahneman and Tversky 2000).

In general, the buyers of an IRS contract want to purchase IRS contracts to convert a floating (e.g., LIBOR) interest rate (option of uncertainty) to a fixed interest rate (option of certainty). The psychological driver is risk hedging, or in other words, a motivation of acquiring certainty and sure gains. Many studies on prospect theory have supported that investors tend to prefer a sure gain over a probability-based uncertain gain, even if the expected utility of the probability-based option is larger than that of the sure-gain option. Therefore, the payment to purchase an IRS contract measures the motivation to acquire a sure gain (the fixed-rate interest).

In Figure 12.10, the straight line OG represents the classical expected utility function, which suggests that the relationship between the mental value and probability of an event (interest-rate payout) is linear. Line $OCHG$ represents a hypothetical weighting function of the prospect theory for valuing IRS contracts. A fixed-rate IRS option is represented as point G with 100 percent probability of payment. A floating-rate IRS option is represented as a point on line $OCHG$, where the fluctuation of LIBOR may produce uncertainty of the floating-rate payment.

Let us assume that a floating-rate payment has a probability of E payout. The buyer of the IRS contract wants to convert it to a fixed interest rate at F (100 percent). With the classical utility function, the value of the

IRS contract is represented as the distance from A to M (AM), namely, the value difference of LG. With the weighting function of prospect theory, the value of the IRS contract is represented as AB, the value difference of HG. Based on these settings, we derive that $AB > AM$. We argue that the value of the IRS contract is AB, not AM.

To summarize, we have proposed a new theory of pricing IRS contracts with the prospect theory. The values of IRS contracts are manifestations of the weighting function of prospect theory for the IRS contracts. In other words, the IRS contracts may be priced as the value difference from a floating (uncertainty) point (H) to a sure-gain (certainty) point (G).

BEHAVIORAL INVESTING BASED ON BEHAVIORAL ECONOMICS

So far we have discussed three instances of behavioral investing: (1) loss aversion in option pricing (see Chapter 5); (2) sentiment asset pricing engine (see Chapters 10, 11); and (3) valuing interest rate swaps with prospect theory (see Figure 12.10).

In all three instances, we define behavioral investing as a type of investment management strategy that engages behavioral economics models for valuing securities. These securities include equity and derivatives contracts such as options and swaps. Figure 12.11 shows the three instances

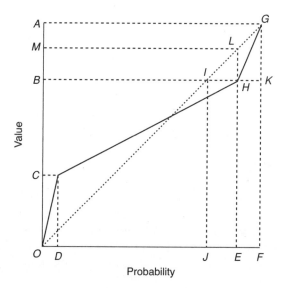

FIGURE 12.10 Pricing IRS Contracts with Prospect Theory

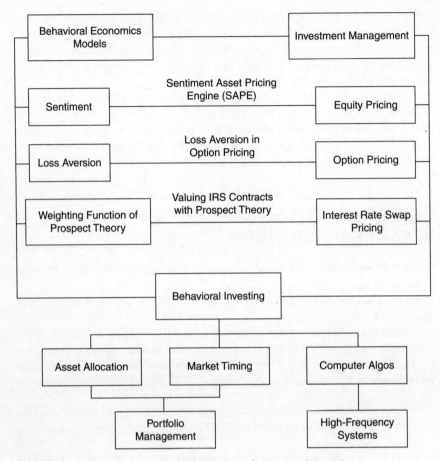

FIGURE 12.11 Instances and Mechanism of Behavioral Investing

and the mechanism of behavioral investing based on the principles of behavioral economics.

CONCLUSION

In this chapter, we discussed various types of derivatives, including mortgaged-backed securities, credit default swaps, options, futures and forwards, and interest rate swaps. We also proposed a new theory on pricing interest rate swaps based on prospect theory. The new theory becomes one of the three cornerstones to establishing the discipline of behavioral investing based on behavioral economics.

CHAPTER 13

Technology Infrastructure for Creating Computer Algos

I n this chapter, we discuss computing infrastructure and languages for high-frequency trading and a popular computing platform for building computer algos. This will serve as the foundation for developing API code that implements quantitative models in the next chapter.

In the past, computer algos were developed as standalone programs that focused on implementing quantitative formulas or trading ideas. The input and output may go through text-based user interfaces such as UNIX, LINUX, or DOS consoles. Due to the development of social media and the need to share the output lately, one would prefer the flexibility to share the input and output over the Internet or Intranet. This gives rise to the need to engage an end-to-end solution for algo developers and others to share the data over networks. Web servers for computer algos are the end-to-end solution with one end as users from anywhere and the other end as the computer algos hosted on Web servers that are accessible from anywhere.

WEB HOSTING VERSUS DEDICATED WEB SERVERS

A Web server is computer software that holds Web applications accessible to many people on the Internet. As opposed to Web hosting where a Web server is shared by many applications and developers, a dedicated Web server means that the Web server is fully controllable by the owners and developers.

A commonly used Web server is the Apache Web server. The Apache server extends the first generation of HTTP servers. And it is free. The server is solid, which is proved by its wide adoption by business and academic web sites. According to a survey disclosed at Apache foundation's web site, 67 percent of web sites in the world run on the Apache Web server.

The Apache Web server can be installed separately, or together with MySQL database server and PHP engine. To enable more functionality such as database and Web development, we engage Fireserv. Fireserv is an open source software package that packages Apache Web server, PHP engine, and MySQL database. PHP engine enables the use of PHP,[1] the popular Web programming language that is used to build Facebook, YouTube, and many others. Database management systems hold the information permanently and enable the search, update, and deletion of information with structured languages such as SQL (structured query language). There are various types of databases such as Oracle, MySQL, DB2 from IBM, and Sybase. MySQL is an open source database management system.

SETTING UP A DEDICATED WEB SERVER

After executing Fireserv.exe, a setup process will start to automatically install three components, namely the Apache Web server, a PHP engine, and a MySQL database. The following is the process of installing and testing the three components of the Fireserv package.

- Make sure that system settings are Windows XP, 2000, or NT.
- Acquire Fireserv.exe setup file.
- Click on Fireserv.exe to install Fireserv software package.
- Click "Startup Fireserv" to bring up the three components (Figure 13.1 shows the start menu of Fireserv).
- Test the three components.

The three components may be tested separately. After the Fireserv package is started, we may test whether the Apache Web server is running. Generally, the Web server should be running on "localhost," which is the hostname of the computer where the Fireserv package is installed and started. The Web server should use port 80 as the default port. In this case, there is no need to specify the port number in the URL (Universal Resource Locator) to access the Apache Web server. Figure 13.2 shows a successful launch of an Apache web server. Both the browser and server are running

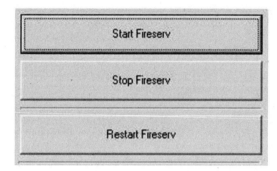

FIGURE 13.1 Fireserv Menu

on the same computer where the server is installed. Figure 13.2 also shows that access to the Apache server is successful at http://localhost.

Testing the PHP engine can be done by clicking on the link to "Click Here to test PHP." Figure 13.3 shows a successful Web access to a PHP file named phpinfo.php. This demonstrates that the PHP engine has been installed and the Web server is working.

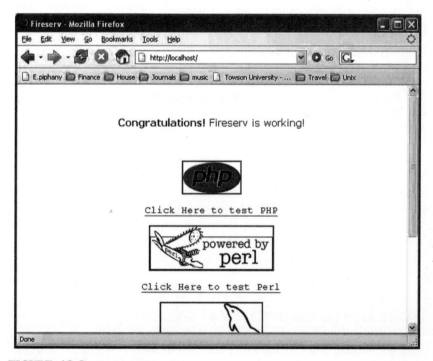

FIGURE 13.2 Fireserv Home Page

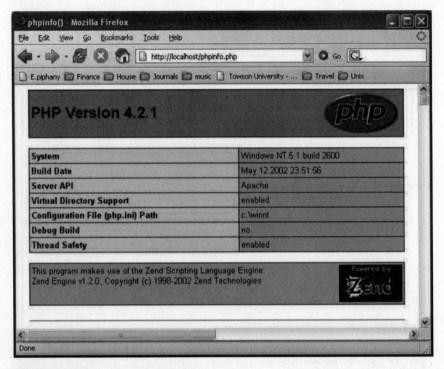

FIGURE 13.3   Active PHP Engine

Figure 13.4 shows a successful installation of the MySQL database. The URL http://localhost/phpMyAdmin/exhibits the primary page for the Web administration of the MySQL database.

Once the Apache server is installed and started, our computer algos and Web pages may be moved to a directory named c:\fireserv\www for Web publishing. The computer algos and Web pages may be PHP programs, which are flat files coded in the PHP language with an extension .php. By default, the directory c:\fireserv\www is the primary access point of the Web space. In other words, files within the directory or subdirectories are accessible to Internet browsers locally or globally. Files outside of the directory cannot be accessed through the Internet.

DEVELOPING COMPUTER ALGOS

With the availability of the first generation of Web servers, the standard server functions are widely used and received. The standard functions

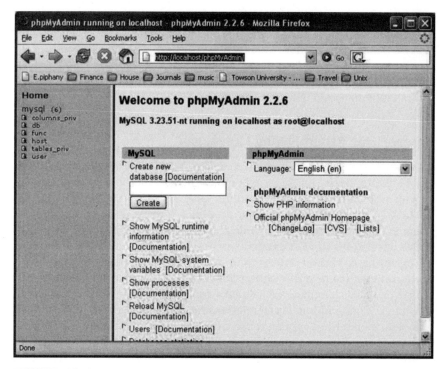

FIGURE 13.4   Active MySQL

encompass the offerings of static HTML files that can be interpreted as Web pages on browsers.

A standard HTML file enables a static Web page. This means that the communication between Web servers and browsers is unidirectional, from servers to browsers only. Web users can view information provided by the Web servers. However, the users cannot interact with Web servers that only offer static Web pages. For example, users cannot submit information contained in a form that requires server side processing.

Bidirectional Web communication means that the users can send data back to servers in addition to acquiring data from servers. There are two ways of sending data. One way starts with Web users who submit a form or e-mail to the server and then the server side applications can process the information. The other way of communication starts with Web servers that send back information to Web users.

For example, server-side applications can use cookies to track user activities and record the data of the cookies files on the server databases. A cookie is pertinent to Web technology. A cookie is a text file sent by server side applications to Web browsers and stays in the local computer that runs the browsers. The text file can record surfers' activities such as URLs browsed. The data in the cookie files can be retrieved by server applications and stored on a server side database.

To extend the standard server functions that offer static HTML pages, server side applications or extensions are needed. These extensions can be written in Web programming languages such as Java and PHP.

Categorizing Programming Languages

Web programming languages can be categorized based on various criteria. For example, based on the perspectives to describe objects and actions, they can be categorized as procedural languages or object-oriented (OO) languages. A procedural language describes objects and actions in a sequential and separate matter, while an object-oriented language uses principles of relationship. For example, to describe the relationship of Car and FordCar that is a brand (type) of Car, a procedural language may have separate routines (to describe actions) and objects for a car and a Ford car. However, an OO language such as Java and C++ views a Ford car as an extension of a car and builds the relationship between them so that routines and objects of a Ford car can reuse what has been implemented for a car.

Another criterion to categorize Web programming languages is the platform (operating systems) in which the applications are running. If the application can run in various platforms such as Windows and UNIX, the language of the application is known as a cross-platform language. If the application cannot run across platforms, the languages of the applications are known as platform-dependent languages such as C and C++. Table 13.1 shows a 2×2 matrix to categorize the languages.

Object-Oriented Features of Java

Java is an object-oriented programming (OOP) language that is frequently used in Web development. It is also platform-independent, which means that the application built with Java is portable across different platforms.

The OOP features of Java suggest that Java has the following functionalities: inheritance, encapsulation, and polymorphism.

TABLE 13.1 Types of Programming Languages

	Object-Oriented	Procedural
Platform-independent	Java	PHP
Platform-dependent	C++	C

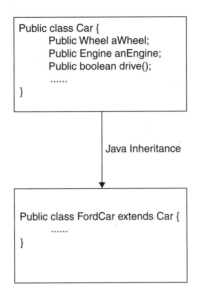

FIGURE 13.5 Example of Inheritance

Inheritance means that properties and functions of a Java object can be passed on to a new object. For example, Object Car contains generic configurations of a car such as four wheels and an engine and the action of driving. A new object FordCar can inherit the features of Object Car so that we do not need to redo the work for FordCar.

Figure 13.5 illustrates the example of inheritance. Class defines the type of object of a Car. Wheel is a class that defines features and functions of Wheels of cars. Object aWheel is an instance of Wheel. Similarly, the class of anEngine is an instance of class Engine. Drive is a method member of class Car that executes a series of actions such as starting engine. Boolean indicates the return value of drive() (i.e., the result of the execution of drive()). The return value can be *true* or *false. True* means success of executing function drive(); *False* means failure of executing function drive(). Inheritance is implemented by having FordCar extend to the class of Car.

Encapsulation is the practice of hiding portions of computer programs that do internal things. This is accomplished by defining different types of data such as public and private. Public data and functions of a parent object are accessible to a child object while private data and functions of the parent object are not accessible to the child object. Hence, private data and functions deal with internal operations that are not viewable from outside of the object scope. The private data and functions are then encapsulated within the scope. The benefit of the encapsulation is simplifying the features of an object so that the private data and functions are not overused and therefore confusing. Encapsulation also enables a component-based design methodology. The methodology advocates the use of interfaces or abstract function definitions for external uses. As a result, external objects have no access to the internal data and functions while the functions of the internal objects undergo routines performed by interfaces. A non-OO language may not have a private data type so the data and functions are wide open to external routines.

Polymorphism accomplishes the maximum degree of reusing previous work. It enables the variations of extended objects on the basis of a core parent object. *Poly* means multiple. For example, FordCar inherits Car's basic features. Another variation of Car, say BMWCar, also inherits the basic features of a Car. Therefore, FordCar and BMWCar are multiple variant instances of a Car. The process of generating multiple variants is known as polymorphism.

We use a simple Java example to illustrate the basic executions of computer programs. A java file called HelloWorldApp.java is coded as follows. It attempts to display "Hello World!" on the console after execution.

```
class HelloWorldApp {
    public static void main(String[] args) {
        System.out.println("Hello World!"); //Display the string.
    }}
```

Figure 13.6 shows the process of compiling a Java source file in a DOS environment.

Figure 13.7 shows the execution of the .class file in a UNIX environment.

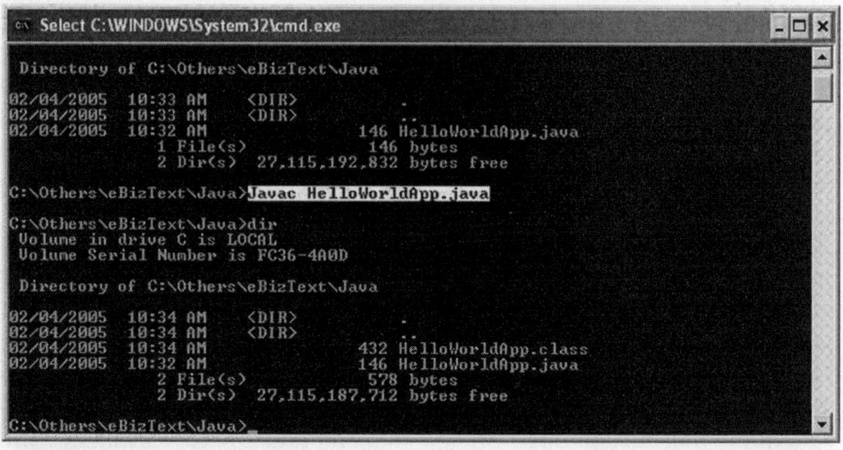

FIGURE 13.6 DOS Console

FIGURE 13.7 UNIX Console

What Does a Java Algo Look Like?

Computer algos are written in various languages such as Java, C, C++, and PHP. Let's look at a computer algo coded in Java. The following program implements the formulas of the multinomial decision model that we will discuss in detail. The program accepts input of the favorite ratings through an object called sharedValues. Then it estimates the input values for the six parameters of the MDP model with the computing functions of the LMPredictor.

```java
import java.io.*;
import Java.text.*;
import sharedValues;
import LMPredictor;
public class EstimateParms
{
static double i=0.00; static double a2=0.00; static double e2=0.00; static double
e4=0.00; static double g1=0.00; static double g2=0.00; double n31=0.00; double
ratioNew = 0.00; double red = 0.00; double §green = 0.00; double blue = 0.00;

public void Estimate()
{
    sharedValues estVal = new sharedValuesQ;
    red = estVal.redValue;
    green = est.Val.greenValue;
    blue = estVal.blue Value;
    i = (red-blue)/(100-blue);
    a2 = blue/100;
    e2 = 1 - (100 - red)/100 * (1-i)*(1-31 a2);
    e4 = 1 - (100 - green)/100 * (1-i)*(1-a2);
    ratioNew = blue/(100 - blue);
    n31 = blue*ratioNew/(1+ratioNew);
    g1 = n31/blue;
    g2 = n31/100 * (1-a2);
    String tablename = "MODELPARMVALUES";
    String mysessionid = null;

try{
    getSessionld myObjSessionld = new getSessionld(tablename);
    mysessionid = myObjSessionld.retSessionld;
}
catch (Exception e)
{
    System.out.println("Error in getSession!d( ). ");
}
```

```
estVal.sessionId = mysessionid;

try{
    loadData Id = new loadData(tablename, mysessionid., e2, e4, g1, g2);
}
catch (Exception e) System.out.println("load Data failed...");
}

public static void main(String[ ] args)
{
    EstimateParms est = new EstimateParms();
    est.Estimate();
}
}
```

In this Java program, we first create a class named EstimateParms and then define a few class variables. There is a method defined as Estimate(). When the class is used, we first initialize it with "new EstimateParms()", and then call the method with the class instance.

Developing a PHP Application

PHP originally stood for personal home page. It evolved into the term for a widely used Web programming language. PHP is used for more than building personal home pages now.

PHP is easy to learn and easy to use and it does not cost much to run an Internet solution. It is also a platform-independent language and the newer version is object-oriented. Therefore, PHP code written for Windows can be ported to UNIX in a seamless manner.

The difference between PHP and Java is that PHP is an interpreted language while Java is compiled before being executed. An interpreted language is a programming language whose programs may be executed from sources by an interpreter. As a result, it is not necessary to compile the PHP code before running it. This makes the process of execution easier. However, the performance (e.g., response latency to users) of the Web applications developed by interpreted languages may be less compared to those compiled a priori.

We will describe a project that shows the use of PHP to develop a simple Web application. This Web application displays a login page of "Online Brand Equity Aid Tool" that accepts user name and password. It then checks against a list of prerecorded usernames and passwords in a MySQL database. If the input is in the list, it will respond with a success judgment. Otherwise, messages of failed login will be displayed.

To successfully complete the project, we have to set up a Web server, a database server, and a PHP interpreter. These three components are bundled in a software package known as Fireserv. A copy of the open source software is accessible from http://www.yeswici.com/fireserv.exe.

The installation of Fireserv is not challenging. Clicking on Fireserv.exe will start the installation process. Following the standard instructions, the three components can be installed under a directory of the C drive of a computer, namely, c:\fireserv.

To start Fireserv, click on the icon on the desktop and then the "start Fireserv" button. After the three components are started, we copy the two PHP files to c:\fireserv\www folder, which is the root directory of the Apache Web server. The two PHP files are login.php and LoginCheck.php.

To access the login page from the Web, we open a browser and type in the following URL: http://localhost/login.php. This should display the login Web page.

The next step is to support LoginCheck.php, which takes the user input of user name and password and checks against a MySQL database. Therefore, we need to set up a table in the database. The name of the table is "web_user" which should be consistent with the SQL statement of the PHP code as follows.

```
select pass, user_type from web_user where user = '$user'
```

The "web_user" table contains three columns, that is, user, pass, and user_type. User stands for user names. Pass stands for password. User_type stands for the type of the user, either "manager" type or "customer" type. A few records (i.e., list of user names and passwords) should be inserted into the "user" table so that the input from the Web can be checked.

After the table is set and populated, clicking on "submit" of the login page will trigger logincheck.php. The result will be displayed. Two additional PHP files "mgr_index.php" and "csr_index.php" may be created to display the results of LoginCheck. Figure 13.8 shows the login page.

The following PHP source code is part of the programs that enable the basic functionalities of a login page. A database table has to be created to support the code.

Online Brand Equity Aid Tool (BEAT)

Manager or Customer Login

Username: _____
Password: _____
Submit   Reset

FIGURE 13.8   Sample PHP Page

How could one write such code? We need to have a crash course in PHP programming.

```
<?
$db = "MyDB";
$admin = "";
$adpass = "";
$mysql_link = mysql_connect("localhost", $admin, $adpass);
mysql_select_db($db, $mysql_link);
?>
<HTML><BODY background="bg.gif">
<font color="#0000FF" size="2" face="Arial, Helvetica, sans-serif"><center><strong>
<p> Online Brand Equity Aid Tool (BEAT)
</strong><p><u><b>Manager or Customer Login</u></b>
<form method="POST" action="LoginCheck.php">
UserType: <input type="text" name="user" size=10><br>
Password: <input type="text" name="pass" size=10><br>
<input type="submit" value="Submit">
<input type="reset" value="Reset">
</form><p></BODY></HTML>

<?
$db = "MyDB";
$admin = "";
$adpass = "";
$mysql_link = mysql_connect("localhost", $admin, $adpass);
mysql_select_db($db, $mysql_link);
$user = $_REQUEST['user'];
$pass_entered = $_REQUEST['pass'];
?>
<html><BODY background="bg.gif">
<font color="#0000FF" size="2" face="Arial, Helvetica, sans-serif">
<strong><script language="php">
$query = "select pass, user_type from web_user where user = '$user' ";
$result = mysql_query($query, $mysql_link);
$reason_str=(string) "";
$reason_ct_str=(string) "";
$tot_ct = 0;
if(mysql_num_rows($result)) {
while($row = mysql_fetch_row($result))
        {       $pass_saved .= $row[0];
                $type .=$row[1];
                if($pass_saved == $pass_entered){
                        if($type == 'mgr'){include('mgr_index.php');}
                        else{include('csr_index.php');       }
                }//end of if
        }//end of while
} //end of if
else { print("No user selected yet");       }
 </script></body></html>
```

JUMP-STARTING ALGO DEVELOPMENT WITH PHP PROGRAMMING

In this section, we go through the basic knowledge of PHP programming, including the basic PHP syntax on strings, numbers, arrays, and functions to develop simple computer algos.

Can PHP Code Live with HTML?

Yes. A PHP code section starts with <? and ends with ?>. The code inside <? ?> is interpreted with the PHP interpreter, while the code outside the <? ?> may be HTML code. The HTML code follows the standard HTML syntax. For example, it starts with <html> and ends with </html>. The tags such as <p> for new paragraphs, <br> for new lines, <table> for creating HTML tables are parsed the exactly the same as they are treated in Web pages.

The file extensions must be .php in order for the PHP interpreter to recognize that there is PHP code inside the flat file. In the meantime, the HTML code is treated the same as if they are in .html files.

Where Should PHP Files Live for Internet Access?

In general, the PHP files should live under the root directory of a Web server. With the Fileserv package, the default root directory is c:\fireserv\www. The PHP files must be placed under the c:\fireserv\www to be accessible through the Internet.

For example, let's assume that you have a PHP file called test.php and you have started Fireserv on your local machine. In order to make it accessible as a URL, it must be placed under c:\fireserv\www. Say you copy it to c:\fireserv\www. How to run test.php?

Accessing PHP Files on Web Browsers

First, bring up a Web browser: Internet Explorer, Firefox, or Chrome. Second, under the URL location of the browser, you type http://localhost/test.php. This should execute the test.php file and display the output of the file on the browser.

The rule of thumb is: You may replace c:\fireserv\www with localhost to form a URL for a PHP file to be accessed on browsers. Let us say that you have the test.php file live under a subfolder (named "my") of c:\fireserv\www. Then the URL to access the file from a browser is http://localhost/my/test.php.

If your colleagues from other computers want to access the PHP file, you will have to figure out what your machine name is or what your machine's IP (Internet Protocol) address is. Let us say that your machine's name is "server123." Then the URL for your friend to access the PHP file is http://server123/my/test.php.

If you want to publish the URL with IP address, then you may replace the machine name ("server123") with the IP address. You may use "ipconfig" on a DOS console to find out the IP address of your machine. Let's say the IP address is 192.168.1.102. Then the URL could be http://192.168.1.102/my/test.php.

If the default port number (80) is changed, then the URL will change to reflect this. Let's say that the default port number is changed to 8080. Then the new URL to access the PHP file is http://192.168.1.102:8080/my/test.php.

Finding a Substring

Let's assume that you have a string variable; how are you going to locate the position of a part of a string? This is especially useful if you want to extract an HTML document for specific texts because the first question is how to find out the location to start the extraction. We use a PHP function, **strpos()**, to locate the position.

```
strpos($whole, $part, $offset);
```

The function returns the numeric position of the first occurrence of $part in the $whole string, starting from $offset. If $part is not found, **strpos()** will return boolean FALSE. Let us look at a simple example.

```
<?
$wholestring = 'abcdef abcdef';
$pos = strpos($wholestring, 'a', 1);
echo $pos;
?>
```

We find that the value of $pos is 7, not 0. This is because the starting position (offset) is 1, which has passed the first "a" at position 0. Therefore, the position 7 for the second "a" is returned. Note that the counting of the positions starts at 0.

Extracting Substrings

When we know the position of a specific character inside a whole string, we may want to extract a section of the whole string, starting from the position. We use **substr()** to achieve this.

```
$sub = substr($whole, $start, $length);
```

substr() returns $length characters in the string $whole, starting at $start. The first character in the $whole is at position 0.

```
<?
$wholestring = 'abcdef abcdef';
$start = 7;
$length = 3;
$sub = substr($whole, $start, $length);
echo $sub;
?>
```

This will return "abc" for $sub.

Checking Whether a Variable Contains a Valid Number

When we parse a token from a large data set, sometimes we would like to know whether the token contains a number. We could use **is_numeric()** to do this. The function returns Boolean true or false. These are examples.

```
<?
is_numeric(6); /* true */
is_numeric('6'); /* true */
is_numeric('six'); /* false */
?>
```

Rounding Floating-Point Numbers

Computer algos sometimes display a numeric output with long digits after decimal points. We would like to shorten the digits. This may be achieved with **round()**.

```
<?
$total = 12.34546;
echo round($total, 2);
?>
```

This will present 12.34; only two digits after the decimal point are returned.

Creating a Random Number within a Range

In Monte Carlo simulations for forecasting, a random number has to be generated within a range. **mt_rand()** does this.

```
<?
$l = 0; $u = 100;
$rand_num = mt_rand($l, $u);
?>
```

This will generate a random number between 1 and 100.

Taking Logarithms

In many financial models, a compound continuous return normally uses the natural logarithmic return. This can be taken with **log()** with base e (natural log). For logs using base 10, use **log10()**. For logs using other bases, we pass the base as the second parameter to **log()**.

```
<?
$log = log(10);        // 2.30
$log10 = log10(10);       // 1
$log2 = log(10, 2);  // 3.32
?>
```

Calculating Exponents

In statistical models engaging Gaussian distributions, we need to use exponents that raise a number to a power. To raise *e* (2.71828) to a power, we use **exp( )**. To raise a number to any power, we use **pow( )**. For example:

```
<?
$exp = round(exp(2),3);   // = 7.389
$exp = round(pow(M_E, 2),3); //= 7.389 M_E is a constant approximating e
$pow = round(pow(2,2.5),3);       // =5.657
?>
```

Formatting Monetary Values

In financial modeling, sometimes the outputs are monetary values that need to display with a specific currency format. For example, we would like to display 8900.25 in U.S. currency format. We use **money_format()**.

```
<?
$v = 8900.25;
setlocale(LC_MONETARY, "en_US");
echo money_format('%n',$v);  // $8,900.25
echo money_format('%i',$v);        // USD 8,900.25
?>
```

Note that %n indicates that the output follows national currency format, and %i follows international format.

Converting between Bases

Normally we use numbers with base 10. Sometimes we need to use numbers with bases other than 10 or need to convert numbers from other bases (e.g., 2, 8, 16) to base 10. We use **base_convert( )** method. For example:

```
<?
$hex = 'a1'; // hex refers to hexadecimal number (base 16)
// convert from base 16 to base 10
$dec = base_convert($hex,16,10); // $dec is now 161 at base 10
?>
```

Finding Current Date and Time

Date and time are often used when an algo is executed for recording. **date( )** may present the current date and time. If we just need time without date, we may use **localtime()**. For example:

```
<?
echo date('r');
$now = localtime();
echo "<br>$now[2]:$now[1]:$now[0]";
?>
```

This prints the following output:

```
'Sat, 02 Jan 2010 16:26:13 -0500'
16:26:13
```

Using Arrays

There are two types of arrays in PHP: a numeric array and an associative array. For a numeric array, if we want to find an entry, we need to know the entry's position, or index of the entry. The positions start at 0 and add up one by one. For an associative array, also known as a **hash**, the indexes are not integers but meaningful strings. An entry of the array is a pair of key (index) and value. Hence, an associative array contains a list of key/value pairs.

For example, a numeric array of automobiles is:

```
$autos[0] = 'Car';
$autos[1] = 'Truck';
$autos[2] = 'Van';
$autos[3] = 'SUV';
```

or

```
$autos[] = 'Car';
$autos[] = 'Truck';
$autos[] = 'Van';
$autos[] = 'SUV';
```

An associative array of automobiles with colors is:

```
$autos['red'] = 'Car';
$autos['blue'] = 'Truck';
$autos['yellow'] = 'Van';
$autos['black'] = 'SUV';
```

Each associative array can hold only one unique value for a key. The more we program in PHP, the more likely we tend to use associative arrays than numeric arrays. We use **foreach as** to loop through an associative array to retrieve keys and values. For example:

```
foreach($autos as $color => $auto)
{
      echo "$auto is $color.<br>";
}
```

This would print:

```
Car is red.
Truck is blue.
Van is yellow.
SUV is black.
```

We may also use **list( )** to assign the values of the key/value pairs to individual variables. For example:

```
list($auto1, $auto2, $auto3, $auto4) = $autos;
```

Iterating through an Array

There are two ways to do this: **foreach as** or **for** loop. Inside the foreach() round brackets (or parentheses), each entry of the array is parsed (**as**) into key/value variables for use inside the {}, curly brackets (braces). The autos-array example in the above section has illustrated the use of **foreach** for an associative array. Let's look at an example of numeric arrays.

```
<?
$a = array(1, 2, 3, 4);
foreach ($a as $v)
{
        echo "Current value: $v.<br>";
}
?>
```

In the above example, inside the round brackets (), the entry of array $a is parsed into an individual variable $v each time when the loop moves to the next entry of the array. Then the variable $v, populated each time with the value of the entry, is used inside the curly brackets {}.

foreach as is designed to simplify the looping through arrays. A traditional approach to loop through arrays is to use **for** loops. For example, the above example can be rewritten as below with the same result:

```
<?
$a = array(1, 2, 3, 4);
for ($i=0; $i<sizeof($a); $i++)
{
    $v = $a[$i];
    echo "Current value: $v.<br>";
}
?>
```

Deleting Elements from an Array

We use **unset( )** to delete single elements and **array_splice( )** to delete multiple elements. For example:

```
<?
$a = array(1,2,3,4);
unset($a[3]);
$offset = 0;
$length = 2;
array_splice($a, $offset, $length);
?>
```

What should be left in the $a? The answer is 3.

Merging Arrays

We use **array_merge( )** to combine two arrays. The keys of the arrays may be renumbered. For example:

```
<?
$a = array(1,2);
$b = array(3);
$c = array_merge($a, $b);
print_r($c);
?>
```

The output should be:

```
Array
(
        [0]=>1
        [1]=>2
        [2]=>3
)
```

Note that we use **print_r( )** to output the content of an array, as opposed to using echo or print for String or number variables.

Turning an Array into a String

We may use **join( )** or **foreach-as** loop to obtain the values of an array $a with a string $s.

```
<?
$a = array(1,2,3,4);
//the string has a comma delimiter
$s = join(',',$a);

foreach($a as $v)
{
        $s=$s.",".$v;
}
?>
```

Searching an Array

array_search( ) returns the index position or key of the value in an array. If the value is not found in the array, the function returns false:

```
<?
$a = array(11,12,13,14);
$pos = array_search(14, $a);
echo "pos is: ".$pos?
?>
```

What is the output for $pos? The answer is 3. We may also use **in_array( )** to check if an array contains a known value.

Finding Largest and Smallest Values in an Array

We may use **max()** for the largest value and **min()** for the smallest value in an array. Or we use **arsort()** to find the largest value and **asort()** for the smallest value. For example:

```
<?
$a = array(10, 11, 8, 15);
$largest = max($a);
$smallest = min($a);

//or
$b = $a;
arsort($b);
$largest = $b[0];
?>
```

    arsort() does a descending sort (ar stands for reverse ascending) with the largest value on top, namely, position [0]. **asort()** produces the smallest value at position [0].

Using Functions

When we build computer algos for financial models, sometimes we want to reuse the algos in a collective way. This gives rise to collecting the pieces of algos as functions for library files. A library PHP file normally looks like this.

```
<?
include "otherlibs.php";
function algo1($a, $b)
{
        $d = "";
...
        return $d;
}

function algo2($c)
{
}
?>
```

    We declare a function with **function** key word, followed by the name of the function with its parameters in parentheses. A function may or may not return a value back to where it is called.

Passing Value by Reference

Normally, the variables declared inside a function are local to the function and may not be accessible outside the function. The communication between the result of the function and the outside is through returned variables. Sometimes we have a variable outside the function with its value designed for change by the function. We can use a technique called passing value by reference.

Passing value by reference is common in many programming languages. The variable passed into the function may keep the changes inside the function. As a result, we do not need to redeclare and return a new variable.

To pass a variable by reference, we add & before the parameter name. For example, if the variable name is $s, then we use &$s to pass $s into a function by reference. After calling the function, the value of the variable will be changed inside the function and be accessible outside the function.

```
<?
$s = "bold me";
add_bold($s);
function add_bold(&$s, $tag='b')
{
    $s = "<$tag>$s</$tag>";
}
echo $s;
?>
```

The output will be:

```
<b>bold me</b>
```

Creating Functions That Take a List of Arguments and Return a List of Results

We use arrays to achieve this. First, we declare an array outside the function. Second, populate the array with a list of arguments. Third, pass the array as the parameter of the function.

```
<?
$a = array(1,2,3,5);

function sumAverage($a)
{
    $tot = 0;
    $avg = 0;
    foreach($a as $v)
    {
        $tot = $tot + $v;
    }
    $avg = $tot/sizeof($a);
    return array($tot, $avg);
}

list($total, $average) = sumAverage($a);
?>
```

The function **sumAverage()** will take the array and compute the sum and average for all the elements. For returns, a new array is used to return the two results. **list()** may decompose the array into two numeric variables.

Accessing a Global Variable Inside a Function

We may pass the value of the variable by reference and into the function. What if we have a list of global variables? Can we use them without passing in? We may bring the global variable into local scope with the **global** key word, or with **$GLOBALS['name']**:

```
<?
$spot = 100;
$strike = 120;
...
function runBlackScholes()
{
    global $spot;
    $GLOBALS['strike'];
...
}
?>
```

JUMP-STARTING ALGO DEVELOPMENT WITH JAVA PROGRAMMING

Java is a popular, industry-standard, object-oriented programming language used in computing for many industries due to its features such as portability and scalability. J2EE, Java enterprise edition, focusing on enterprise computing, is the foundation of many commercial systems. Open source frameworks such as Struts and Spring have extended Java's capabilities for Web computing. Implementations of service-oriented architecture such as REST and SOAP have extended Java's capabilities of enterprise computing. To summarize, Java may satisfy various needs of industrial computing. We may see more and more financial algos being developed in Java language.

Compared to PHP, Java has overhead, or more infrastructure preparation for end-to-end computing. For example, to enable Web programming for Java, we may have to add servlet or Struts capacities to the Web server, which is complex compared to enabling PHP with the PHP engine (interpreter) that comes out of the box (e.g., in Fireserv or LAMP[2] or WAMP[3] packages). Table 13.2 compares the pros and cons of the PHP and Java programming languages for algo developments. The + sign indicates pros and − sign indicates cons according to the author's opinion.

To conclude, we use PHP for most of the algo development in this book due to its features such as parsimonious syntax and ease of use. However, in this section we will provide a jump-start introduction for Java, as some of our readers may start algo development with Java.

TABLE 13.2 Comparing PHP to Java

Features	PHP	Java
Ease of use	+ straightforward syntax and execution on Web servers	− more disciplined syntax and the execution on Web servers could be challenging for beginners
Infrastructure	+ out of box with Fireserv, WAMP, or LAMP packages	− needs custom configurations (e.g., Websphere, RAD, Tomcat, Eclipse) and may not be enabled by default in many hosting services; challenging to beginners in computing
Web programming	+ most popular in Web computing, used by Facebook, YouTube, and other popular sites	− popular for many corporate sites
Enterprise adoption	− popular for front-end (Web) developments; used less in the back end	+ popular in enterprise computing engaging databases and extensive messaging

The Development Environment

Java has a comprehensive syntax system and libraries with which a developer or architect may need additional real-time assistance to be productive. This gives rise to IDE (Integrated Development Environment) tools such as Eclipse (an open source IDE donated by IBM) and RAD (Rational Application Developer, an Eclipse-based commercial IDE from IBM). Let us look at Figure 13.9, which shows some of the features of Eclipse.

In Figure 13.9, the IDE screen is divided into several sections (panels). Each section has tabs to provide different views. On the left panel of the package, the structure is organized as projects. Inside each project, the files and resources may be explored. This facilitates the navigation of the file system.

In the middle section, the opened files are presented as different tabs. Each tab is indicated by the name of the opened file. The main body of the middle section displays the content of the present Java file that is being edited (coded).

In the right section of the screen, the outline panel displays the structure of the Java file that is being coded in the middle panel. For example, the outline panel may display the import declarations and the names of each method declared in the Java file.

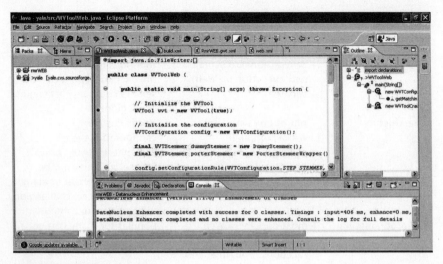

FIGURE 13.9 Eclipse IDE

At the middle-bottom section, the problem and console tabs may display the results and issues of executions. If we click on "run" from the menu on the top, a properly coded Java program may be executed. The result would display on the console tab. If the code has issues such as a coding error, the issues would be displayed on the problem tab of the middle-bottom panel.

The majority of the Java programming work happens in the middle section where the Java files are coded. This requires the familiarity with the basic syntax such as variable types (e.g., strings, numbers, and arrays) and methods. These are similar to PHP syntaxes from a functional perspective, but the actual syntaxes are different.

Note that Java and PHP have different terminology systems. For example, the functions of PHP are called methods in Java. As Java is designed to be an object-oriented programming language, the methods are called from the object where the methods are declared.

Extracting Substrings

Java uses **substring()** method of a string object. For example, here is a code snippet:

```
String a = "life is great";
System.out.println(a);
String b = a.substring(5);
System.out.println(b);
```

The one argument 5 for **substring( )** indicates the new substring is formed from the starting position 5 to the end of the original string. Therefore, the output in the console of an IDE should be:

```
is great
```

Note that Java does not use $ as the prefix of a variable name, while PHP uses $ as the prefix of variables.

Breaking a Sentence into Words

Java uses **StringTokenizer( )** to break a sentence. Here is an example:

```
String sent = "this is a sentence to be split into words";
StringTokenizer st = new StringTokenizer(sent);
while(st.hasMoreTokens())
{
    System.out.println(st.nextToken());
}
```

Lately, StringTokenizer has been replaced with the **split( )** method of a string object in newer versions of Java compilers. For example:

```
String s = "Life is good.";
String[] tokens = s.split(" ");
System.out.println(Arrays.toString(tokens));
```

produces the following output:

```
[Life, is, good.]
```

Putting Strings Together

There are three ways to do this: the + **operator** for string concatenation; the StringBuffer (synchronized) class; and the StringBuilder (not synchronized). Here is the code snippet to show the usage:

```
String s1 = "life" + " is" + " good.";
System.out.println(s1);

StringBuffer sbf = new StringBuffer();
sbf.append("life").append(" is").append(" good.");
System.out.println(sbf.toString());

StringBuilder sbd = new StringBuilder();
sbd.append("life").append(" is").append(" good.");
System.out.println(sbd.toString());
```

Table 13.3 compares the pros and cons of StringBuffer and String-Builder.

TABLE 13.3 Comparing StringBuffer to StringBuilder

	Pros	Cons
StringBuffer	Synchronized	Unnecessary overhead in single-threaded use
StringBuilder	Faster and preferable for single-threaded use	Not thread safe; not available prior to JDK 1.5

Controlling Cases of Strings

The two methods of string class, **toUpperCase** and **toLowerCase**, may do the conversion. For example:

```
String s = "Life Is Good.";
System.out.println("Original: "+s);
System.out.println("UPPER: "+s.toUpperCase());
System.out.println("lower: "+s.toLowerCase());
```

This will output three lines: the original, the uppercase, and the lowercase ones.

```
Original: Life Is Good.
UPPER: LIFE IS GOOD.
lower: life is good.
```

How to Remove Blanks at the Beginning or the End of Strings

In order to remove leading or trailing white spaces of a string, the trim() method of string object may be used. For example:

```
String s = " life is good. ";
System.out.println(s.trim());
```

This will output a string without leading or trailing blanks.

Checking If a String Is a Valid Number

As high-frequency trading needs quite a bit of computing with numbers, we may look at the inventories in Java for the computing. In general, Java has seven built-in types of numbers: 4 types of signed numbers (byte, short, int, long) without fractional parts; 2 types of floating numbers (float and double) with fractional parts; and a type of char numbers for Unicode characters.

One may convert any types of numbers to a string in Java. If a number is in String format, how to find out if it is a valid number? We may use proper wrapper class's translating routine and catch the exception if the string cannot be converted to a valid number. For example:

```
String num = "212.56";
double res;
try{
      res = Double.parseDouble(num);
}
catch(NumberFormatException e) {
      System.out.println(num+" is an invalid number");
      return;
}
```

Translating a Primitive Number into an Integer Object

In financial computing, we may need to hold a sequence of data (such as daily volumes of equity trades) in a collection. Java uses a class called Collection to achieve this. In order to translate back and forth between a primitive number and an Integer object, we use new Integer() or **intValue()** method. For example:

```
Integer numTradesObj = new Integer(89890); // from primitive type to objectint
numTrades = numTradesObj.intValue(); //from Integer object to primitive type
```

Rounding Floating Numbers

When we display a floating number, the fractional parts may be too long. In this case, we like to use **Math.round()** to round the floating number. For example:

```
System.out.println(Math.round(25.5f));
System.out.println(Math.round(-18.1f));
System.out.println(Math.round(-25.5f));
```

returns:

```
26
-18
-25
```

Generating Random Numbers

In Monte Carlo simulations, we need to generate random numbers. We use java.util.Random object to generate a random number. Here is an example to generate many random numbers with the **nextInt()** method and **nextGaussian()** method. Note that the random numbers generated by nextGaussian() method may produce a normal distribution.

```
java,util.Random r = java.util.Random();
for(int i=0; i<100;i++){
      r.nextInt();
```

```
}
for (int j=0; j<1000; j++){
     r.nextGaussian();
}
```

Creating Date Objects from Strings

Java uses a formatter instance of SimpleDateFormat class to convert strings into Date objects. The format of the conversion may be defined at the beginning of initialization. Then the formatter may parse the string input into a Date object. Here is how to do this:

```
SimpleDateFormat formatter = new SimpleDateFormat("yyyy-mm-dd");
Date t = formatter.parse("2010-01-10");
```

Instead of using Date alone, we may use GregorianCalendar class to hold date objects and more, and then use **getTime()** method to retrieve the date object. For example, the code snippet below initiates a Gregorian-Calendar object and populates the beginDate object with the getTime() method. It then gets the milliseconds for beginDate and today and computes the difference between the two dates.

```
Date beginDate = new GregorianCalendar(2009, 11, 29, 23, 59).getTime();
Date today = new Date();
long diff = today.getTime() - beginDate.getTime();
```

Using Array and ArrayList to Store Data

Similar to PHP programming, Java uses **Array** and **ArrayList** to store collections of data. Compared to Array class, ArrayList does not need to specify the size a priori. Here is an example to define an Array and an ArrayList. In the example, an array int[12] has to set the size of the data collection, while ArrayList is dynamic with the size. To sort an array, we use static **Arrays.sort()** method. To sort a collection such as ArrayList, we use **Collections.sort()** method.

```
Int[] months = new int[12];
Arrays.sort(months);
List monthsList = new ArrayList();
...
Collections.sort(monthList)
```

Finding an Object in an Array

After an array or a collection is sorted, we may want to find an object inside. The **binarySearch()** method is available in both Arrays and Collections classes. Therefore, we may do the search to find an object in an array or a collection. The example below shows the binarySearch on an array of banks.

```
String[] banks = new String[3];
banks[0] = "Morgan Stanley";
banks[1] = "JP Morgan";
banks[2] = "Goldman Sachs";
Arrays.sort(banks);
int i = Arrays.binarySearch("JP Morgan");
```

Converting an Arraylist to an Array

In Java, an array may be created by converting a collection such as ArrayList. Therefore, a dynamically sized collection may become a fixed-size array. For example, the following code converts an ArrayList to an Array of objects or strings.

```
ArrayList list = new ArrayList();
list.add("Morgan Stanley");
list.add("JP Morgan");
list.add("Goldman Sachs");
Object[] objs = list.toArray();
String[] sBanks = (String[]) list.toArray(new String[0]);
```

Difference between Hashtable and Hashmap

In PHP, we use associate arrays to hold key value pairs. In Java, we use **HashMap** objects to do so. Hashtable is an older class used for the same purpose. Here is an example of using HashMap:

```
HashMap hCorpAndCity = new HashMap();
hCorpAndCity.put("Goldman Sachs","New York City");
hCorpAndCity.put("CME","Chicago");
```

JUMP-STARTING ALGO DEVELOPMENT WITH C++ PROGRAMMING

In general, there are two reasons that many financial applications are using C++ nowadays. First, they were started with C++ when Java and other languages were not mature. Second, it is because of performance considerations. It is perceived in the industry that C++ and C applications run faster than Java applications.

There are quite a lot of books and online resources on C++ that explain the basic syntaxes, objects, and advanced topics. For starters on algo development, the O'Reilly book (by Steve Oualline) entitled *Practical C++ Programming* is recommended. For experienced C++ developers, the book by Bruce Eckel entitled *Thinking in C++* is always an expert's favorite.

JUMP-STARTING ALGO DEVELOPMENT WITH FLEX PROGRAMMING

The recent Web computing sees the rapid adoption of Flex as the default choice as RIA (Rich Internet Application) programming language for user interfaces (UI) of financial algos. Major investment banks such as Morgan Stanley are beginning to adopt Flex as the UI programming language for investment apps for traders and portfolio managers. The intent is to increase their productivity by leveraging Flex's features of ease of use and visual appeal.

There are two main components of Flex language: MXML and Action-Scripts. MXML is designed to build a slick user interface with a standard XML-based UI definition language. The standard definition language is created by Mozilla called XUL. For example, the XML-based tag <vbox> for a vertical box is commonly used and implemented in various XUL-based languages.

Another major component of Flex is the object-oriented ActionScript (AS) that looks a lot like Java. The AS code is normally wrapped inside a code block of <mx:script> ... </mx:script>. It communicates with the MXML components with MXML IDs and binding variables. For starters, a book by Adobe Press entitled *Training from the Source* may be helpful.

JUMP-STARTING ALGO DEVELOPMENT WITH SQL

SQL, or structured query language, is used by many types of database management systems such as Oracle, DB2, and MySQL. Database management systems may hold financial information permanently. Therefore, data such as ticker quotes over a period of many years may be stored in a database and may be retrievable for use by SQL.

SQL is a standardized data retrieval and manipulation language, normally being used in the back-end operations for computer algos that are built in PHP, Java, C++, or Flex. There are four major operations that SQL can complete for data, namely, CRUD: create, retrieve, update, and delete.

Creating a Table

One may use the **create table** command to create a database table (see Table 13.4) like this:

```
create table employees (first varchar(15), last varchar(20),
id varchar(10), age number(3), state varchar(20));
```

TABLE 13.4 Employees Table

First	Last	ID	Age	State
Henry	Smith	111	55	Maryland
Larry	Jackson	222	35	DC
Kerry	Carlson	333	28	New York

varchar is a type of SQL variable that defines a string-like column with flexible length.

Dropping a Table

If we do not want to keep a table and the data in the table, then we can drop the table. For example:

```
drop table employees
```

Using a Select Statement

Here is a simple select SQL statement:

```
select last, first from employees where firs]t LIKE 'Er%';
```

This SQL statement returns records with first names that start with 'Er'. Note that the strings are in single quotes.

```
select last, first from employees where last LIKE '%s';
```

This SQL statement will return records with last names that end in 's'.

```
select * from employees where first = 'Eric';
```

This SQL statement selects rows where the first name equals 'Eric' exactly.

Inserting Data into a Table

To add a new line to a table, we use insert into command:

```
insert into employees (first, last, id, age, state) values
('Jason', 'Kid', '32478', 45, 'Georgia');
```

Deleting Records in a Table

If we want to remove a record from a table, then we can use delete command. For example:

```
delete from employees where last = 'Smith';
```

Updating a Record

Sometimes we want to change the value of a record in a table. The update command may be used here:

```
update employees set state = 'Virginia' where id = 111;
```

COMMON UNIX/LINUX COMMANDS FOR ALGO DEVELOPMENT

Most of the computer algos for high-frequency trading are running on UNIX or LINUX operating systems. Compared to Windows operating systems, UNIX and LINUX are more stable in performance and security. Hence, production systems and mission-critical applications are normally running on UNIX or LINUX as opposed to Windows.

Here is a list of common UNIX/LINUX commands for computer algo development and deployment.

- cat: create or display files to console
- chmod: change access permissions of files or directories
- cd: change from current directory to another directory
- cp: copy files
- date: show current date
- echo: display to console
- ftp: transfer (download or upload) files to a remote machine
- grep: search files
- head: display first part of file
- lpr: print files
- ls: display current files and directories
- more: read files
- mkdir: create a directory
- mv: move or rename files
- ncftp: download files through anonymous ftp
- print: print to printer
- pwd: find out current directory
- rm: remove a file
- rmdir: remove a directory
- setenv: set environment variables
- sort: sort a file
- tail: display last part of a file
- tar: create, add, or extract tar files
- telnet: log in to a machine
- vi: edit files
- wc: count a file's characters, words, lines

CONCLUSION

This chapter covered the technology infrastructure and computing languages used in creating computer algos for high-frequency trading. We included the procedure for setting up a computing environment with dedicated Web servers and jump-start courses on Java and PHP for algo development.

Creating Computer Algos for High-Frequency Trading

S tarting from the last quarter of 2008 until the end of 2009, the $600 trillion U.S. derivatives market had been almost frozen because of the lack of liquidity. High-frequency trading brings in the liquidity to equities markets in that investors can buy and sell securities almost instantly. Therefore, in order to bring liquidity to the derivatives market, introducing high-frequency trading with computer algos to trade derivatives securities would be an appropriate solution with a reasonable expectation that it would be successful. I predict that in a few years the derivatives market will be flooded with electronic trading or high-frequency trading operations, just as the equities market was in 2008 and 2009. In order to prepare for its coming, let us look at some basic computer algos that may be used for high-frequency trading operations in derivatives trading. These computer algos may be applicable to electronic trading of other securities.

GETTING PROBABILITY FROM Z SCORE

Instead of checking statistical tables for converting Z scores to probabilities manually, we may write an algo to do this conversion on the Web. This function has to be available for the Black-Scholes algos because the cumulative normal distribution formula is needed in the Black-Scholes model for the Z-to-probability conversion. I single out the cumulative normal distribution function of the Black-Scholes algos from the SAPE library for enabling high-frequency trading of derivatives.

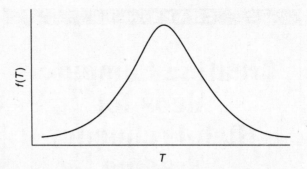

FIGURE 14.1 A Normal Distribution
Note: μ = mean of the normal distribution; σ = standard deviation of the distribution.

The introduction to the statistical formula for the normal distribution density function (see Figure 14.1) may be found in an advanced statistical textbook. Let's just look at its formula:

$$f(T) = \frac{1}{\sigma_T\sqrt{2\pi}}e^{-\frac{1}{2}\left(\frac{T-\mu}{\sigma_T}\right)^2}$$

$$f(T) \geq 0, \quad -\infty < T < \infty, \quad -\infty < \overline{T} < \infty, \quad \sigma_T > 0$$

The formula is coded as follows. Note that $T is the Z score for a standard normal distribution.

```
function CND ($T) {
        $Pi = 3.141592653589793238;
        $a1 = 0.319381530;
        $a2 = -0.356563782;
        $a3 = 1.781477937;
        $a4 = -1.821255978;
        $a5 = 1.330274429;
        $L = abs($T);
        $k = 1 / (1 + 0.2316419 * $L);
        $p=1-1/pow(2*$Pi,0.5)*exp(-pow($L,2)/2)*($a1*$k+$a2*pow($k,2)+$a3*pow($k,3)+
        $a4*pow($k,4)+$a5*pow($k,5));
        if ($x >= 0)
        {    return $p;
        }
        else
        {    return 1-$p;}
}
```

Given an observed value $X, we may convert the observed value to a Z score at first. Thus we use the following algo to compute probabilities from observed values.

```
<?php
//NORMDIST
////Returns the normal cumulative distribution for the
```

```
//specified mean and standard deviation. This function
//has a very wide range of applications in statistics,
//including hypothesis testing.
////Syntax
//NORMDIST(x,mean,standard_dev)
////X is the value for which you want the distribution.
//Mean is the arithmetic mean of the distribution.
//Standard deviation is the standard deviation of the distribution.
////Example

//NORMDIST(42,40,1.5,TRUE) equals 0.908789

function normdist($X, $mean, $sigma)
{
        $res = 0;
        $x = ($X - $mean) / $sigma;
        if ($x == 0) {
                $res = 0.5;
        }
        else {
                $oor2pi = 1 / (sqrt(2 * 3.14159265358979323846));
                $t = 1 / (1 + 0.2316419 * abs($x));
                $t *= $oor2pi
                * exp(-0.5 * $x * $x)
                * (0.31938153 + $t
                * (-0.356563782 + $t
                * (1.781477937 + $t
                * (-1.821255978 + $t * 1.330274429)))));
if ($x >= 0)
        {
                $res = 1 - $t;
        }
        else {
                $res = $t;
        }
        }
        return $res;
} //function end
?>
```

GETTING Z SCORES FROM PROBABILITY

This following algo is handy for computing standardized Z scores from probabilities.

```
<?php
/*****************************************************************************
*                          getZScoreFromProbability
*       copyright            : 2004 Michael Nickerson; 2009 Gewei Ye
*****************************************************************************/

function getZScoreFromProbability($p) {
 //Inverse ncdf approximation by Peter J. Acklam, implementation adapted to
 //PHP by Michael Nickerson, using Dr. Thomas Ziegler's C implementation as
 //a guide. http://home.online.no/~pjacklam/notes/invnorm/index.html
 //I have not checked the accuracy of this implementation. Be aware that PHP
 //will truncate the coeficcients to 14 digits.
```

```php
//You have permission to use and distribute this function freely for
//whatever purpose you want, but please show common courtesy and give credit
//where credit is due.
//Input parameter is $p - probability - where 0 < p < 1.

  //Coefficients in rational approximations
  $a = array(1 => -3.969683028665376e+01, 2 => 2.209460984245205e+02,
             3 => -2.759285104469687e+02, 4 => 1.383577518672690e+02,
             5 => -3.066479806614716e+01, 6 => 2.506628277459239e+00);
  $b = array(1 => -5.447609879822406e+01, 2 => 1.615858368580409e+02,
             3 => -1.556989798598866e+02, 4 => 6.680131188771972e+01,
             5 => -1.328068155288572e+01);
  $c = array(1 => -7.784894002430293e-03, 2 => -3.223964580411365e-01,
             3 => -2.400758277161838e+00, 4 => -2.549732539343734e+00,
             5 => 4.374664141464968e+00, 6 => 2.938163982698783e+00);
  $d = array(1 => 7.784695709041462e-03, 2 => 3.224671290700398e-01,
             3 => 2.445134137142996e+00, 4 => 3.754408661907416e+00);
  //Define break-points.
  $p_low = 0.02425;                  //Use lower region approx. below this
  $p_high = 1 - $p_low;              //Use upper region approx. above this
  //Define/list variables (doesn't really need a definition)
  //$p (probability), $sigma (std. deviation), and $mu (mean) are user inputs
  $q = NULL; $x = NULL; $y = NULL; $r = NULL;
  //Rational approximation for lower region.
  if (0 < $p && $p < $p_low) {
    $q = sqrt(-2 * log($p));
    $x = (((((($c[1] * $q + $c[2]) * $q + $c[3]) * $q + $c[4]) * $q + $c[5]) * $q
      + $c[6]) / (((($d[1] * $q + $d[2]) * $q + $d[3]) * $q + $d[4]) * $q + 1);
  }
  //Rational approximation for central region.
  elseif ($p_low <= $p && $p <= $p_high) {
    $q = $p - 0.5;
    $r = $q * $q;
    $x = ((((($a[1] * $r + $a[2]) * $r + $a[3]) * $r + $a[4]) * $r + $a[5]) * $r
      + $a[6]) * $q / ((((($b[1] * $r + $b[2]) * $r + $b[3]) * $r + $b[4])
      * $r + $b[5]) * $r + 1);
  }
  //Rational approximation for upper region.
  elseif ($p_high < $p && $p < 1) {
    $q = sqrt(-2 * log(1 - $p));
    $x = -((((($c[1] * $q + $c[2]) * $q + $c[3]) * $q + $c[4]) * $q
      + $c[5]) * $q + $c[6]) / (((($d[1] * $q + $d[2]) * $q + $d[3])
      * $q + $d[4]) * $q + 1);
  }
  //If 0 < p < 1, return a null value
  else {
      $x = NULL;
  }
  return $x;
}
//echo "<br>Probability to z for .95 = ". getZScoreFromProbability(.95);
?>
```

ALGOS FOR THE SHARPE RATIO

The Sharpe ratio is named after William Sharpe, who won the Nobel Prize in Economics in 1990, along with Harry Markowitz. The Sharpe ratio is a measure of the excess return (or risk premium) per unit of risk for an asset, a trading strategy, or a portfolio. The excess return is the difference

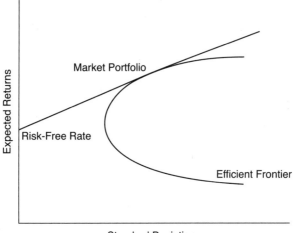

FIGURE 14.2 Efficient Portfolio Frontier

between the asset return and the return of a benchmark asset. Here is the formula for computing the Sharpe ratio (Sharpe 2000):

$$S = \frac{R - R_f}{\sigma} = \frac{E\left[R - R_f\right]}{\sqrt{\text{var}\left[R - R_f\right]}},$$

where R is the asset return, R_f is the return on a benchmark asset, such as the risk free rate of return, $E[R - R_f]$ is the expected value of the excess of the asset return over the benchmark return, and σ is the standard deviation (volatility) of the asset excess return.

The statistical formula for computing the Sharpe ratio was proposed in 1966. Since then, it has been used as the standard for assessing portfolio performance. For example, in the efficient portfolio frontier (see Figure 14.2), a curve to describe portfolio returns and risks, the Sharpe ratio for the market (tangency) portfolio is the largest. Therefore, the market portfolio is regarded as the optimized asset allocations based on modern portfolio theory (Markowitz 1952).

Due to its frequency of usage, the Sharpe ratio may be programmed as a computer algo for derivatives trading. Here is the code in PHP.

```
function calcSharpeRatio($arr1){
    $m = calcMean($arr1);
    $std = standard_deviation_population($arr1);
    $tb = calcAvgTBillRate($arr1);
    $ret = 0;
    if($std > 0){
        $ret = ($m - $tb)/$std;
    }
```

```
//      echo "<br>Daily Sharpe Ratio: ".round($ret,3);
        return $ret;
}
function calcAvgTBillRate($arr1){
//According to http://able.harvard.edu/rates/ca004q/, FY2008 T-Bill rates,
// 4.94, 4.36, 3.99, 3.99, 3.33, 3.05 2.82, 2.16, 1.22%
        $tot = 2.82 + 2.16 + 1.22;
        $avg = $tot/300; //3 months
//      $days = count($arr1);
        $days = 365; //yearly T-bill rate to daily rate
        $avg1 = $avg/$days;
        $avg2 = round(100 * $avg1, 3); //percent
//      echo "<br>average daily T-bill return: ".$avg2."%";
        return $avg1;
}
function standard_deviation_population ($a)
{
  //variable and initializations
  $the_standard_deviation = 0.0;
  $the_variance = 0.0;
  $the_mean = 0.0;
  $the_array_sum = 0;
  $number_elements = count($a); //count the number of elements
  if($number_elements>0){
        $the_array_sum = array_sum($a); //sum the elements
        //calculate the mean
        $the_mean = $the_array_sum / $number_elements;
  }
  //calculate the variance
  for ($i = 0; $i < $number_elements; $i++)
  {
    //sum the array
    $the_variance = $the_variance + ($a[$i] - $the_mean) * ($a[$i] - $the_mean);
  }
  if($number_elements>0){
    $the_variance = $the_variance / $number_elements;
  }
  //calculate the standard deviation
  $the_standard_deviation = pow($the_variance, 0.5);
  return $the_standard_deviation;
}

function calcMean($arr1){
        $the_array_sum = 0;
        $avg = 0;
        $number_elements = count($arr1); //count the number of elements
        if($number_elements>0){
                $the_array_sum = array_sum($arr1); //sum the elements
                //calculate the mean
                $avg = $the_array_sum / $number_elements;
        }
        $avg1 = 100 * $avg;
        return $avg;
}
```

COMPUTING NET PRESENT VALUE

Calculating net present value is normally the introductory portion of a financial modeling class. Microsoft Excel is a commonly used tool. However, in many high-frequency trading settings, including derivatives trading, engaging Excel for computing becomes a challenge because of the interoperability issues between Microsoft windows and UNIX, and Excel macros and the computing languages used for high-frequency trading operations. Therefore, a computer algo that implements the net present value formula would be helpful for an easier adaption by a high-frequency trading operation.

The net present value is the difference between the present value of cash inflows and the present value of cash outflows (Sharpe 2000). The present value of cash inflows is the summation of the discounted future values of an asset, a project, or a portfolio. The formula for computing the net present value is:

$$NPV = \sum_{t=1}^{T} \frac{C_t}{(1+r)^t} - C_o$$

Where C_o: cash outflow
           C_t: cash inflow
           r: interest rate
           t: a point of a time series

The code below implements the summation of the net present value.

```
function getNPV($cf, $cfn, $n, $r){
        $npv = 0;
        $npv = $cf + getSum($cfn, $n, $r);
        return $npv;
}

$cf0 = $_REQUEST['cf0'];
$cf1 = $_REQUEST['cf1'];
$n = $_REQUEST['n'];
$cfn = $_REQUEST['cfn'];
$cfn1 = $_REQUEST['cfn1'];
$r = $_REQUEST['r'];
$r1 = $_REQUEST['r1'];
$incr = 0;
$res = "";

if($cf0!="" && $n!=""){
$npvsoa = getNPV($cf0, $cfn, $n, $r);
$npvbench = getNPV($cf1, $cfn1, $n, $r1);
$incr = $npvsoa - $npvbench;
$res = "<br><font color=\"#000000\"><b>Result: $".$incr."K is the added value for
SOA over benchmark strategies.</font></b>";
}

function getSum($cfn, $n, $r){
$sum = 0;
for($i=0;$i<=$n;$i++){
        $rate = 1 + $r;
        $div = pow($rate,$n);[1]
        $sum = $sum + $cfn/$div;
//      echo "<br>sum: ".$sum;
}
return round($sum,3);
}
```

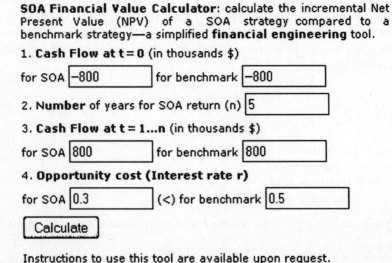

SOA Financial Value Calculator: calculate the incremental Net Present Value (NPV) of a SOA strategy compared to a benchmark strategy—a simplified **financial engineering** tool.

1. **Cash Flow at t = 0** (in thousands $)

for SOA -800   for benchmark -800

2. **Number** of years for SOA return (n) 5

3. **Cash Flow at t = 1...n** (in thousands $)

for SOA 800   for benchmark 800

4. **Opportunity cost (Interest rate r)**

for SOA 0.3   (<) for benchmark 0.5

[Calculate]

Instructions to use this tool are available upon request.

FIGURE 14.3 Computing Net Present Value

The preceding code works with a user interface on the Web for calculating the present value of the investment on a service-oriented architecture. Figure 14.3 shows a screen shot of the UI.

DEVELOPING A FLEX USER INTERFACE FOR COMPUTER ALGOS

In his book entitled *My Life as a Quant*, Emanuel Derman describes his contributions when working with Fischer Black at Goldman Sachs. He developed a nice UNIX user interface for traders. UNIX is a text-based operating system that does not provide graphic user interface (GUI). In the early days of computing, Unix UIs were well received by traders. With the advent of GUI and rich Internet application (RIA), a nicer GUI for trading would help traders and portfolio managers improve productivity. One of the advanced RIA technologies for building sleek GUI on the Web or desktop is Flex programming language.

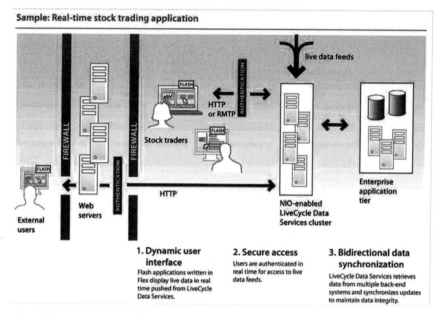

FIGURE 14.4 Web Architecture with Flex and LiveCDS
Source: Adobe web site.

Flex includes two sets of languages: ActionScript and MXML. MXML defines the UI components and ActionScript code handles the complex logic of the UI components.

Figure 14.4 describes the architecture of a typical trading application with Flex and LiveCycle Data Services (LiveCDS for short). In this architecture, the Flex UI may be used for internal users or external users. Stock traders inside the two firewalls are authenticated internal users who may access the real-time data pushed from the LiveCDS server. The LiveCDS server may obtain the real-time data from enterprise applications such as trading algos server written in C++, or with live data feeds such as Bloomberg. For external users who have to pass the firewall to access the Flash application, they hit the Web server first (between the two firewalls), and then use HTTP protocol to interact with the LiveCDS server.

Adobe has recently introduced a set of advanced methodologies and architectures for Flex to develop visually appealing Web or desktop applications. One methodology is model-driven development or application modeling technology (AMT) that extends the object-oriented design. The premium module of the AMT is LiveCycle Data Services that adds data model view to the integrated development environment (IDE), that is, the

Flash Builder 4. The LiveCDS server, together with a database server, backs the data model view in the Flash 4 builder's workbench.

Here is an example of how an AMT application works. Let's say we would like to display the content of a contact table (having data of first name, last name, e-mail, address, see Figure 14.5) of a MySQL database on the Web or on a desktop. We first visually create a data model for the contact table by dragging the database object to the data model view of the workbench of Flash Builder 4. The functions of getters and setters to operate on the contact table will be automatically generated. The objects in the workbench are now tied to the database table, which provides many advantages for the model-driven development.

In traditional application development, database view is always separate from the programming IDE. For example, DB visualize for DB2 is separate from Rational Application Developer (RAD) for Java programming. Therefore, using LiveCDS inside Flex IDE is a revolutionary step for application development and architecture.

With the data model view binding to the database table and accessible in the Flex IDE, a read-only display of the database table requires a further binding between a UI element (e.g., DataGrid) and the data model methods generated by LiveCDS (e.g., getAll). A technologist (developer or architect) may drag the getAll method of LiveCDS to the DataGrid element of a MXML file inside the design view of the Flash Builder 4. The binding between the data and the UI occurs after redeploying the data model changes to the LiveCDS server. As a result, the sleek Flex UI may access the database

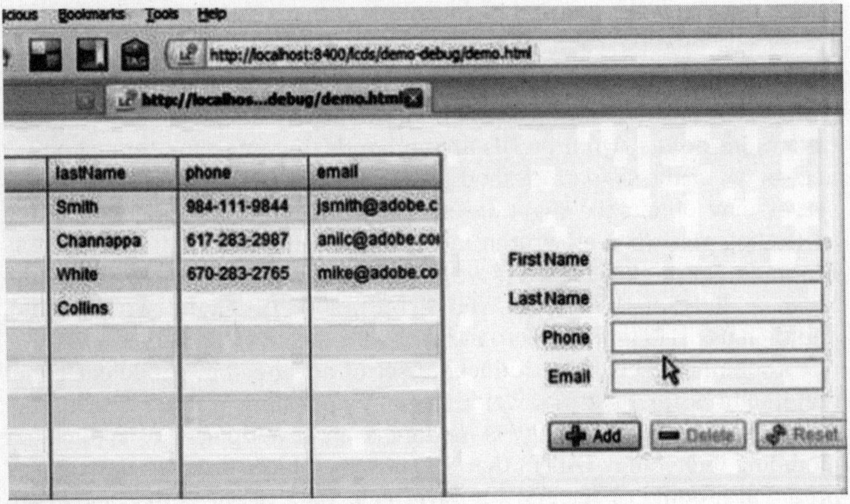

FIGURE 14.5 User Interface Built by Flex with LiveCDS

table (contact) without going through complicated database wiring. The display of the database table is part of (i.e., the read function) the CRUD (create, read, update, and delete) and search functions that are offered by Web or desktop GUI applications.

There is a demo video from Adobe that provides the details of using LiveCDS data model view to build a CRUD and search GUI application with Flex (Adobe 2009).

Recall the PHP and Flex code for calculating option prices with the Black-Scholes model. Flex UI normally uses an HTTP service or a SOA technology such as REST to pull database data. As a result of adding the LiveCDS data view to Flash Builder 4, the Flex UI does not need to use SOA (REST or HTTP service) to access the database data. The database tables are accessible inside Flex Builder 4 as data model view.

We use Flex to build user interfaces for computer algos. For example, a Black-Scholes algo may use Flex UI to accept parameter values and present results. Below is the picture that shows the screens to accept the values of five parameters. When a user clicks on the calculate button, the Flex UI component takes in the five values, converts them to XML format, and then sends the XML data to a PHP program that does the Black-Scholes algo computing. After the PHP program gets the result, it sends the result back to the Flex UI. The UI then displays the result to the user.

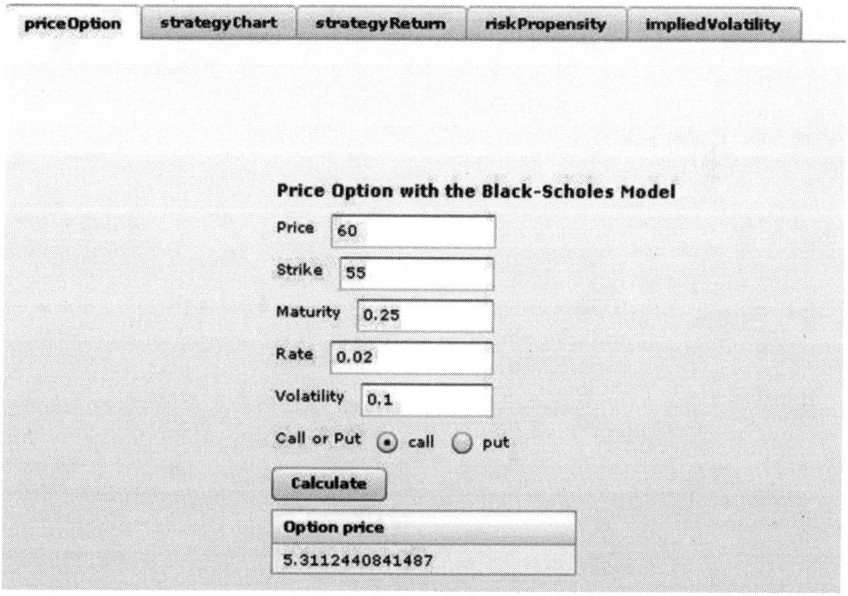

FIGURE 14.6 User Interface Built by Flex for the Black-Scholes Model

ALGOS FOR THE BLACK-SCHOLES MODEL

We discussed the Black-Scholes formula in Chapter 10. The following code implements a typical Black-Scholes formula for European options. **CND( )** computes the cumulative probability from a Z score. **runBlackScholes( )** calculates the option prices based on six parameter values as input.

```php
<?php
/* Use these to replace the hard-coded value if you take input from the arguments of
a URL
$S = $_POST['price'];
$X = $_POST['strike'];
$T = $_POST['year'];
$r = $_POST['rate'];
$v = $_POST['vola'];
$call = $_POST['call'];
$put = $_POST['put'];
$call_put_flag = $_POST['callput'];
*/
$S = 60;
$X = 55;
$T = 0.25;
$r = 0.02;
$v = 0.1;
$call = 'c';
$put = 'p';
$call_put_flag = "";

$ret = "<response>";
$optP = runBlackScholes($call_put_flag, $S, $X, $T, $r, $v);
$ret.= "<option>".$optP."</option>";
$ret.= "</response>";
echo $ret;

function CND ($x) {
  $Pi = 3.141592653589793238;
  $a1 = 0.319381530;
  $a2 = -0.356563782;
  $a3 = 1.781477937;
  $a4 = -1.821255978;
  $a5 = 1.330274429;
  $L = abs($x);
  $k = 1 / (1 + 0.2316419 * $L);
  $p=1-1/pow(2*$Pi,0.5)*exp(-pow($L,2)/2)*($a1*$k+$a2*pow($k,2) + $a3*pow($k,3) +
      $a4*pow($k,4) + $a5*pow($k,5));
  if ($x >= 0)
  { return $p;}
  else
  { return 1-$p;}
  }
}
function runBlackScholes ($call_put_flag, $S, $X, $T, $r, $v) {
  // $call_put_flag: c
  // $S: present stock price: 60
  // $X: strike price, 55
  // $T: years of maturity, 0.25
  // $r: interest rate:
  // $v: volatility
  $d1 = (log($S / $X) + ($r + pow($v, 2) / 2) * $T) / ($v * pow($T, 0.5));
  $d2 = $d1 - $v * pow($T, 0.5);
```

```
  if ($call_put_flag == 'c') {
    return $S * CND($d1) - $X * exp( -$r * $T ) * CND($d2);
  }
  else {
    return $X * exp( -$r * $T ) * CND(-$d2) - $S * CND(-$d1);}
}
?>
```

Figure 14.6 shows the user interface for the Black-Scholes formula. Here is the Flex code for the user interface. HTTPService collects the data input from the Flex UI and sends the data to http://www.yeswici.com/wici/bs/BSmodel.php to compute option prices. The response is captured and displayed by dataProvider with userRequest.lastResult.response.

```
<?xml version="1.0" encoding="utf-8"?>
<mx:Application xmlns:mx="http://www.adobe.com/2006/mxml" layout="absolute">
    <mx:HTTPService id="userRequest" url="http://www.yeswici.com/wici/bs/BSmodel.php"
        method="POST">
      <mx:request xmlns="*">
          <price>{in_price.text}</price>
          <strike>{in_strike.text}</strike>
          <year>{in_year.text}</year>
          <rate>{in_rate.text}</rate>
          <vola>{in_vola.text}</vola>
          <call>{in_call.value}</call>
          <put>{in_put.value}</put>
          <callput>{callput.selectedValue}</callput>
      </mx:request>
    </mx:HTTPService>
    <mx:Script>
      <![CDATA[
          private function send_data():void {
              userRequest.send();
          }
      ]]>
    </mx:Script>
    <mx:Form x="169" y="65" width="349" height="301">
        <mx:Label text="Price Option with the Black-Scholes Model" width="279"
            fontWeight="bold" fontFamily="Verdana" fontSize="11" color="#050505"/>
        <mx:HBox width="100%">
            <mx:Label text="Price"/>
            <mx:TextInput width="112" id="in_price" text="60" enabled="true"
            editable="true"/>
        </mx:HBox>
        <mx:HBox width="100%">
            <mx:Label text="Strike"/>
            <mx:TextInput id="in_strike" text="55" displayAsPassword="false"
            editable="true" enabled="true" width="105"/>
        </mx:HBox>
        <mx:HBox width="100%">
            <mx:Label text="Maturity"/>
            <mx:TextInput id="in_year" text="0.25" editable="true" enabled="true"
            width="93"/>
        </mx:HBox>
        <mx:HBox width="100%">
            <mx:Label text="Rate"/>
            <mx:TextInput width="111" id="in_rate" text="0.02" editable="true"
            enabled="true"/>
        </mx:HBox>
        <mx:HBox width="100%">
            <mx:Label text="Volatility"/>
            <mx:TextInput width="90" id="in_vola" enabled="true" text="0.1"/>
```

```
        </mx:HBox>
        <mx:HBox width="100%">
            <mx:Label text="Call or Put"/>
    <mx:Script>
        <![CDATA[
            import mx.controls.Alert;
            import mx.events.ItemClickEvent;
            private function handleRBGClick(event:ItemClickEvent):void {
                if (event.currentTarget.selectedValue == "c") {
                    //callput.selectedValue="c";
                    Alert.show("You selected Call: "+callput.selectedValue);
                } else if (event.currentTarget.selectedValue == "p") {
                    Alert.show("You selected Put: "+callput.selectedValue);
                    //callput.selectedValue="p";
                }
            }
        ]]>
    </mx:Script>
            <mx:RadioButtonGroup id="callput" itemClick="handleRBGClick(event)"/>
            <mx:RadioButton label="call" groupName="callput" id="in_call" value="c"
            selected="true" enabled="true"/>
            <mx:RadioButton label="put" groupName="callput" id="in_put" value="p"
            selected="false" enabled="true"/>
        </mx:HBox>
        <mx:HBox width="100%">
            <mx:Button label="Calculate" id="calc" click="send_data()"/>
        </mx:HBox>
        <mx:HBox width="100%" height="45">
            <mx:DataGrid id="dgUserRequest" x="22" y="128"
            dataProvider="{userRequest.lastResult.response}" height="43" width="208">
                <mx:columns>
                    <mx:DataGridColumn headerText="Option price" dataField="option"/>
                </mx:columns>
            </mx:DataGrid>
        </mx:HBox>
    </mx:Form>
</mx:Application>
```

COMPUTING VOLATILITY WITH THE ARCH FORMULA

In Chapter 12, we discussed the formula of the ARCH(1,1) model. The formula computes forward volatilities from historical volatilities and returns (Engle 1982; Hull 2008). Here is a sample algo that computes the volatility from the ARCH(1,1) model. In the algo, **inverse_ncdf()** computes the standardized Z scores from probabilities; **getArchSigma()** uses the ARCH formula to compute the volatility.

```
function getVaR_Arch()
{
    $p = 0.01;
    $z = - inverse_ncdf($p); // -2.33 for 1%; -1.65 for 5%
    $arr = getLogRetArr($arr_price);
    $whichDay = 2; //0, 1, 2
    //get Garch sigma
    $sigma = getArchSigma($arr, $whichDay);
    //get standard sigma
    //$sigma = standard_deviation_population($arr); //daily sigma
```

```
    //monthly sigma
    //$t = 20; //20 business days in a month
    //$sigma_mon = $sigma * sqrt($t);
    $mean = calcMean($arr);
    $var = $mean + $z * $sigma;
    return $var; //$var is a percentage of losing the sum of the portfolio
}

function getArchSigma($arr, $whichDay)
{
    $arr_var = getArchSigmaSquare($arr);
    $sigma = sqrt($arr_var[$whichDay]);
    return $sigma;
}
```

ALGOS FOR MONTE CARLO SIMULATIONS

Monte Carlo simulations are useful for forecasting with uncertain variables. The values of these uncertain variables may be simulated with random numbers within a range.

We discuss a simple algo to conducting Monte Carlo simulations. In the following code, **runMCS()** starts with two random variables. Based on the random variables, two expected future returns are computed. With about 3,000 trials, the two returns are compared for each trial. At the end, the percentage of one return better than the other is calculated and returned by the function.

```
function runMCS($arra, $arrb){
    $count = 0;
    $tot = 3000;
    $beta_a=getBetaZ($arraa[0]);
    $exp_a=$arra[1];
    $ret_a=getRetZ($arra[2]);
    $beta_b=getBetaZ($arrb[0]);
    $exp_b=$arrb[1];
    $ret_b=getRetZ($arrb[2]);

for($i=0; $i<$tot; $i++){
    $randa = getRand();
    $fra = calcFutureRate($ret_a, $beta_a, $randa);
    $randb = getRand();
    $frb = calcFutureRate($ret_b, $beta_b, $randb);
    if($fra > $frb){
        $count++;
    }
} //end of for
    $pct = 100*$count/$tot;
    return round($pct,2)."%";
}
function calcFutureRate($ret, $beta, $rand){
    $fr = $ret + $beta * $rand;
    return $fr;
}
function getRand(){
```

```
//$rand is between 0 and 100%
    $rand = rand(-100,100);
    return $rand/100;
}
```

ALGOS FOR AN EFFICIENT PORTFOLIO FRONTIER

Figure 14.2 shows an efficient portfolio frontier with a market portfolio that has the largest Sharpe ratio of the frontier. The following code comes from the library of SAPE algos. Each function has its own purpose:

- **calcPortfolioRisk()** computes the volatility of the portfolio with two assets.
- **getPortfolioAvg()** computes the average returns of the portfolio.
- **getAvgAbdVarCovMatrix()** computes the portfolio return and covariance of assets.
- **getCovMx()** and **getCov()** compute covariance of assets.
- **calcVar()** computes the variance of an asset.
- **getRetByPrice()** compute an array of log returns from an array of prices.

```
function calcPortfolioRisk($p, $var1, $var2, $cov)
{
    $sp1 = $p*$p*$var1;
    $sp2 = (1-$p)*(1-$p)*$var2;
    $sp3 = 2*$p*(1-$p)*$cov;
    $sp = $sp1 + $sp2 + $sp3;
    return sqrt($sp);
}
function getPortfolioAvg($arr_avg, $arr_x){
    //$arr_x is the envelope proportions;
    //$arr_x = getEfficientPortfolioVectorX($arr_data);
    //arr_avg is the average return for each assets of the portfolio
    //$arr_avg = $arr_data[0];
    $size = sizeof($arr_x);
    $avg_p = 0;
    for($i=0; $i<$size; $i++)
    {
        $avg_p = $avg_p + $arr_x[$i] * $arr_avg[$i];
    }
    return $avg_p;
}

function getAvgAndVarCovMatrix($arrTicks){
    //number of assets
    $sizeAssets = sizeof($arrTicks);
    $arr_mx = array();
    $arr_avg = array();
    //portfolio x for the assets: mean return and var
    for($i=0; $i<$sizeAssets; $i++)
    {
```

```
        //get return for each asset
        $tick = $arrTicks[$i];
        $arr_price = getPriceByTick($tick);
        //get return from price for recent 3 month
        $arr_ret = getRetByPrice($arr_price);
        //get avg for the return arr
        $avg = calcMean($arr_ret);
        //get variance of an asset
        $var = calcVar($arr_ret, $avg);
        $arr_avg[$i] = $avg;
        $arr_mx[$i][$i] = $var;
        //get covariance of an asset with the rest of the assets
        $arr_mx = getCovMx($arr_mx, $arr_ret, $avg, $arrTicks, $i);
    }
    $arr_assets_data = array();
    $arr_assets_data[0] = $arr_avg;
    $arr_assets_data[1] = $arr_mx;
    return $arr_assets_data;
}

function getCovMx($arr_mx, $arr_ret_i, $avg_i, $arrTicks, $i)
{
    $size = sizeof($arrTicks);
    for($j=$i+1; $j<$size; $j++){
        //get return for each asset
        $tick = $arrTicks[$j];
        $arr_price = getPriceByTick($tick);
        //get return from price for recent 3 month
        $arr_ret_j = getRetByPrice($arr_price);
        //get avg for the return arr
        $avg_j = calcMean($arr_ret);
        $cov = getCov($arr_ret_i, $avg_i, $arr_ret_j, $avg_j);
        $arr_mx[$i][$j] = $cov;
    }
    return $arr_mx;
}

function calcVar($arr, $avg)
{
    $var = 0;
    $n = sizeof($arr);
    $tot = 0;
    for($i=0; $i<$n; $i++)
    {
        $tot= $tot + ($arr[$i]-$avg)*($arr[$i]-$avg);
    }
    $var = $tot/$n;
    return $var;
}

function getCov($arr1, $avg1, $arr2, $avg2){
    $n = sizeof($arr1);
    $tot = 0;
    for($i=0; $i<$n; $i++)
    {
        $tot= $tot + ($arr1[$i]-$avg1)*($arr2[$i]-$avg2);
    }
    $cov = $tot/$n;
    return $cov;
}

function getRetByPrice($arr){
    $len = count($arr);
    for ($i=0; $i<$len; $i++){
```

```
        if($arr[$i+1]!=0){
            $ret = $arr[$i]/$arr[$i+1];
            $arr1[$i] = log($ret);
        }
    }
    $len--;
    unset($arr1[$len]);
    return $arr1;
}
```

ALGOS FOR SIGNAL DETECTION THEORY

In Chapter 8, we discussed the risk propensity surface with respect to signal detection theory (SDT). We also discussed that SDT may assess a portfolio manager's performance in detail, as opposed to a single Sharpe ratio. Can we develop some basic SDT algos? Here are some code snippets to get us started.

calcHit() computes number of hits for the hit rate (probability of responding signal to signal trials) with an array of data input. **calcFA()** computes number of false alarms for the false alarm rate (probability of responding signal to noise trials) with the array input. **calcYesRatio()** calls **calcHit()** and **calcFA()**, takes Z scores from the two probabilities, and then returns the difference between the two Z scores, which is the d' value of the SDT. d' measures the sensitivity of operators' responses to risk stimuli.

```
function calcHit($arr){
    $len = count($arr);
    $h = 0;

    for($i=0; $i<$len; $i++){
        if($arr[$i]>$arr[$len-1]) $h++;
    }
    return $h;
}
//FA: expect up (response), but actual price went down (stimulus)
function calcFA($arr){
    $len = count($arr);
    $f = 0;
    for($i=0; $i<$len; $i++){
        if($arr[$i]<$arr[$len-1]) $f++;
    }
    return $f;
}
function calcYesRatio($arr){
    $h = calcHit($arr);
    $f = calcFA($arr);
    $de = 2*($h+$f); //expectation ratio for up and down: 50%
    $hp = 0;
    $fp = 0;
    if($de>0){
        $hp = $h/$de;
        $fp = $f/$de;
    }
```

```
$z_h = inverse_ncdf($hp);
$z_f = inverse_ncdf($fp);
$yesratio = $z_h - $z_f;
return $yesratio;
}
```

These computer algos may get us started in assessing the performance of portfolio managers from two aspects, that is, sensitivity and bias. A sample Web app has used these algos to compare fund performances with the SDT measures. Figure 14.7 shows that the performances of two

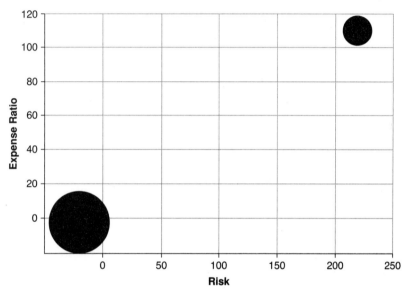

Mouse over balloon for detail; balloon size represents return; ticker with negative return does not display

Table Compare with YesWici Indicator Scores

Ticker	Fund Name	Quote	Beta_z	Ret_z	Exp_z	**dprime**	bias_c
CGMFX	CGM FOCUS FUND		−0.19	3.14	−0.03	3.33	−1.48
BFOCX	BERSHIRE FOCUS FUND		2.19	1.49	1.09	−0.69	−1.84

YesWici is an investing utility based on a pending patent.

FIGURE 14.7 Portfolio Managers' Performances in SDT's d' and β
Source: All rights reserved © YesWici.com.

California mutual funds are compared in sensitivity d' (as **dprime**) and bias (as **bias_c**). Both the chart and the table in Figure 14.7 are produced automatically by the computer algos of Yeswici.com.

CONCLUSION

In this chapter, we discussed how to create basic computer algos for high-frequency trading on derivatives such as pricing options. In addition, we discussed the basic computer algos that implemented the formulas for Sharpe ratio, net present value, Monte Carlo simulation, and signal detection theory.

Notes

CHAPTER 1 HIGH-FREQUENCY TRADING AND EXISTING REVENUE MODELS

1. A graduate of Johns Hopkins University.

CHAPTER 3 HISTORY AND FUTURE OF HIGH-FREQUENCY TRADING WITH INVESTMENT MANAGEMENT

1. By a graduate student of Johns Hopkins University; used with permission.

CHAPTER 4 BEHAVIORAL ECONOMICS MODELS ON LOSS AVERSION

1. We use "investors" and "consumers" interchangeably in this chapter, as the finding is applicable to investment management.
2. A fund name is the brand of the fund.

CHAPTER 5 LOSS AVERSION IN OPTION PRICING: INTEGRATING TWO NOBEL MODELS

1. See Part IV for the details on the concept of options and the types of options.

CHAPTER 7 MULTINOMIAL MODELS FOR EQUITY RETURNS

1. Multinomial modeling is a different technique from the multinomial logit model in the sense that the former deals with laboratory data collected from human subjects to investigate judgment formation for individual decision making, classified as psychological modeling. The multinomal logit model deals mostly with survey or simulation data, classified as econometric modeling.

2. In Analysis 1, estimates using Equation 7.6 are not correlated with S&P 500 returns; however, estimates using Equation 7.7 do. This suggests that Equation 7.7 provides a better approximation of the implicit component of consumer confidence. If the data is a percentage rather than an index, no approximations are needed.

3. Without removing the January data, the Pearson correlation is not significant; $r = 0.13$, $n = 200$, $p = 0.067$.

4. There was no significant correlation between the ICC ratio estimated with Equation 7.6 and the MARR. The reason is that there is a lack of approximation to $(N - Vn)$ with $(100 - Vn)$ in Equation 7.6.

5. The reference value for estimating the Conference Board ICC ratio is 110. This is because the average of the Conference Board index between 1985 and 2002 (102.91) is approximately 10 points greater than that of the Michigan index (92.41).

6. Since the χ^2 is smaller than the degrees of freedom (4), this indicates a good fit.

CHAPTER 8 MORE MULTINOMIAL MODELS AND SIGNAL DETECTION MODELS FOR RISK PROPENSITY

1. I would like to thank Dr. Fred van Raaij's valuable comments on an earlier version of this section.

2. A logarithmic function that creates a diminishing marginal utility is assumed between utility and wealth by Bernouli (1738). The implicit utility function still hypothesizes a logarithmic relationship between the conscious component of utility (preference) and gains of wealth. Therefore, the Bernouli's *utility* is interpreted as a proportion of the choice process, namely, the rational (conscious) component of the

preference. It is argued that implicit processes operate under different rules in decision and choice processes.

3. For $H \geq FA$, $A' = 0.5 + [(H - FA)(1 + H - FA)]/[4H(1 - FA)]H < FA$, $A' = 0.5 - [(FA - H)(1 + FA - H)]/[4FA(1 - H)]$

   For $H \geq FA$, $B'' = [H(1 - H) - FA(1 - FA)]/[H(1 - H)+FA(1 - FA)]H < FA$, $B'' = [FA(1 - FA) - H(1 - H)]/[FA(1 - FA)+H(1 - H)]$

CHAPTER 11 SAPE FOR PORTFOLIO MANAGEMENT—EFFECTIVENESS AND STRATEGIES

1. This relates to the new HIT economy. As part of the 2010 federal budget, $18 billion to $27 billion from the federal government may be the startup fund for the HIT economy. The sustainability of the HIT economy may come from proper investment banking and portfolio management in life sciences.

2. Employment contracts that forbid employees to compete with the employer within a fixed period of time after the end of the employment relationship.

CHAPTER 12 DERIVATIVES

1. In architecture, mezzanine refers to an intermediate floor between the main floors.

2. A measure of an asset's value based on the present spot price of the asset.

3. Swaps contracts are especially helpful in hedging financial institutions' risk exposure. For interest rate swaps, the risk of a floating rate may be converted to a stable fixed rate. In the case of CDSs, the risk of credit defaults is hedged or insured with the CDS contract.

4. LIBOR stands for London Interbank Offered Rate.

CHAPTER 13 TECHNOLOGY INFRASTRUCTURE FOR CREATING COMPUTER ALGOS

1. PHP initially stood for personal home page. Now it means Hypertext Preprocessor.

2. Linux, Apache, MySQl, PHP.
3. Windows, Apache, MySQL, PHP.

CHAPTER 14 CREATING COMPUTER ALGOS FOR HIGH-FREQUENCY TRADING

1. pow is a PHP function for exponential expression.

References

Aaker, D. 1996. *Building strong brands*. New York: Free Press.

Adobe. 2009. LiveCycle Data Services. http://www.adobe.com/devnet/livecycle/articles/lcdses2v3_videos/lcds3_demo.html.

Aldridge, I. 2009. Quant hedge funds poised to benefit from high-frequency trading. FIN Alternatives, http://www.finalternatives.com/node/10055.

Ambler, T. 2001. What does marketing success look like? *Marketing Management* 10 (1): 12–19.

Ambler, T., C.B. Bhattacharya, J. Edell, K.L. Keller, K. Lemon, and V. Mittal. 2002. Relating brand and customer perspectives on marketing management. *Journal of Service Research* 5 (1): 13–26.

Ariely, D., G. Loewenstein, and D. Prelec. 2003. Coherent arbitrariness: Stable demand curves without stable preferences. *Quarterly Journal of Economics* 118 (1): 73–105.

Arkes, H.R. 1991. Costs and benefits of judgment errors: Implications for debiasing. *Psychological Bulletin* 110 (3): 486–498.

Ashok, K., W.R. Dillon, and S. Yuan. 2002. Extending discrete choice models to incorporate attitudinal and other latent variables. *Journal of Marketing Research* 39 (1): 31–46.

Atkinson, R., R. Herrnstein, G. Lindzey, and D. Luce. 1988. *Stevens' handbook of experimental psychology*. 2nd ed. New York: John Wiley & Sons.

Bagozzi, R. 1982. A field investigation of causal relations among cognitions, affect, intention, and behavior. *Journal of Marketing Research* 19: 562–584.

Barberis, N., A. Shleifer, and R. Vishny. 1998. A model of investor sentiment. *Journal of Financial Economics* 49: 307–343.

Barberis, N., and R. Thaler. 2001. A survey of behavioral finance. Working paper.

Barberis, N., and W. Xiong. 2009. What drives the disposition effect? An analysis of a long-standing preference-based explanation. *Journal of Finance* 64: 751–784.

Bargh, J. 2002. Losing consciousness: Automatic influences on consumer judgment, behavior and motivation. *Journal of Consumer Research* 29: 280–285.

Bargh, J.A., and T.L. Chartrand. 1999. The unbearable automaticity of being. *American Psychologist* 54: 462–479.

Bargh, J.A., and M. Ferguson. 2000. Beyond behaviorism: On the automaticity of higher mental processes. *Psychological Bulletin* 126 (6): 925–945.

Bass, F. 1969. A new product growth model for consumer durables. *Journal of Marketing Research* 15 (5): 215–227.

Bass, F. 1998. Multinomial processing tree models and psychological assessment. *Psychological Assessment* 10 (4): 331–344.

Bass, F. 2004. The Bass model: A commentary. *Management Science* 50 (12): 1833–1840.

Batchelder, W.H. 1998. Multinomial processing tree models and psychological assessment. *Psychological Assessment* 10: 331–344.

Batchelder, W.H., and D.M. Riefer. 1990. Multinomial processing model of source monitoring. *Psychological Review* 97, 318–339.

Bell, D., and P. Fishburn. 2000. Utility functions for wealth. *Journal of Risk and Uncertainty* 20: 5–44.

Ben-Akiva, M., and S. Lerman. 1985. *Discrete choice analysis.* Cambridge: MIT Press.

Bernouli, D. 1738. Translated by L. Sommer, 1954, as exposition of a new theory on the measurement of risk. *Econometrica* 22: 23–36.

Bettman, J.R. 1979. *An information processing theory of consumer choice.* Reading, MA: Addison-Wesley.

Black, F., E. Derman, and Bill Toy. 1991. A one-factor model of interest rates and its application to treasury bond options. *Financial Analysts Journal* 46 (1): 33–39.

Black, F., and M. Scholes. 1973. The pricing of options and corporate liabilities. *Journal of Political Economy* 81 (3): 637–654.

Block, M.P., and B.G. Vanden Bergh. 1985. Can you sell subliminal messages to consumers? *Journal of Advertising* 14 (3): 59–62.

Bolton, R., K. Lemon, and M. Bramlett. Modeling repeat purchase decision: How customers' experiences over time influence their renewal of service contracts, unpublished manuscript.

Bornstein, R. 1989. Exposure and affect: Overview and meta-analysis of research, 1968–1987. *Psychological Bulletin* 106: 265–289.

Buchner, A., E. Erdfelder, and P.B. Vaterrodt. 1995. Toward unbiased measurement of conscious and unconscious memory processes within the process dissociation framework. *Journal of Experimental Psychology: General* 2: 137–160.

Burnkrant, R., and T. Page. 1982. An examination of the convergent, discriminant, and predictive validity of Fishbein's behavioral intention model. *Journal of Marketing Research* XIX: 550–561.

Casey, J. 1995. Predicting buyer-seller pricing disparities. *Management Science* 41 (6): 979–999.

Chapman, G.B., and E.J. Johnson. 1999. Anchoring, activation, and the construction of value. *Organizational Behavior and Human Decision Processes* 79 (2): 115–153.

Chapman, G.B., and E.J. Johnson. 2002. Incorporating the irrelevant: Anchors in judgments of belief and value. In *Heuristics and biases: The psychology of intuitive judgment*, ed. Thomas Gilovich, Dale Griffin, and Daniel Kahneman, 120–138. Cambridge University Press.

Chenev, A., and G.S. Carpenter. 2001. The role of market efficiency intuitions in consumer choice: A case of compensatory inferences. *Journal of Marketing Research* 38 (3): 349–361.

Cohen, J. 1988. *Statistical power analysis for the behavioral sciences* (2nd ed.). Hillsdale, NJ: Erlbaum.

Cradit, J., A. Tashchian, and C. Hofacker. 1994. Signal detection theory and single observation designs. *Journal of Marketing Research* 31: 117–127.

Daniel, K., D. Hirshleifer, and A. Subrahmanyam. 1998. Investor psychology and security market under- and overreactions. *Journal of Finance* 53 (5): 1839–1886.

Daniel, K., and S. Titman. 1997. Evidence on the characteristics of cross-sectional variation in stock returns. *Journal of Finance* 52 (1): 1–33.

De Bondt, W., and R. Thaler. 1985. Does the stock market overreact? *Journal of Finance* 40: 793–807.

DeCarlo. 2002. Signal detection theory with finite mixture distributions: Theoretical developments with applications to recognition memory. *Psychological Review* 109: 710–721.

Dhar, R., and I. Simonson. 2003. The effect of forced choice on choice. *Journal of Marketing Research* 40: 146–160.

Dhar, R., and K. Wertenbroch. 2000. Consumer choice between hedonic and utilitarian goods. *Journal of Marketing Research* 37 (1): 60–71.

Engle, R. 1982. Autoregressive conditional heteroskedasticity with estimates of the variance of U.K. inflation. *Econometrica* 50: 987–1008.

Epley, N., and T. Gilovich. 2001. Putting adjustment back in the anchoring and adjustment heuristic. *Psychological Science* 12 (5): 391–396.

Fama, E.F. 1970. Efficient capital markets: A review of theory and empirical work. *Journal of Finance* 25 (2): 383–417.

Fama, E.F., and K. French. 1992. The cross-section of expected stock returns. *Journal of Finance* 47: 427–465.

Fazio, R.H., D.M. Sanbonmatsu, M.C. Powell, and F.R. Kardes. 1986. On the automatic activation of attitudes. *Journal of Personality and Social Psychology* 50: 229–238.

Fiedler, K., S. Nickel, and T. Muehlfriedel. 2001. Is mood congruency an effect of genuine memory or response bias? *Journal of Experimental Social Psychology* 37: 201–214.

Fitzsimons, G.J., and B. Shiv. 2001. Nonconscious and contaminative effects of hypothetical questions on subsequent decision making. *Journal of Consumer Research* 28: 224–238.

French, C.W. 2003. The Treynor capital asset pricing model. *Journal of Investment Management* 1 (2): 60–72.

Garner, A. 2002. Consumer confidence after September 11. *Economic Review of Federal Reserve Bank of Kansas City* (second quarter): 5–25.

Goetzmann, W. 1996. *An Introduction to Investment Theory.* Internet book, http://viking.som.yale.edu/will/web_pages/will/finman540/classnotes/class1.html.

Graf P., and D. Schacter. 1985. Implicit and explicit memory for new associations in normal and amnesic subjects. *Journal of Experimental Psychology: Learning, Memory, and Cognition* 11: 501–518.

Graves, P.M., and K.F. Thompson. 1970. Habituation: A dual process theory. *Psychological Review* 77: 419–450.

Green, D.M., and J.A. Swets. 1966. *Signal detection theory and psychophysics.* New York: John Wiley.

Greenwald, A., and M.R. Banaji. 1995. Implicit social cognition: Attitudes, self-esteem, and stereotypes. *Psychological Review* 102: 4–27.

Greenwald, A.G., M. Banaji, L. Rudman, S. Farnham, B. Nosek, and D. Mellot. 2002. A unified theory of implicit attitudes, stereotypes, self-esteem, and self-concept. *Psychological Review* 109 (1): 3–25.

Greenwald, A.G., D.E. McGhee, and J.K.L. Schwartz. 1998. Measuring individual differences in implicit cognition: The implicit association test. *Journal of Personality and Social Psychology* 74: 1464–1480.

Grewal, D., and H. Marmorstein. 1994. Market price variation, perceived price variation, and consumer's price search decisions for durable goods. *Journal of Consumer Research* 21 (3): 453–460.

Grier, J. 1971. Nonparametric indexes for sensitivity and bias: Computing formulas, *Psychological Bulletin* 15 (6): 424–429.

Groves, P.M., and R.F. Thompson. 1970. Habituation: A dual process theory. *Psychological Review* 77: 419–450.

Guadagni, P.M., and J.D.C. Little. 1983. A logit model brand choice calibrated on scanner data. *Marketing Science* 2: 203–238.

Gupta, S., D. Lehmann, and J. Stuart. 2004. Valuing Customers. *Journal of Marketing Research* 41 (1): 7–18.

Hanselman, D., and B. Littlefield. 2001. Mastering MATLAB 6. Upper Saddle River, NJ: Prentice Hall.

Hardie, B., E. Johnson, and P. Fader. 1993. Modeling loss aversion and reference dependence effects on brand choice. *Marketing Science* 12 (4): 378–394.

Hendershott, T., C.M. Jones, and A.J. Menkveld. In press. Does algorithmic trading improve liquidity? *Journal of Finance* (forthcoming).

Howard, J., and J.N. Sheth. 1969. *The theory of buyer behavior.* New York: John Wiley & Sons.

Hsee, C.K., G.F. Loewenstein, S. Blount, and M.H. Bazerman. 1999. Preference reversals between joint and separate evaluations of options: A review and theoretical analysis. *Psychological Bulletin* 125 (5): 576–590.

Hu, X. 1991. Statistical inference program for *multinomial* binary tree *models* (Version 1.0) [Computer program], University of California, Irvine, CA, USA.

Huber, J., J. Payne, and C. Puto. 1982. Adding asymmetrically dominated alternatives: Violations of regularity and the similarity hypothesis. *Journal of Consumer Research* 9: 90–98.

Hull, J. 2008. *Options, futures, and other derivatives.* 7th edition. Prentice Hall.

Jacoby, J., G.V. Johar, and M. Morrin. 1998. Consumer research: A quadrennium. *Annual Review of Psychology* 49: 319–344.

Jacoby, L.L. 1991. A process dissociation framework: Separating automatic from intentional uses of memory. *Journal of Memory and Language* 30: 513–541.

Jacoby, L.L. 1998. Invariance in automatic influences of memory: Toward a user's guide for the process-dissociation procedure. *Journal of Experimental Psychology: Learning, Memory, and Cognition* 24: 3–26.

Janiszewski, C., and T. Meyvis. 2001. Effects of brand logo complexity, repetition, and spacing on processing fluency and judgment. *Journal of Consumer Research* 28: 18–32.

Jöreskog, K.G. 1973. A general method for estimating a linear structural equation system. In *Structural equation models in the social sciences,* ed. Arthur S. Goldberger and Otis Dudley Duncan. New York: Seminar Press.

Kahneman, D., J.L. Knetsch, and R. Thaler. 1991 The endowment effect, loss aversion, and status quo bias. *Journal of Economic Perspectives* 5: 193–206.

Kahneman, D., and A. Tversky. 1979. Prospect theory. *Econometrica* 47: 263–292.

Kahneman, D., and A. Tversky. 2000. *Choices, values, and frames.* New York: Cambridge University Press.

Kamen, J., and R. Toman. 1970. Psychophysics of prices. *Journal of Marketing Research* 7: 27–35.

Kanninen, B. 2002. Optimal design for multinomial choice experiments. *Journal of Marketing Research* 39 (2): 214–227.

Katona, G. 1975. *Psychological economics.* New York: Elsevier.

Keller, K. 2002. *Strategic brand management.* Upper Saddle River, NJ: Prentice Hall.

Kelley, H.H. 1973. The processes of causal attribution. *American Psychologist* 28: 107–128.

Keown, A.J., J.D. Martin, W. Petty, and D.F. Scott Jr. 2003. *Financial management,* 9th ed. Upper Saddle River, NJ: Prentice Hall.

Kivetz, R., and I. Simonson. 2002. Earning the right to indulge: Effort as a determinant of consumer preferences toward frequency program rewards. *Journal of Marketing Research* 39 (2): 155–170.

Kruger, J., and D. Dunning. 1999. Unskilled and unaware of it: How difficulties in recognizing one's own incompetence lead to inflated self-assessments. *Journal of Personality and Social Psychology* 77: 1121–1134.

Lazarus, R. 1991. Cognition and motivation in emotion. *American Psychologist* 46 (4): 352–367.

Lee, A. 2002. Effects of implicit memory on memory-based versus stimulus-based brand choice. *Journal of Marketing Research* 39: 440–456.

Lee, A., and A. Labroo. 2004. The effects of conceptual and perceptual fluency on brand evaluation. *Journal of Marketing Research* XLI: 151–165.

Lei, V., C. Noussair, and C. Plott. 2001. Nonspeculative bubbles in experimental asset markets: Lack of common knowledge of rationality vs. actual irrationality. *Econometrica* 69: 831–859.

Leibenluft, J. 2008. $596 trillion! http://www.slate.com/id/2202263. Slate.com.

Leising, M., and T. Seeley. May 13, 2009. Geithner urges electronic OTC derivatives trading. Bloomberg news, http://www.bloomberg.com/apps/news?pid=20601009&sid=a1Yy1SLxmCwo.

Loewenstein, G. 2001. The creative destruction of decision research. *Journal of Consumer Research* 28 (3): 499–505.

Loewenstein, G., E. Weber, C. Hsee, and N. Welch. 2001. Risk as feelings. *Psychological Bulletin* 127 (2): 267–286.

Markowitz, H.M. 1952. Portfolio selection. *Journal of Finance* 7 (1): 77–91.

McFadden, D. 1999. Rationality for economists? *Journal of Risk and Uncertainty* 19: 73–105.

Mellers, B. 2000. Choice and the relative pleasure of consequences. *Psychological Bulletin* 126 (6): 910–924.

Monroe, K. 1971. Psychophysics of pricing: A reappraisal. *Journal of Marketing Research* 8 (2): 248–250.

Monroe, K. 2003. *Pricing: Making profitable decisions*. 3rd ed. New York: McGraw-Hill.

Morrin, M., J. Jacoby, G. Venkataramani Johar, H. Xin, and D. Mazursky. 2002. Taking stock of stockbrokers: Exploring momentum versus contrarian investor strategies and profiles. *Journal of Consumer Research* 29: 188–199.

Mussweiler, T., and F. Strack. 2001. The semantics of anchoring. *Organizational Behavior and Human Decision Processes* 86: 234–255.

NASDAQ. 2009. Flash Functionalities. http://www.nasdaqtrader.com/content/ProductsServices/Trading/Flash_factsheet.pdf.

Nijkamp, J., H.J. Gianotten, and W.F. van Raaij. 2002. The structure of consumer confidence and real value added growth in retailing in the Netherlands. *The International Review of Retail, Distribution and Consumer Research*.

Nunes, J.C., and P. Boatwright. 2004. Incidental prices and their effect on willingness to pay. *Journal of Marketing Research* 41 (1): 457–466.

Nunes, J., and C.W. Park. 2003. Incommensurate resources: Not just more of the same. *Journal of Marketing Research* 40: 26–38.

O'Donoghue, T., and T. Banin. In press. Self awareness and self control. In *Now or later: Economic and psychological perspectives on intertemporal choice*, ed. R. Baumeister, G. Loewenstein, and D. Read. New York: Russell Sage Foundation Press.

Papoulis, A. 1984. *Probability, random variables, and stochastic processes*. 2nd ed. New York: McGraw-Hill.

Patterson, S., and G. Rogow. 2009. What's behind high-frequency trading. *Wall Street Journal* (August 1), http://online.wsj.com/article/SB124908601669298293.html.

Pratkanis, A.R., and A.G. Greenwald. 1988. Recent perspectives on unconscious processing: Still no marketing applications. *Psychology & Marketing* 5 (4): 337–353.

Pronin, E., J. Kruger, K. Savitsky, and L. Ross. 2001. You don't know me, but I know you: The illusion of asymmetric insight. *Journal of Personality and Social Psychology* 81: 639–656.

Rabin, M. 1998. Psychology and economics. *Journal of Economic Literature* 36: 11–46.

Rayport, J., and B. Jaworski. 2003. *e-Commerce strategies*. 2nd ed. New York: McGraw-Hill/Irwin.

Riefer, D.M., and W.H. Batchelder. 1988. Multinomial modeling and the measurement of cognitive processes. *Psychological Review* 3: 318–339.

Roediger, H.L., III. 1990. Implicit memory: Retention without remembering. *American Psychologist* 45: 1043–1056.

Rust, R., K.N. Lemon, and D. Narayandas. 2005. Customer equity management. Upper Saddle River, NJ: Prentice Hall.

Rust, R.T., K.N. Lemon, and V.A. Zeithaml. 2004. Return on marketing: Using customer equity to focus marketing strategy. *Journal of Marketing* 68: 109–127.

Rust, R., C. Moorman, and P.R. Dickson. 2002. Getting return on quality: Revenue expansion, cost reduction, or both. *Journal of Marketing* 66: 7–24.

Samuelson, P.W., and R. Zeckhauser. 1988. Status quo bias in decision making. *Journal of Risk and Uncertainty* 1: 7–59.

Saunders, A., and M. Cornett. 2008. *Financial institutions management: A risk management approach*. New York: McGraw-Hill/Irwin.

Schacter, D.L. 1987. Implicit memory: History and current status. *Journal of Experimental Psychology: Learning, Memory, and Cognition* 13: 501–518.

Schacter, D.L., and R. Badgaiyan. 2001. Neuroimaging of priming: New perspectives on implicit explicit memory. *Current Directions of Psychological Science* 10 (1): 1–4.

Schiffman, L., and L. Kanuk. 2001. *Consumer Behavior*. Upper Saddle River, NJ: Prentice Hall.

Shankar, V., and R.N. Bolton. 2004. An empirical analysis of determinants of retailer pricing strategy. *Marketing Science* 23 (1): 28–49.

Sharpe, W. 1992. Asset allocation: Management style and performance measurement. *Journal of Portfolio Management* (Winter): 7–19.

Sharpe, W. 2000. *Portfolio theory and capital markets.* New York: McGraw-Hill.

Sharpe, W., G.J. Alexander, and J.V. Bailey. 1999. *Investments.* Upper Saddle River, NJ: Prentice Hall.

Sharpe, W.F. 1963. A simplified model of portfolio analysis. *Management Science* 9: 277–293.

Sharpe, W.F. 1964. Capital asset prices: A theory of market equilibrium under conditions of risk. *Journal of Finance* 19 (3): 425–442.

Shiller, R. 2000a. *Irrational exuberance.* Princeton, NJ: Princeton University Press.

Shiller, R. 2000b. Measuring bubble expectations and investor confidence. *Journal of Psychology and Financial Markets* 1 (1): 49–60.

Shiv, B., and A. Fedorikhin. 1999. Heart and mind in conflict: The interplay of affect and cognition in consumer decision making. *Journal of Consumer Research* 26 (December): 278–292.

Simon, H. 1955. A behavioral model of rational choice. *Quarterly Journal of Economics* 69: 99–118.

Simonson, I. 1989. Choice based on reasons: The case of attraction and compromise effects. *Journal of Consumer Research* 16: 158–174.

Simonson, I., Z. Carmon, R. Dhar, A. Drolet, and S.M. Nowlis. 2001. Consumer research: In search of identity. *Annual Review of Psychology* 52: 249–275.

Simonson, I., and A. Drolet. 2004. Anchoring effects on consumers' willingness-to-pay and willingness-to-accept. *Journal of Consumer Research* 31 (4): 681–690.

Simonson, I., T. Kramer, and M.J Young. 2004. Effect propensity. *Organizational Behavior and Human Decision Processes* 95 (2): 156–174.

Snodgrass and Corwin. 1988. Perceptual identification thresholds for 150 fragmented pictures from the Snodgrass and Vanderwart picture set. *Perceptual and Motor Skills* 67: 3–36.

Sommerville, I. 1996. *Software engineering.* 5th ed. Harlow, England: Addison-Wesley.

Spicer, J., and J. Kwan. 2009. High-frequency trading surges across the globe. Reuters, http://www.reuters.com/article/idUSTRE5B110520091202.

Srivastava, R.K., T.A. Shervani, and L. Fahey. 1999. Marketing, business processes, and shareholder value: An organizationally embedded view of marketing activities and the discipline of marketing. *Journal of Marketing* 63: 168–180.

Srull, T.K., and R. Wyer. 1989. *Memory and cognition in its social context.* Hillsdale, NJ: Erlbaum.

Stevens, S.S. 1961. To honor Fechner and repeal his law. *Science* 133: 80–86.

Swensen, D. 2000. *Pioneering portfolio management: An unconventional approach to institutional investment.* New York: Free Press.

Swensen, D. 2005. *Unconventional success: A fundamental approach to personal investment.* New York: Free Press.

Tabachinick, B., and L. Fidell. 1996. *Using multivariate statistics.* 3rd ed. Harper-Collins College Publishers.

Tashchian, A., D. White, and S. Pak. 1988. Signal detection analysis and advertising recognition: An introduction to measurement and interpretation issues. *Journal of Marketing Research* 25: 397–404.

Thaler, R. 1980. Toward a positive theory of consumer choice. *Journal of Economic Behavior and Organization* 1: 39–60.

Thaler, R. 1985. Mental accounting and consumer choice. *Marketing Science* 4 (3): 199–214.

Thaler, R. 1991a. Mental accounting matters. *Journal of Behavioral Decision Making* 12: 183–206.

Thaler, R. 1991b. *The winner's curse: Paradoxes and anomalies of economic life.* Princeton, NJ: Princeton University Press.

Thaler, R.H. 1993. Advances in behavioral finance: Introduction. *Advances in Behavioral Finance,* xv–xxi. New York: Russell Sage Foundation.

Thaler, R. 1999. The end of behavioral finance. *Financial Analysts Journal* (November): 12–17.

Tversky, A., and D. Kahneman. 1974. Judgment under uncertainty: Heuristics and bias. *Science* 185: 1124–1130.

Tversky, A., and D. Kahneman. 1992. Advances in prospect theory: Cumulative representations of uncertainty. *Journal of Risk and Uncertainty* 5: 297–323.

van Heerde, H., S. Gupta, and D.R. Wittink. 2003. Is 75% of the sales promotion bump due to brand switching? No, only 33% is. *Journal of Marketing Research* XL (November): 481–491.

van Raaij, F. 1984. Micro and macro economic psychology. *Journal of Economic Psychology* 5 (4): 385–401.

van Raaij, W.F. 1989. How consumers react to advertising. *International Journal of Advertising* 8: 261–273.

van Raaij, W.F., and H.J. Gianotten. 1990. Consumer confidence, expenditure, saving, and credit. *Journal of Economic Psychology* 11 (2): 269–290.

von Neumann, J., and O. Morgenstern. 1944. *Theory and games and economic behavior.* Princeton, NJ: Princeton University Press.

Wyer, R.S., Jr., and T.K. Srull. 1986. Human cognition in its social context. *Psychological Review* 93 (July): 322–359.

Xu, M., and F. Bellezza. 2001. A comparison of the multimemory and detection theories of know and remember recognition judgments. *Journal of Experimental Psychology: Learning, Memory, and Cognition* 27: 1197–1210.

Ye, G. 2003. Formulas of decision service and the process of using the formulas. Patent of United States Patent and Trademark Office (No. 09/852,337).

Ye, G. 2005. The locus effect on inertia equity. *Journal of Product and Brand Management* 14 (3): 206–210.

Ye, G.W. 2000. Modeling the unconscious components of marketing communication. Dissertation, Tilburg University, The Netherlands.

Ye, G.W. 2002. Formulas of intelligent decision service and the process of using the computerized formulas. United States Patent and Trademark Office, publication reference number 30280172, approved December 2002.

Ye, G., and W.F. van Raaij. 1997. What inhibits the mere-exposure effect: Recollection or familiarity? *Journal of Economic Psychology* 18: 629–648.

Ye, G., and W.F. van Raaij. 2002. A multinomial decision process model with implicit and affective components. Unpublished manuscript.

Ye, G.W., and W.F. van Raaij. 2003. Feeling bias as status quo: A signal detection analysis. Unpublished manuscript.

Ye, G.W., and W.F. van Raaij. 2005. Modeling preference formation: A multinomial decision process model. Unpublished manuscript.

Yonelinas, A.P. 1994. Receiver-operating characteristics in recognition memory: Evidence for a dual-process model. *Journal of Experimental Psychology: Learning, Memory, and Cognition* 20: 1341–1354.

Yonelinas, A.P. 1999. The contribution of recollection and familiarity to recognition and source-memory judgments: A formal dual-process model and an analysis of receiver operating characteristics. *Journal of Experimental Psychology: Learning, Memory, & Cognition* 25: 1415–1434.

Zajonc, R.B. 1968. Attitudinal effects of mere exposure. *Journal of Personality and Social Psychology* Monograph Supplement 9 (2, Pt. 2): 1–27.

Zajonc, R.B., and H. Markus. 1982. Affective and cognitive factors in preference. *Journal of Consumer Research* 9: 123–131.

About the Author

D r. Gewei Ye is the president of Yeswici.com, a research platform for investment modeling and computing. He teaches graduate-level courses in financial engineering, derivatives, institutions, portfolio management, and program trading strategies at Johns Hopkins University, a well-respected training camp. With the teaching notes that are part of this book, he is training Hopkins graduate students to be top portfolio managers, high-frequency trading technologists, quantitative traders, financial advisors, and so forth. He hopes that in the future some of these Hopkins graduates will be very successful in investment management and choose to give back to society.

His research interests include high-frequency trading and behavioral investing with the Sentiment Asset Pricing Engine (SAPE), option pricing in stocks and bonds, and behavioral economics for investment research. He earned a PhD from the University of Tilburg, the Netherlands (ranked top 5 in economics and business research in Europe). He has published about 40 articles in peer-reviewed journals or conference proceedings. He has spent more than 10 years building financial models and computing systems. Recently he has released the SAPE, a Web-based strategy builder for algorithmic trading and high-frequency trading systems. For a live demo on SAPE, see Yeswici.com. The SAPE algorithms have been used to construct SAPE funds that have repeatedly outperformed the market indexes.

Dr. Ye has been a senior architect and consultant for investment and technology companies and agencies including Citigroup, IBM, T. Rowe Price, and Federal Reserve Banks.

Index

Edinburgh ?

Books may I
if so you wi

Due Da

University Edinburgh

30150   027699526